ARTISTRY IN NATIVE AMERICAN MYTHS

Artistry in Native American Myths

KARL KROEBER

University of Nebraska Press
Lincoln and London

Portions of chapter 2 were previously published in "Unaesthetic Imaginings: Native American Myth as Speech Genre," *boundary 2* 23, no. 2 (summer 1996): 171–98. Portions of chapter 5 were previously published in *Religion and Literature* 26, no. 1 (spring 1994); reprint permission granted by the University of Notre Dame.

♾ The paper in this book meets the minimum requirements of American National Standard for Information Sciences – Permanence of Paper for Printed Library Materials, ANSI Z39.48-1984.

Library of Congress Cataloging-in-Publication Data. Kroeber, Karl, 1926– . Artistry in Native American myths / Karl Kroeber. p. cm. Includes bibliographical references (p.) and index. ISBN 0-8032-2737-X (cl: alk. paper). – ISBN 0-8032-7785-7 (pa: alk. paper) 1. Indian mythology – North America. 2. Legends – North America. 3. Animals – North America – Folklore. 4. Trickster – North America. I. Title.
E98.R3K76 1998 398.2'08997 – DC21 97-51506 CIP

To the memory of
Juan Dolores,
who hoped to make me
an honorary Papago

CONTENTS

4
Trickster-Transformer's Orality

5
Myth as Historical Process

PREFACE

This collection of Native American myths illustrates the extraordinary artistry of the narratives that embodied and kept alive traditional Indian cultures. Because all these diverse peoples were without written language, their mythic tellings constituted the primary connective tissue of their lifeways. Contemporary readers educated within a print-dominated culture, however, usually fail to recognize the skill with which oral myths are constructed and underestimate the emotional and intellectual power transmitted through their performance. I have, therefore, appended to the translations commentaries pointing up rhetorical features in individual stories and describing characteristics of myth performances in preliterate societies, as well as some cultural causes for our difficulties in appreciating oral narrative discourse.

Although these myths represent the full range of cultural areas of Indian North America, each was selected for its individual power. Some evoke complex emotions, some are intellectually stimulating, some are hilarious, some almost painfully beautiful – and the majority combine most of these qualities. From my experience in teaching this material and for a decade editing the journal *Studies in American Indian Literatures*, I have learned that internalized cultural prejudices often block modern readers' enjoyment of Indian stories' moral, intellectual, and emotional richness. Ironically, the most obstructive prejudices have been fostered by recent literary criticism, especially that influenced by European structuralist and poststructuralist ethnological theorizing.

I begin my essays, consequently, by distinguishing my purpose and method of presentation from those of a collection published thirty-five years ago by an eminent folklorist. It just preceded the development within American anthropology of new understandings of the formal characteristics of Indian narratives and new ideas as to how they should be translated. This emergence of "ethnopoetics" accompanied, and was stimulated by, a dramatic resurgence of Native Americans' self-awareness of – and self-confidence in – the viability of their cultures. The interconnection illustrates a unique feature of twentieth-century American anthropology, which was from the first shaped by its special engagements with Native Americans. I therefore sketch the originating orientation of Boasian anthropology, which enabled American ethnographers and linguists in the 1960s to recognize the sustaining *forms* of traditional Indian myths. The sketch permits me also to present a hypothesis for understanding myths as imaginative acts.

In each chapter the myths come first because they are primary. I will be surprised, however, if most readers can without assistance fully enjoy these stories – although each one has richly rewarded every hour of attention I have devoted to it. I would like to awaken others to the emotional excitement and intellectual satisfaction they offer, especially because there are preserved (and still being enunciated) other Indian myths as remarkable as these. Yet, as I've said, experience has taught me how difficult it is for readers today, even with the best will in the world, to appreciate traditions of imaginative forms so alien to our own. I have come to recognize, for a cogent example, that my own earlier attempts to understand these myths as "oral literature" were mistaken; that well-meant approach in fact obscures the artistry responsible for the unique power of mythic enactments.

My pleasure in working with these materials has been enhanced by the possibility of making them accessible to others. To that end I have tried to help nonspecialists by including in the notes brief sketches of the cultures from which the myths emerged and suggesting introductory ethnographic descriptions and histories. Given my aims, it seemed distracting to discuss special problems of ethnopoetic translation, although these are both inherently fascinating and central to remarkable advances in American anthropology since the 1960s (I hope to address these problems in subsequent work). I have been able to include a few representatively contemporary translations, notably those of Dell Hymes, Barre Toelken, and Nora and Richard Dauenhauer. By mere happenstance, however, there is no example in this volume of the work of Dennis Tedlock, who is perhaps the scholar most influential in changing ideas about translating Indian myths.

Listing the indebtedness I have compiled in arriving at this volume would be longer than my commentaries, so I must be appallingly selective. Too substantial a group to list individually are the scholars, several of them American Indians, who over the past twenty-five years have criticized my work in this field; they have stimulated me to think again – and they at least will recognize the beneficence of their suggestions, although I fear a few may find new grounds for further critiques. To the innocent enthusiasm of the Columbia students who have taken my course on traditional American Indian discourse, I owe an even more profound debt. Their readiness to admit, when challenged, that they do in fact approach such material on the basis of unexamined prejudices, then to throw these off and push blindly but hopefully into unexplored realms of imagination has bolstered my courage and kept my aging mind from shutting down completely. It has been a privilege to share classrooms with these young people. A subtler gratitude is owing to my son Paul, whose knowledge, primarily linguistic but also ethnological, has through various conversations seeped into my thinking to give it a little of the substance, rigor, and detailed precision it desperately needs. I happily acknowledge the generosity of the editors of *boundary 2 and Religion and Literature* for permission to use portions of essays that appeared in those journals in, respectively, chapters 2 and 5, and to the National Endowment for the Humanities for a grant that enabled me to visit locations important in some of the myths. I am indebted, finally, to the enthusiasm for this project and the practical help in its accomplishment offered by staff of the University of Nebraska Press and especially to Patricia Sterling, the best copyeditor in the world.

1
Anthropological Roots of Ethnopoetics

Iroquois[1]

Excerpt from *Concerning the League*

JOHN ARTHUR GIBSON

After Tekanwita had departed in that direction he came to a house belonging to a cannibal who had his house there. Then Tekanawita went close to the house. Then, when he saw the man coming out, departing, sliding down the hill to the river, and dipping water, thereupon Tekanawita hurriedly climbed onto the house to the place where there was a chimney for the smoke to escape; he lay down on his stomach and looking into the house he saw that the task of breaking up meat and piling it had been completed. Then the man returned, and he was carrying a drum with water in it. Thereupon he poured it into a vessel, put meat into the liquid, and hung the vessel up over the fire until it boiled. Moreover, the man watched it, and when it was done, he took down the vessel, placing it near the embers. Thereupon he said, "Now indeed it is done. Moreover, now I will eat." Thereupon he set up a seat, a bench, thinking that he will put it there when he eats. Thereupon he went to where the vessel sat, intending to take the meat out of the liquid, when he saw, from inside the vessel, a man looking out. Thereupon he moved away without removing the meat, and sat down again on the long bench, for it was a surprise to him, seeing the man in the vessel. Thereupon he thought, "Let me look again." Thereupon he, Tekanawita, looked again from above where the smoke hole was, again causing a reflection in the vessel, and then the man, standing up again, went to where the vessel sat, looked into the vessel again, saw the man looking out, and he was handsome, he having a nice face. Thereupon the man moved away again, and he sat down again on the long bench, and then he bowed his head, pondering and thinking: "I am exceedingly hand-

Concerning the League: The Iroquois Tradition as Dictated in Onondaga by John Arthur Gibson, ed. and trans. Hanni Woodbury in collaboration with Reg Henry and Harry Webster, Algonquian and Iroquois Linguistics Memoir 9 (Winnipeg, 1992), 78–83.

some and I have a nice face; it is probably not right, my habit of eating humans. So I will now stop, from now on I ought not to kill humans anymore." Thereupon he stood up again, went to where the vessel sat, picked up the vessel with the meat in it, and then he went out, sliding straight down the slope beside the river and near an uprooted tree he poured out the vessel full of meat.

COMMENTARY

A historical survey of the many collections of Native American tales (each gathered, translated, and edited in a different way for different readers) would dramatically illuminate the shifting attitudes of white Americans toward the Indians they have relentlessly dispossessed. Contrast with a single anthology, that edited by Tristram P. Coffin, published in 1961 by the American Folklore Society in Philadelphia under the title *Indian Tales of North America: An Anthology for the Adult Reader*, will help to define my purpose in this collection – as well as illustrate in what directions both folkloristic and literary studies have evolved in less than four decades. Coffin's subtitle, for example, might mislead today, because far from presenting X-rated tales he edited out "unprintable words and concepts"; what he extends to "the intelligent adult reader" is "the opportunity to enjoy and profit from one of the richest literary traditions in the human heritage." At the conclusion of his introductory remarks Coffin speaks even more forcefully of this Native American tradition: "it is never too late to profit from and enjoy the art they left us far more willingly than they left us their hunting grounds. It is a great art, and it will not take the reader long to realize the tales below have stood the test of time because they are great tales" (xvii).

Yet other remarks contradict this praise, Coffin's inconsistency manifesting the confusions that marked the early 1960s, when forces counteractive to modernism were beginning to crystallize into what we now call postmodernism. He weirdly contradicts himself because he is caught within confusing changes of direction in two modes of discourse. His identification of himself as an editor who is a "folklorist trained in the history of literature" highlights the confluence of doubly shifting currents, which sucks him into denigrating an "alien" artistry he enthusiastically praises.

For Coffin, literary accomplishment of the highest order is an exclusive possession of Western civilization. The stories he has collected, he warns us, show that "the primitive mind is incapable of the subtleties and probings we have come to expect of our own narrators" (ix). The "Indian tale's purpose is clearly to entertain," and tellers rely on the form of the "single incident" plot because "it needs no pattern of organization, no characterization, or real setting, it can spring up even in the most naive of minds" (x). The "primitive" Indians, he tells us, "are not capable of unifying their tales in the fashion described by Aristotle" (x–xi). To enjoy Indian tales, we must take them "at the level of which their authors were capable," which does not include "scientific, logical accuracy" (xii).

This condescending attitude toward formal qualities of Indian narratives accompanies equivalent moral pronouncements that were commonplaces in the 1950s. Although Coffin remarks that whites were wrong to call the Indians "sneaky and cowardly," their stories show them, he says, "like most primitives . . . more interested in the end than in the means and, providing the job was successfully done," indifferent to "whether deceit and knavery were used to accomplish it" (xvi). Coffin remains trapped in the modernist conception of "primitivism," even when responding to something in the Indian narratives that might have liberated him from that imperialistic, colonial mind-set. Evidence of his entrapment is his refusal to credit any individual Indian teller with artistic gifts, even though he wants the tales recognized as "great art." Coffin follows modernists who pretended to admire "the primitive" while denying there could be a meaningful primitive "tradition" of art because there were no individualistically self-conscious primitive artists; tradition and individual talent are the sole possession of Western civilization.

Running counter to these pronouncements are Coffin's observations about qualities in the Indian stories that subvert his modernist assumptions. In contrast to European painters and writers (Picasso and D. H. Lawrence are conspicuous exemplars) who exploited "the primitive" to enhance their own artistry, Coffin calls attention to characteristics in the Indian tales whose *absence*, he claims, weakens the art of Chekhov, Woolf, Joyce, Faulkner. Unlike these writers, the Indian teller "trusts life itself" and shows the importance of a "relationship between religious faith in a culture and acceptance of life" (xiv). Coffin fails, however, to identify more precisely the qualities that justify calling Indian stories "great art," because he is unable to develop a valid intuition of the difference between Western written literature and Indian oral narratives. He recognizes, for example, that the Indian tales function not alogically but according to "a completely different logical system from the one we are used to using" (xiii). But he cannot specify what that different system might consist of. And although he deliberately excluded from his collection all stories that were not myths, his concept of myth as a naive explanation of natural phenomena is itself uselessly naive. What we read in his anthology, he tells us, "are the ancient and revered legends of a primitive people," even though he has just observed that some are mere "adventure stories taking place in a by-gone era" (xvi).

My radically different collection takes advantage of advances in both literary criticism and ethnology or folklore achieved since 1961. Coffin assumed that whatever was worth understanding in Indian myths his readers could comprehend without assistance. I have more respect for the difficulties the myths pose to us. They were created out of conditions about which we remain largely ignorant. The nature of their special artistry differs radically from what we unthinkingly assume constitutes literary art. My experience in studying and teaching this material has taught me how baffling Indian myths are for readers today. They are, indeed, built upon unfamiliar kinds of "logic," and they arise out of and sustain oral cultures, the experience of which is alien to our print-dominated society.[2]

In making use of intellectual developments since 1961, I hope to enhance understanding of the difficulties intrinsic to what is now called ethnopoetics, study of the artistry of discourse in oral cultures. To do so requires me to say a little about the history of anthropology in America, which currently suffers some distortion by popular theoreticians of ethnology who confuse European and American anthropological traditions.[3] The differences needing emphasis are epitomized in *The Writing of History* by the French scholar Michel de Certeau. He begins his chapter on the sixteenth-century anthropological writer Jean de Lery by announcing that "in a primitive society, a timeless land as it were, is displayed before the observer's eye ("Things have always been like this," remarks the native).[4] What one makes of the phrase "a timeless land *as it were*" is an interesting question, but it is Certeau's parenthetical sentence that I wish to dwell on here: "'Things have always been like this,' remarks the native." "*The* native" – not a Tupinamba, not a Zuni, not a Japanese, but an abstract being – all too appropriate a member of that equally abstract "primitive society." At moments like this one recognizes the truth of Charlie Chan's caution: "Theory like mist on eyeglasses. Obscures facts."

The fact is that in all the anthropological literature of American Indians I have read, I cannot recall any member of any tribal group ever being quoted as saying "things have always been like this." To the contrary, a majority of American Indian mythological stories refer, usually quite explicitly, to a time when things were different. American anthropologists have regularly followed Indian practice in distinguishing myths from other kinds of tales according to whether a story referred to the present or a time when things were different – when, for instance, animals talked.[5]

Certeau's gross empirical error is not unusual among European intellectuals who comment on Native Americans, but it is useful because it so glaringly reveals its source: a conception of "primitive society." "Primitive society" is a nineteenth-century colonialist conception that has never had more than a tenuous connection to any real society. Its disconnection is signaled by its hallucination of a changeless social order – something that has never existed, that never could have existed, on this earth. The societies that Certeau patronizingly calls "primitive," in fact, tended to be unusually mobile and changeable. American Indian cultures have survived largely by being self-transformative and hence highly adaptable to new conditions. But for Certeau the French historian, history is something that happens only to Europeans. In his elaborate analysis of Jean de Lery's wonderful sixteenth-century account of the Tupinamba people in Brazil, Certeau never considers the possibility that the Tupinambas might have reached the Brazilian coast not very long before the French – although from the opposite direction – in the course of driving out the prior inhabitants, another timelessly primitive society in which things never change.

American anthropology has followed the beat of a different drum, whose rhythm we may suggest by looking at what seems to have been the first spectacular public display of its findings – at the Chicago world's fair of 1893, celebrating the anniversary of Columbus's discovery of a new world inhabited by what he called Indians. The World's Columbian Exposition came a year late because it was promoted less to commemorate Columbus than to discover to the rest of the world an unprecedented greatness in the future of American civilization. To a degree the exposition succeeded in selling America, if not always in the manner the promoters intended. It was here that Henry Adams was inspired to learn to ride a bicycle and began articulating his ideas about dynamos, and here that Frederick Jackson Turner announced his thesis on the closing of the American frontier. And it was here, I suggest, that a distinctively American anthropology began successfully to establish itself publicly, not only in contradistinction to European imperialist anthropologies but also through resistance to some powerful Americanizing ideals.

The distinctively American school of anthropology has come to be called Boasian, and Franz Boas, working as Frederick Putnam's assistant and in keeping with Putnam's own intellectual program, was in good part responsible for the ethnological displays at the Chicago exposition.[6] These presentations helped to crystallize American anthropological endeavors and give them a popular foundation, concretely embodied in the Chicago Field Museum, whose basic collections derive from the 1893 exposition. This private museum joined other private philanthropies in becoming important sponsors of American anthropological research.

The sequence is significant. The Chicago Exposition of 1893 was funded and organized by wealthy citizens such as Marshall Field; it was not a government project. Boasian anthropology, to a surprising degree, was in its early years heavily supported by wealthy individuals or privately endowed museums, at crucial times defining itself *against* the chief quasi-governmental organ of anthropological studies, the Bureau of American Ethnology of the Smithsonian Institution – and in every feasible way opposing the principal instrument of federal control of Native Americans, the Bureau of Indian Affairs.

I emphasize the antigovernmental orientation of Boasian anthropology because recent commentators, working metahistorically, have overlooked this distinction between American and European anthropology.[7] All nineteenth- and twentieth-century European anthropology has served directly or indirectly as an instrument of colonialist governments, a tool for official exploitations cultural, political, and economic. This partly explains why in the approved fiction of Communist regimes sustained by the Soviet Union, ethnologists so often appeared as villains. In our non-Communist country the two major battles in the profession of anthropology, the first following the First World War and the second near the end of the Vietnam War, arose from attacks by professional anthropologists on alleged governmental manipulation of anthropological work.

Boasian anthropology was by no means ideologically innocent, but the nature of its ideological slant is obscured if we ignore its originating bias toward the private as antagonistic to the governmental – a bias revealed in the exposition of 1893, which helped to popularize ethnology. The exposition, after all, was not merely a creation of private businesses but also a product of fierce competition; there had been a severe contest as to where it should take place, the principal combatants being New York and Chicago. Chicago won out because more of its businessmen were willing to give more money to fund the fair. They were willing because they truly believed that Chicago was the westernmost culmination of European civilization but, simultaneously, was superseding the Europeanism from which America had derived.

The promoters of the exposition presented it as an expression of America as the New World, not in the sense in which it was new for Columbus and his contemporaries but in the sense in which politically and economically and socially 1893 America embodied an improved, reconstituted Western civilization and showed how it could work – if one ignored the embarrassing fact that in 1893 this country was entering probably the worst economic depression in its history. Not only Boston but even New York, in the jovially myopic perspective of Chicago's business tycoons, were too "Old World" to be appropriate sites for the celebration of modern America as the harbinger of a New World.

Even as Frederick Jackson Turner announced the closing of the "traditional" frontier, which had in his view represented the essence of the American experience and whose disappearance foreboded important socioeconomic changes, the fair's promoters proclaimed the opening of a new technological frontier. More quietly, the Boasian anthropological exhibits offered a different way of *conceiving* frontiers. The intricacies of this innovation in understanding culture, which would ultimately subvert patriotic boosterism, were brought to sharp focus by William Dean Howells's comments on the Chicago fair. These appeared in his *Letters from an Altrurian*, which purport to be comments of an observer from an advanced nation distinguished by its dedication to altruistic social behavior. Such an observer, of course, serves Howells's aim of criticizing the selfishness of American business culture, the exposition's sponsor. Howells nonetheless praises the White City, as the exposition was called, in a fashion that may remind us that when he wrote, the great critic of urban architecture Jane Jacobs had not even been born:

[It] is like our own [Altrurian] cities in being a design, the effect of a principle, and not the straggling and shapeless accretion of accident. . . . Very few who visit this gala town . . . realize that it has its own system of drainage, lighting and transportation and its own government, which looks as scrupulously to the general comfort and cleanliness, as if these were private concerns of each member of the government. This is, as with us, military in form, and the same precision and discipline which give us the ease and freedom of our [Altrurian] civic life proceed here from the same spirit and same means. The Columbia guards, as they are called, who are here at every turn, to keep order and to care for the pleasure as well as the welfare of the people, have been trained by officers of the United States Army, who still command them.[8]

Howells's cheery reliance on the virtues of a police state (which he sees as founded in a military ideal of selfless service) is peculiarly interesting because so contradictory to his simultaneous idealization of individuality. The contradiction arises, I believe, from his lack of appreciation for what some people call the problematic of otherness. For Howells – and I wonder if he is not characteristic of a good many Americans in this – there is no mediation between individual and society, no suggestion of some kind of intermediate community. He never refers to a unity more intimate than that of state, never mentions other kinds of bondings among people differentiated by age, ethnicity, gender, or occupation. His altruism as a social ideal of individuality simply transcends the intrinsically dialectical, if not conflictual, character of any psychology responsive to practical social diversities. He does not address the possibility of a people consisting of different peoples.

Howells' altruism seems to me inadequate (and dangerous) because it is merely the reverse of the most selfish kind of colonialism or robber-baronism. What makes multiculturalism as we today conceive it a threatening yet necessary possibility is that it pays little attention to any altruistic abnegation of self. Contemporary multiculturalism appears to be the product of narcissistic forces that insist on a dynamic and productive confrontation, even antagonism, between othernesses. Something like that view, I propose, was given an early intellectual form by Boasian anthropology. There was a logicality in this anticipation. The significant peculiarity of American anthropology emerged from its coming into being through dual resistance to both liberal altruism and the simple assimilatory ideals epitomized in the concept of the American melting pot.

As European anthropology has not been able to do, American anthropology has in the past few decades dramatically renewed itself, not least in revising its understanding of mythic narratives through the development of ethnopoetics. This success is rooted in American anthropology's complex evolution in resistance (instead of mere nonproductive hostility) to the Americanist culture that, as the promoters of the Chicago exposition hoped, has become the dominating model of our postmodern world. Boasian anthropology's resistance consisted in working both with and against the grain of the dominating social ideals of its era. Given an opportunity for popular publicity at the White City, it focused on the difference of Native American peoples from their white successors through exhibitions prepared by a naturalized American, Franz Boas. His premier student was my father, Alfred Kroeber, the son of immigrants, reared in one kind of classic immigrant environment. It would take too long to pursue in detail how the anthropological study of Native Americans worked as a naturalizing tool for immigrant Americans, but even the names of some leading Boasians – Robert Lowie, Edward Sapir, Paul Radin, and Jaime de Angulo – suggest the efficacy of the process. The intense Americanism of American anthropology depended, like the Chicago exposition itself, upon superseding unconcealed European origins through the valorizing of a new conception of how cultures could function interactively.

The foregoing mite of history may suggest that it was no accident that Tristram Coffin's anthology appeared under the aegis of the *Journal of American Folklore*, a primary vehicle for the publication by ethnologists of Native American myths. It is in good measure due to the evolution of American anthropological studies of mythic narratives since 1961, moreover, that we feel such discomfort at Coffin's condescending naiveté in claiming artistic merit for Native American narratives. In Europe there is still no equivalent for the extensive development of aesthetic revaluation of narratives from oral cultures, which – through the labors of Dell Hymes, Dennis Tedlock, Barre Toelken, and many others – has initiated fruitful interactions among the current generation of American anthropologists, literary critics, folklorists, and linguists. The colonialist-imperialist mind-set that has dominated European ethnology for so long, especially in its tendency toward abstract theorizing and its dependence on the Eurocentric construct of "the primitive," could not encourage interdisciplinary efforts to affirm the unique significance of small-scale preliterate cultural achievements. Such affirmations have been fostered primarily by American anthropologists and folklorists responding to the growing influence of resurgent Native American tribal groups.

We should not underestimate the advantages created by the resistance to a Eurocentric mind-set whereby Boasian American anthropology defined itself in its diversified practices. To take one very crude example: from Columbus into the nineteenth century, many Europeans visiting the New World were more impressed by new flora and fauna and mineral resources than by new peoples, an emphasis that flowered into climatological theories of culture – culture as determined by topography and meteorology.[9] This imaginative bias spectacularly climaxes in Joseph Conrad's novel *Nostromo*, in which there is no hint of any native culture within brilliantly imagined topography. Boasian conceptions of culture arise out of a determination to understand people and their beliefs as just as important as physical environment, even to emphasize how peoples shape environments.

Such generalized contrasts of course oversimplify complex intellectual history, but they direct us toward important orientations in anthropological traditions. Only by recognizing these differences can we establish on a sound basis methods of interpretation and comment that will, given the conditions of today's culture, encourage real understanding of mythic narratives' finest accomplishments.

I have observed that Boas was himself an immigrant, a "naturalized" American. For such a scientist, the nativeness of American Indian populations almost necessarily took on a different cast from that dominating the thinking of transient, government-sponsored European observers of aboriginal societies in colonies far from their own hearthsides. For people such as Boas and my father and Robert Lowie, the understanding and describing of native cultures was part of the process of naturalizing themselves as Americans – of finding themselves at home in an America created by dispossession of native cultures. This painful and ambiguous naturalizing depended, obviously enough, not on an assimilation but upon articulation of differences – which led to a bias of American anthropology toward some interesting but rather tangled reconceptions of the discipline as a problematic science.[10]

For my purposes, only one strand of this intricate tangle needs to be teased out, a strand illuminated by the *form* of some of the anthropological exhibits at the Chicago Exposition. Exemplary is the Kwakiutl village that Boas was responsible for establishing. Putnam and Boas wanted to dramatize pre-European native life, and the "characteristic" village not only exhibited a different "ordinary" life in its unspectacular commonplaceness but also affirmed the unique, self-sufficient, and enduring integrity of Kwakiutl culture. The Kwakiutl village might be said to embody the essence of Boas's argument against the scientific principles underlying Smithsonian anthropological exhibitions in his day, principles that Boas had debated with Otis Mason, the Smithsonian curator, a few years previously in the pages of *Science*.[11]

Boas objected to Smithsonian exhibits that were "scientifically" arranged to display the overarching evolutionary development of human cultures; for example, arrow points would be laid out in a sequence of their "progressive" refinement, rather than collected according to their culture area or tribal provenance. The Smithsonian's "Darwinian" approach explained cultural phenomena in the metacultural terms of evolutionary development – as then understood. This led Otis Mason and his fellow curators to account for parallel accomplishments or characteristics in different peoples as due to similar responses to like physical, environmental, and social situations. Boas argued explicitly that, to the contrary, *unlike* circumstances often produce cultural similarities – and the reverse, that similar circumstances often produce cultural differences.

Boas's paradox is a cornerstone of American anthropology. It undermines the basis of late-nineteenth-century scientific reasoning by denying direct cause-effect connections in cultural phenomena. The "paradox" that different people in similar situations may behave differently, or that different people may arrive at similar modes of behavior through confronting unlike conditions, makes "culture" intrinsically problematic. With Boas, anthropology must address the question of what culture is, instead of taking it as an understood given whose variations are to be explained by appeal to some metacultural principle. Boas therefore directed American anthropology into two simultaneous activities: the massive collection of all possible empirical information about the multitude of distinct American Indian cultures (a data-gathering accomplishment without parallel), along with intellectual exploration into the nature of culture, conceived of as something not yet understood, still enigmatic – in good measure because it constitutes the very medium that gives rise to the questioning impulse itself.

Although the accomplishment of the Boasian questioning of the nature of culture is not generally recognized, I know of no contemporary "cultural criticism" or investigation into "multiculturalism" that does not derive (however unwittingly) from the Boasian principle that culture is important because it enables human beings to be fully human in so many diverse ways. How the Boasians established the basis for our current understanding of culture is dramatized by Alfred Kroeber's early formulation of it as "superorganic," a term he quickly discarded as misleadingly oversimple. "Superorganic," however, does focus attention on culture as functioning by systems that, although rooted in evolutionary biology, are not explicable by "laws" of that more primary level, just as biological phenomena themselves, although dependent on physical laws, are not explicable by physics. Today's commonplace of a "cultural construct" (gender difference, for example, being understood as a phenomenon decisively shaped by social systems, even though founded on physiological differences) originates in the American anthropological problematizing of "culture" a century ago.

In some respects Boasian anthropology thus worked against the grain of the Enlightenment-based, "progressive" social thinking of modernism, not only in "salvaging" marginal and dying cultures but also in resisting the universalizing tendencies that characterize all forms of modernism – political, economic, intellectual, aesthetic. Explanations of cultural phenomena must in the Boasian view be entirely cultural, and therefore culturebound, explanations. Boasians, in striking contrast to Freudians, for example, do not recognize the validity of metacultural explanations; they do not explain cultural phenomena by appeals to principles, or fantasies, of some universal "human nature." Implicitly, the Boasian explanation represents itself as one among other possible perspectives rather than a universal truth. For the Boasian, there are no metacultural (or acultural) "primal scenes" but only cultural singularities, whether of event or explanation of event. This approach characterizes the best American "revisionist" studies of Native American myths since the 1960s, especially those concentrating on ethnopoetic problems.

The cross-grainedness of American anthropology is rooted not merely in the biographical circumstances of the leaders of Boasian anthropology but, ironically, in the source of their basic ideas, the German originators of the modern concept of culture in the later eighteenth century. Probably the most important source was Johann Gottfried von Herder's counter-Enlightenment suggestions that different cultures are not merely distinguishable but even incommensurate.

The Herderian-Boasian view of cultures as not only equidistant from God (as Leopold von Ranke phrased it) but also not intermeasurable allows us to reconceive of a frontier, for example, not as civilization's outward edge meeting the unformed and undeveloped "primitive" but, instead, as a zone of interactions between equally real and equally articulated, though probably not equally powerful, social entities. This idea is the foundation of the contemporary, excruciating self-doubts of anthropologists about the propriety of their endeavors to collect and publish "translations" of the myths of Native Americans. Once we liberate our minds from modernism's disguised commitment to metahistorical explanations, however, and assume that cultures are not intermeasurable, we clear the ground for more complex understanding – and an authentically respectful appreciation – of unfamiliar forms of discourse, such as oral myths.

This excursion into schematized ethnological history explains the basis of my comments about Indian myths. I wish to increase admiration of their "artistry" without confining it to forms and purposes familiar because characteristic of Western, written literature. I range beyond the anthropological and linguistic ethnopoeticists only by concentrating on imagination. I assume that myths, whatever else they may be, are imaginings, and any kind of adequate response to important myths requires us to use our own powers of imagination – but in unfamiliar ways. Imagining, too, differs in different cultures. Approaching myths in this fashion, we may discover something like the rewards Coffin sought in stories that may at first appear to a Western reader simultaneously obscure and pointless. When we assume the necessity of imaginativeness in both myth creation and myth understanding, positing as a problem that cultural differences produce different kinds of imagining, we position ourselves to admire the skills of Indian mythmakers in a manner that neither romantically mystifies them nor confines their accomplishments to the limits of our culturebound prejudices.

It may be helpful at this point to illustrate my approach by commenting on a specific myth that is in some ways fairly accessible to a modern reader. I focus on the episode from the long Iroquois myth of the founding of their Great League. This political structure, probably originating in the fifteenth century to unify five Iroquoian tribal peoples, was attributed by them to the vision and labors of Tekanawita (in some transliterations, Dekanawidah). He, with the help of his convert Hiawatha, persuaded the Mohawk, Oneida, Onondaga, Cayuga, and Seneca to give up making war on one another and enter into a cooperative confederacy whose central political organ was a permanent council of fifty members, with representatives from each tribe. This structure endured for several centuries and made the Iroquois a powerful force, not only in relation to other Indian peoples but also to European invader-colonizers.

The brief cannibal-conversion episode presented here from the long myth of Tekanawita's crusade gains much of its strength from embodying in miniature as a personal psychological event the essence of the prophet's sociopolitical message: abandon the bloodthirsty murdering of your own people. This fundamental lesson will be apparent to any reader. But the episode is recounted in a manner that makes its details resonate with other important Iroquois myths, so that for a native audience this brief episode would evoke the structure of their entire belief system.

In oral cultures, myth tellings normally resonate in this way. Not only episodes as wholes (those that tell, for example, of a familiar character, such as a local Trickster) but even brief phrases echo and recall figures, acts, or circumstances in other myths (as well as, of course, previous tellings of the same myth). Each hearing of a single myth is a reentry into an entire mythological system. The efficacy of such reentry lies in the reciprocality of its effects: the "recollection" of a specific detail not only enriches the story being recounted but also acts upon what it resonates with, the total mythological system, which is in turn thereby revitalized in the imaginations of listeners.

We can scarcely expect to recognize how this telling of the cannibal conversion might impress those for whom Iroquois mythology was a living system, but we can identify some methods by which it evokes the system. At the end of the episode the cannibal returns to the river (from which we first saw him coming) to dispose of the uneaten body in a hole created by an uprooted tree. That detail would for an Iroquois listener bring to mind a basic creation myth in which a sick woman is pushed through a hole in the sky created by the uprooting of a corn-producing tree; the woman falls to earth, where she miraculously gives birth to twins, one good, one evil, who between them shape the world as we know it. The tree was uprooted because one man had dreamed that only this could cure the woman's illness – and it was an accepted practice in Iroquoian culture that what was dreamed had to be carried out in practice, especially if there was illness to be cured. Yet another man, the one who pushes the woman through the hole, justifiably asserts that uprooting the tree destroys the sky people's source of food. Such resonances are strengthened by the fact that the beginning of this myth tells of Tekanawita's miraculous birth as exactly paralleling that of the original twins.[12] His mission to stop internecine warfare has thus been established as a development of the original struggle of good to overcome its twin, evil.

This kind of reinvocation of a mythological matrix is perhaps the determining feature of oral mythic artistry. The allusions, as I have noted, function reciprocally, the resonating power of contextual mythology being activated by a specific retelling. Those effects we miss. But the process does not absolutely exclude some appreciation by a non-Iroquoian listener or reader. Careful attention to the myth's individual features can provide insight into Iroquoian mythological imagining, because the myth treats of experiences that are at the least analogous to those that we, in a very different way, undergo in our own cultural fashion. There are, for instance, plenty of conversion narratives in Western literature, although none I know of that focus on cannibalism. Chief Gibson's dramatization of the psychic and spiritual transformation, because it is shaped to provoke active interpreting by its audience (which may include questioning and judging of what is told), can be evocative even for an outsider like me. My understanding of the episode, like that of an Iroquois, depends on my interpretation of details. I judge, for example, that when the cannibal looks into his pot, he sees what he believes to be the reflection of his own face but what is in fact the reflection of Tekanawita's face from above. Other interpretations than mine, however, are possible. Awareness that this is a story *of* interpretation (how the cannibal "reads" the face he sees) *demanding* interpretation is deliberately provoked by the myth teller. Chief Gibson crafts his telling to make each of his hearers *reflect* on the complex process of a personal conversion crucial to the foundation of the political structure they share.

That appeal to reflective assessing offers even an outsider some access to the power of this mythic enactment. In my interpretation, for instance, what the cannibal mistakes for his self-image is the image of a peacemaker and spiritual leader who seems his absolute antithesis. Literally a mistake, the self-perception is nevertheless valid, because the cannibal sees a potentiality in himself not yet realized but realizable. He comes to believe that his eating people is bad because founded on a misperception of his true being: he perceives himself as a handsome human being, not an ugly one. Such personal experience embodies the process by which Tekanawita leads the Iroquoian peoples away from violence and bloodshed by offering them a vision of themselves as better than their current behavior implies. His ministry is to make Iroquois esteem themselves properly, to perceive their better natures.[13]

This is why the story comes to us from the cannibal's point of view and he is consistently referred to as a man. Seeing things from the cannibal's perspective, we are drawn to regard him as a human being rather than as a monster, totally alien to us. The form of the myth, that is, recognizes our potential to be cannibalistic. The myth is shaped so that we may feel the protagonist's cannibalism as something not abstractly bad but concretely bad because it is a failure to realize a potential for specific behavior truer to his full potentialities as a human being like us. The cannibal's revelation from looking into the pot evokes a parallel revelation in us as we look into his story, as it were, from above Tekanawita, who is looking down with his face reflected upward. As the cannibal's conversion reveals to him a connection between himself and his victim (situated, as he is, midway between the victim in the pot and Tekanawita on the roof), so his understanding dramatizes a connection between us and him: we are all capable of cannibalism and of benefiting from the exemplary anticannibalistic message of Tekanawita.

Whether or not my interpretation seems helpful for understanding how the Iroquois may have responded to this episode, one should notice that the process of the cannibal's conversion is represented through bodily acts and that he himself expresses his psychic revelation in terms of his physical appearance. This manner of presentation (characteristic of Indian myths) is probably required by a conception of the "spiritual" as inseparable from the "natural." Conversion in Indian cultures is not a matter of breaking out of a merely material world into a different, higher order of life. It is, rather, achieving an intensified harmony of participation in the normal processes of natural life. The cannibal eliminates the characteristic that has defined his identity by connecting his "good" appearance with his "bad" habit, accepting the possibility of behaving handsomely in the everyday world of cooking and eating.

As ethnologists have frequently observed, much American Indian religious experience is closely associated with activities of healing –

which is to say, of natural renewal. It should not be surprising, then, that their myth tellings normally function to restore the traditions they enunciate. The transmissive power of each retelling to some degree lies in its remaking (thereby opening to enhanced reapprehension) the texture of a cherished mode of life. I know of no other version, for example, of the Tekanawita myth that contains an account of the cannibal's conversion exactly like Gibson's remarkable dramatization. But the source of its unique effectiveness can be identified with a deliberate refashioning of a commonly imagined story, one whose preciousness resides in its enabling the Iroquois to preserve the vitality of cultural traditions that foster such community-restoring acts of individualized reimagining.

NOTES

1. The Iroquois Confederacy, probably established in the fifteenth century but founded according to legend by Tekanawita (Deganwidah) and Hiawatha, brought into political union five major tribes of Hokan-Siouan linguistic stock – the Mohawk, the Cayuga, the Oneida, the Onondaga, and the Seneca – occupying lands in New York from the Hudson River north to the St. Lawrence and west to the Genesee. In the early eighteenth century a sixth tribe, the Tuscarora, were admitted to the confederation. This political structure made the Iroquois the most powerful Indian political entity in the Northeast after they began to obtain firearms from Dutch traders in Albany. Until the Revolutionary War they dominated the lucrative fur trade, destroying many of their rivals, such as the Hurons. The Iroquois, who generally allied themselves with the British, were a major force in the political and military conflicts of the seventeenth and eighteenth centuries, their power eroding only after the American Revolution.

The Iroquois subjected captives to severe tortures, killing some but adopting many of those tortured into their own tribes, for much of the purpose of attacks on other tribal groups was to replace the population losses that resulted principally from diseases introduced by Europeans. The Iroquois lived in longhouses, pole-frame structures covered with bark, as much as two hundred feet long, sometimes clustered in palisaded towns. Hunting supplemented agriculture, which was carried on by women, who owned the fields (and also nominated the candidates for the confederacy's Great Council, retaining the power to recall incompetent "senators").

Iroquoian religion was deeply concerned with dreams, which were regarded as conveying important messages that had to be acted upon. Someone who had a dream might consult a specialist who would interpret its meaning and tell the dreamer what he or she must do to fulfill the dream's command. Sometimes this was a particular act: if, for example, a man dreamed of eating, he might be required to give a feast. Sometimes "cures" would be prescribed that entailed continued actions over many years. In the early nineteenth century a prophet named Handsome Lake established a new "Longhouse Religion," which combined traditional Iroquoian elements with some features of Christianity and continued to be popular into this century.

A primary source for information on many Native American peoples, their cultures, and the history of their contacts with whites is the *Handbook of North American Indians* (Washington DC: Smithsonian Institution), a multivolume, ongoing series under the general editorship of William Sturdevant; for essays on the Iroquois, see vol.15, ed. Bruce Trigger. Anthony F. C. Wallace, *The White Roots of Peace* (Philadelphia: University of Pennsylvania Press, 1946), synthesizes texts of the founding of the Great League; Daniel K. Richter, *The Ordeal of the Long-House* (Chapel Hill: University of North Carolina Press, 1992), provides a fine historical analysis of the Iroquois; in *The Death and Rebirth of the Seneca* (New York: Knopf, 1970) Wallace describes the historical context of Handsome Lake's prophecies. See also William N. Fenton, "Iroquoian Culture History: A General Evaluation," in *Symposium on Cherokee and Iroquois Culture*, ed. Fenton and John Gulich, Bureau of American Ethnology Bulletin 180 (Washington DC, 1961), 253–77; and for stories, see Jeremiah Curtin and J. N. B. Hewitt, "Seneca Fiction, Legends, and Myths," in the bureau's *Annual Report* 32 (1910–11).

2. The world of an oral culture is, as Bruce A. Rosenberg says, "one that literates can barely imagine" (*Folklore and Literature: Rival Siblings* [Knoxville: University of Tennessee Press, 1991], 31). Studies of oral practices in our culture tend to mislead, because *all* our discourse is significantly contaminated by literacy; see Deborah Tannen, *Spoken and Written Language: Exploring Orality and Literacy* (Norwood NJ: Ablex, 1982). The most sophisticated among the recent spate of studies of literacy is Vlad Godzich, *The Culture of Literacy* (Cambridge: Harvard University Press, 1994). Notable, for example, are Godzich's analysis of the ambiguities and contradictions in the post-Renaissance historical development of literacy in Europe (7–9); his discussion of how today "the story, commodified as it has become, will take on the guise of an object rather than being a process between human beings" (102–08); and his explanation of how social upheavals linked to "decolonization" movements since 1960 have upset the "ideology of universalism" that prevailed on both sides of the Cold War (260–67).

3. Although the recent history of folklore follows a course analogous to that of anthropology, the firmament of folklore has been less afflicted by the vapor trails of high-flying theoreticians. Scholars such as Richard Dorson, Alan Dundes, and Barre Toelken, therefore, have been able to set forth with clarity

and exactness the current nature of the discipline's relations to earlier practices and aspirations. The best recent survey of the vastly complicated field, with judicious representation of its historical developments especially in the past twenty years, is Barre Toelken's splendidly readable *The Dynamics of Folklore*, rev. ed. (Logan: Utah State University Press, 1996). Richard Dorson, *The British Folklorists: A History* (Chicago: University of Chicago Press, 1968), provides a vivid narrative of the emergence of what we now regard as folklore. An excellent collection of wide-ranging essays with fine headnotes was edited by Alan Dundes, *The Study of Folklore* (Englewood CliffsNJ: Prentice-Hall, 1965). Comprehensive commentaries on folklore genres will be found in Jan Harold Brunvand, *The Study of American Folklore: An Introduction*, 3d rev. ed. (New York: Norton, 1986). Of special interest for the shift during the last twenty-five years of folkloristic interest toward issues of performance (paralleling and to a degree inspired by anthropological developments of ethnopoetics) is an essay by J. E. Limon and M. J. Young, "Frontiers, Settlements, and Developments in Folklore Studies, 1972–1986," *Annual Review of Anthropology* 15 (1986): 437–60. An important contributor to the emphasis on performance has been Richard Bauman, whose *Verbal Art as Performance* (Prospect Heights IL: Waveland, 1984) includes his important title essay (from a decade before) and contributions by other folklorists treating various aspects of performance. See also Bauman's *Story, Performance, and Event: Contextual Studies of Oral Narrative*, Cambridge Studies in Oral and Literate Culture 10 (Cambridge: Cambridge University Press, 1986). Elizabeth C. Fine, *The Folklore Text: From Performance to Print* (Bloomington: Indiana University Press, 1984) is comprehensive and judicious. For special topics – such as the creative role of audience in oral performances, which John Miles Foley examines meticulously in *Immanent Art: From Structure to Meaning in Traditional Oral Epic* (Bloomington: Indiana University Press, 1991) – one may consult Toelken's admirable bibliographic essays in *The Dynamics of Folklore*.

4. Michel de Certeau, *The Writing of History*, trans. Tom Conley (New York: Columbia University Press, 1988), 209. As Terence Turner has cogently pointed out, the European assumption that indigenous societies lack historical consciousness accompanies an assumption that their forms of expression make no difference to the content expressed; see his "History, Myth, and Social Consciousness among the Kayapó of Central Africa," in *Rethinking History and Myth*, ed. Jonathan D. Hill (Urbana: University of Illinois Press, 1988), 195–213, esp. 196–97.

5. Although I usually refer to the stories in this collection as myths, discriminations between myth, legend, "true story," and the like vary among cultural

groups, many of which also make important distinctions between kinds of stories *within* such genres and have various restrictions on how, by whom, and when particular myths may be told. As I discuss in the following chapter, all the stories in this collection are important stories, usually "sacred" (although what that term means to Indian peoples is likely different from our conception), wherein the truth of the tale must lie in the telling, because the events narrated antedate any present living witness. Emilienne Ireland in "The Whiteman in Waura Myth" (in Hill, *Rethinking History and Myth*, 157–73), reports encountering among the Waura a quite specific exemplification of the distinction I make: her informants differentiated "true" or "real" mythic narratives of events not witnessed by any living people from stories that were "mere factual accounts," not great myths but "just a fact, something that happened" (163).

6. The premier student of the history of American anthropology is George W. Stocking Jr., among whose many works one may cite as especially relevant his introduction, "The Basic Assumptions of Boasian Anthropology," to his edited volume, *The Shaping of American Anthropology, 1882–1911: A Franz Boas Reader* (New York: Basic Books, 1974). One of Stocking's earliest essays, "Franz Boas and the Culture Concept in Historical Perspective," *American Anthropologist*, n.s., 68, no.4 (1966): 867–82, remains a subtly perceptive analysis of Boas's "transitional" role, although Stocking's later works have added depth and factual richness to his insights. Regna Darnell, "Hallowell's Bear Ceremonialism," *Ethos* 5 (1977): 14–30, derives from Irving Hallowell's first major monograph (discussed in chapter 3) some good insights into Boasianism. Joan Mark, *Four Anthropologists: An American Science in Its Early Years* (New York: Science History Publications, 1980), offers some judicious insights, especially in the chapter on Frederic Ward Putnam. She seems to me correct in asserting that Boas has received all the credit for developing a historical method in opposition to the evolutionary speculations of nineteenth-century anthropologists, yet Putnam, who sponsored Boas in America and was largely responsible for launching his career, had already adopted a historical approach. Mark is also justified in pointing out that Boas and his followers tended not to give adequate credit to the originality of some earlier American anthropologists. "Boasian anthropology," however, has become the appropriate term for distinguishing twentieth-century American anthropological developments from the various European schools, and it is fair to say that it is Boasian anthropology which in the 1960s – with linguists and anthropologists such as Dell Hymes, Barre Toelken, and Dennis Tedlock and critics such as Jarold Ramsey – began "revising" in ways that make possible improved understanding of the form and meaning of American Indian myths.

7. An excellent factual corrective to the romanticizing of French anthropology by metaethnographic commentators – such as George Marcus and Michael Fischer, *Anthropology as Cultural Critique* (Chicago: University of Chicago Press, 1986); James Clifford, *The Predicament of Culture* (Cambridge: Harvard University Press, 1988); and Edward Said, *Culture and Imperialism* (New York: Vintage, 1994) – may be found in Ruth Larson, "Ethnography, Thievery, and Cultural Identity: A Rereading of Michael Leiris's *L'Afrique fantôme*," *PMLA* 112, no.2 (1997): 229–42.

8. William Dean Howells, *Letters of an Altrurian Traveller (1893–94)* (Gainesville FL: Scholars Facsimiles and Reprints, 1961), 24.

9. Fredi Chiappelli, ed., *First Images of America: The Impact of the New World on the Old*, 2 vols. (Berkeley: University of California Press, 1976), is a fine collection, including Antonello Gerbi's valuable "The Earliest Accounts of the New World" (37–43). The climatological explanation of culture reached its first peak with the Scottish Enlightenment, notably manifested in William Robertson's *History of America* (1777), which Edmund Burke praised as displaying simultaneously diverse cultural levels, from barbaric savagery to refined European enlightenment, thus turning history into a "Great Map of Mankind." Edmund Burke's view that cultural hierarchies could then be represented in the same fashion as geographic features appears in many of his contemporaries, Turgot, for example, with its implications succinctly articulated by Sir James Mackintosh's observation in 1798 that History "is now a museum."

10. The contrastive development of contemporaneous Freudian psychology to Boasian anthropology is instructive. Freudian psychology not only was from the first "scientifically" oriented as metahistorical, claiming to articulate principles that transcended sociocultural distinctions, but also tended toward dogmatism. Boas was not himself lacking in paternalistic arrogance, but "Boasians" by the very act of "anthropologizing" in America entered instantly and inescapably into the practice of cultural history – celebrating, for an obvious example, the discovery of unique survivors of distinct cultures. Still more important was their determination to investigate culture even when unsure of what culture might be. This produced not only a bias toward empiricism rather than theorizing but also a healthy self-questioning and examination of their own intellectual practices which undercut dogmatic faiths – contributing usefully to the revisionary translation practices of the last thirty years, which have extended and refined our understanding of the functions of mythic narratives.

11. On the controversy, see (besides Stocking), the excellent study by Curtis M. Hinsley Jr., *The Smithsonian Institution and the Development of American Anthropology, 1845–1910* (Washington DC: Smithsonian Press, 1981). Mark also com-

ments cogently on Boas's changing attitudes toward museums (*Four Anthropologists*, 48–49). Otis Mason described the "Ethnological Exhibit of the Smithsonian Institution at the World's Columbian Exhibition" in *Memoirs of the International Congress of Anthropology*, ed. C. Stanford Walse (Chicago: Schulte, 1894), 208–16 (the congress was held in conjunction with the fair).

The full story of Indians and the 1893 exposition is more complex than my focus on Boas suggests. The fair's "Plaisance" offered several commercialized displays of Indian savagery, including a reenactment of the massacre at Fort Dearborn. The fair's organizers denied a place at the opening ceremonies to the Pottawattamie Chief Simon Pokagon, who made impressive claims to be heard. His father had sold the land upon which Chicago (*She-gog-gong*, Algonquin for skunk) was built, and the Pokagons had camped and hunted on the grounds of the "White City." Simon spent most of his life trying (finally successfully) to get the whites to pay most of what they had promised his father. Barred from speaking at the opening, Pokagon published (on birchbark) "The Red Man's Rebuke," setting forth Indian grievances so effectively that he was invited as principal honoree for "Chicago" day at the exposition. On that occasion Chicago's mayor promised that "Chicago will keep untarnished the site the Indians have given us," and announced that he had Indian blood in his own veins – a remarkable proclamation by a public official in 1893.

12. See the volume edited by Woodbury, Henry, and Webster, *Concerning the League* (from which I have excerpted the episode of Tekanawita and the cannibal), 23–28.

13. The impressive Iroquoian Ritual of Condolence, the ceremony by which a new member of the intertribal council of fifty is installed to replace one who has died (assuming his predecessor's name, so that the council continues to consist of its original "mythic" members), continually emphasizes this relation of physical and individualized perception with "spiritual" and socialized significance. Spiritual or psychic transformation among Indian peoples almost always takes a material form. A reason for this is that each oral enactment of a myth makes the telling situation itself one of transformation in which both the individuals involved and their society can be renewed, remade.

2
Mythic Imagining

Blackfoot[1]

The Sand Hills

ANONYMOUS

Once a man was hunting buffalo near the Sand Hills [Badlands]. That is where the dead go. He killed a buffalo and when he went up to butcher it, he saw a man come towards him, whom he knew to be a dead man. He was very much afraid, so he said to the dead man, "Now I will divide up this buffalo with you, but first I must go back there and bring up my pack-horses. You can go on with the butchering." The man lied, for as soon as he reached his horse he mounted and galloped away. A long time after this, the man was back in the same part of the country, and thought to himself, "I will go to get the arrow-points I left at the place where I killed the buffalo." When he came to the place, he found the skeleton of the buffalo and also his arrow-points. As he looked up he saw the same man he had seen before. The man spoke to him and said, "My friend, where have you been? I have been waiting for you all this time." This frightened the man so much that he sprang upon his horse and galloped away at great speed. Shortly after he returned to his camp, he took sick and died.

Mythology of the Blackfoot Indians, comp. and ed. Clark Wissler and D. C. Duvall, Anthropological Papers of the American Museum of Natural History 2, pt.1 (New York, 1908), 163.

Yurok[2]

Pulekukwerek and Thunder and Blood Money

JULIA WILSON AND KATE OF WAHSEK

There was a flood. Before this the world had been smooth and level; afterwards it was rough. This is how it happened. A young Thunder went out and was killed. The Thunders did not know what had killed him; they had thought that no one was left. They were angry. It began to storm constantly. There was a great wind, the sky was torn, and rocks were flying about.

Then Pulekukwerek went south to Humboldt Bay. Here the man lived who had killed the Thunder. Pulekukwerek wanted to make him pay (blood money). He found him, his house all blown away, lying with one board to cover him. Pulekukwerek told him that he should offer to settle for the Thunder. Then Pulekukwerek went up to the sky to tender the payment. The Thunders saw him coming, thought he was the murderer, and prepared to kill him. He said, "I know what you want to do. but if you try to hurt me, I will swallow the place where you are. Take this pay for the dead one or you will all be killed." Then they accepted his settlement, and the storm stopped. That is why people pay when they have killed. If the Thunders had not accepted there would be no settlement now. Then Pulekukwerek also repaired the rents in the sky.

A. L. Kroeber, *Yurok Myths*, ed. Grace Buzaljko (Berkeley: University of California Press, 1976), 321;

Yurok

Origin of Blood Money Settlement

JACK OF MUREK

Thunder's boy was killed. That is how it came about that those who are killed get paid for. When his son was killed, Thunder took settlement. He said, "I want you all, when your relative is killed, and they come to pay for him, to take those dentalia. That is why I am going to accept it now: I want it to be offered to all of you. When they have paid you, hide the money somewhere. Sometimes, when you want to see your dentalia, and go to look at them, you will feel sorry because you will remember your poor kinsman who was killed.

A. L. Kroeber, *Yurok Myths*, ed. Grace Buzaljko (Berkeley: University of California Press, 1976), 364;

Yurok

Money Eats the Sky

WILLIAM JOHNSON

Once all things were alive. Baskets were people, dentalia were people, and all other things were people. Now the *woge* knew that they must all leave: they were already in the sweathouse talking about it. Some said they were going to the sky. Others said that they would go off to the mountains.

But Dentalium said, "I will not go. I wish to live where I am. I shall stay." Now he who had said they must go asked, "What shall you be able to do? You are very small." Dentalium said, "I know it. I am small, but it would be a bad thing if I went off. People would not live well. They would kill one another, and they would have no way of settling the feud. So I shall remain here." Then he began to suck in and swallow the sky (to show his power) and ate most of it. Then that one said, "Stop!" So Dentalium remained, and is kept in purses by human beings.

A. L. Kroeber, *Yurok Myths*, ed. Grace Buzaljko (Berkeley: University of California Press, 1976), 438;

Pulekukwerek Institutes Blood Money

LAME BILLY OF WEITSPUS

Wohpekumeu was going downstream. Looking back, he saw a man following. That one carried a quiver, drew out arrows, held them in his teeth, took his bow in his hand, and looked about him. Wopekumeu thought, "He looks like Pulekukwerek." He watched him. He saw him approach a man and shoot. The man fell. Then that one went on.

Wohpekumeu followed his tracks. He came to a large tree and the tracks stopped. Wohpekumeu looked on this side and on that side of the tree but could find no more tracks. Then he heard someone above him. "Here I am." Pulekukwerek was in the tree. "Why did you do that?" asked Wohpekumeu. "I did it in order that they may not kill each other too much, that they may not kill all the time," said Pulekukwerek. "Take this and go and tell them to accept it in settlement." He gave him dentalium money.

Then Wohpekumeu went where they were mourning for the dead man. He said, "Accept a settlement. He will give you woodpecker crests and boats and money, whatever you like. Ask for what you want and he will pay you." Then they were persuaded and said, "I want this and that," and received it.

Now Pulekukwerek said, "I have made it that it is good. Now they will not kill often. When they do kill one another, they will settle for it and that will be the end. If anyone does not pay he will die in ten days. Even while they were crying I nearly fell off the tree. I was so weak that I could hardly hold my place."

A. L. Kroeber, *Yurok Myths*, ed. Grace Buzaljko (Berkeley: University of California Press, 1976), 140;

Blackfoot

Scarface: Origin of the Medicine Lodge

CORA M. ROSS

I

In the earliest times there was no war. All the tribes were at peace. In those days there was a man who had a daughter, a very beautiful girl. Many young men wanted to marry her, but every time she was asked, she only shook her head and said she did not want a husband.

"How is this?" asked her father. "Some of these young men are rich, handsome, and brave."

"Why should I marry?" replied the girl. "I have a rich father and mother. Our lodge is good. The parfleches are never empty. There are plenty of tanned robes and soft furs for winter. Why worry me, then?"

The Raven Bearers held a dance; they all dressed carefully and wore their ornaments, and each one tried to dance the best. Afterwards some of them asked for this girl, but still she said no. Then the Bulls, the Kit-foxes, and others of the *I-kun-uh'-kah-tsi*† held their dances, and all those who were rich, many great warriors, asked this man for his daughter, but to every one of them she said no. Then her father was angry, and said: "Why, now, this way? All the best men have asked for you, and still you say no. I believe you have a secret lover."

"Ah!" said her mother. "What shame for us should a child be born and our daughter still unmarried!" "Father! mother!" replied the girl, "pity me. I have no secret lover, but now hear the truth. That Above Person, the Sun, told me, 'Do not marry any of those men, for you are mine; thus you shall be happy, and live to great age'; and again he said, 'Take heed. You must not marry. You are mine.'"

George Bird Grinnell, *Blackfoot Lodge Tales: The Story of a Prairie People* (1892; Lincoln: University of Nebraska Press, 1962, 93–103. Footnotes are Grinnell's unless otherwise identified.

†"All Comrades," an association made up of members of a number of societies whose main function was to punish offenses but which also served to organize military expeditions and to assist the needy. – KK

"Ah!" replied her father. "It must always be as he says." And they talked no more about it.

There was a poor young man, very poor. His father, mother, all his relations, had gone to the Sand Hills. He had no lodge, no wife to tan his robes or sew his moccasins. He stopped in one lodge to-day, and to-morrow he ate and slept in another; thus he lived. He was a good-looking young man, except that on his cheek he had a scar, and his clothes were always old and poor.

After those dances some of the young men met this poor Scarface, and they laughed at him, and said: "Why don't you ask that girl to marry you? You are so rich and handsome!" Scarface did not laugh; he replied: "Ah! I will do as you say. I will go and ask her." All the young men thought this was funny. They laughed a great deal. But Scarface went down by the river. He waited by the river, where the women came to get water, and by and by the girl came along. "Girl," he said, "wait. I want to speak with you. Not as a designing person do I ask you, but openly, where the Sun looks down, and all may see."

"Speak then," said the girl.

"I have seen the days," continued the young man. "You have refused those who are young, and rich, and brave. Now, to-day, they laughed and said to me, 'Why do you not ask her?' I am poor, very poor. I have no lodge, no food, no clothes, no robes and warm furs. I have no relations; all have gone to the Sand Hills; yet, now, to-day, I ask you, take pity, be my wife."

The girl hid her face in her robe and brushed the ground with the point of her moccasin, back and forth, back and forth; for she was thinking. After a time she said: "True. I have refused all those rich young men, yet now the poor one asks me, and I am glad. I will be your wife, and my people will be happy. You are poor, but it does not matter. My father will give you dogs. My mother will make us a lodge. My people will give us robes and furs. You will be poor no longer."

Then the young man was happy, and he started to kiss her, but she held him back, and said: "Wait! The Sun has spoken to me. He says I may not marry; that I belong to him. He says if I listen to him, I shall live to great age. But now I say: Go to the Sun. Tell him, 'She whom you spoke with heeds your words. She has never done wrong, but now she wants to marry. I want her for my wife.' Ask him to take that scar from your face. That will be his sign. I will know he is pleased. But if he refuses, or if you fail to find his lodge, then do not return to me."

"Oh!" cried the young man, "at first your words were good. I was glad. But now it is dark. My heart is dead. Where is that far-off lodge? where the trail, which no one yet has travelled?"

"Take courage, take courage!" said the girl; and she went to her lodge.

II

Scarface was very sad. He sat down and covered his head with his robe and tried to think what to do. After a while he got up, and went to an old woman who had been kind to him. "Pity me," he said. "I am very poor. I am going away now on a long journey. Make me some moccasins."

"Where are you going?" asked the old woman. "There is no war; we are very peaceful here."

"I do not know where I shall go," replied Scarface. "I am in trouble, but I cannot tell you now what it is."

So the old woman made him some moccasins, seven pairs, with parfleche soles, and also she gave him a sack of food, – pemmican of berries, pounded meat, and dried back fat; for this old woman had a good heart. She liked the young man.

All alone, and with a sad heart, he climbed the bluffs and stopped to take a last look at the camp. He wondered if he would ever see his sweetheart and the people again. "*Hai'-yu!* Pity me, O Sun," he prayed, and turning, he started to find the trail.

For many days he travelled on, over great prairies, along timbered rivers and among the mountains, and every day his sack of food grew lighter; but he saved it as much as he could, and ate berries, and roots, and sometimes he killed an animal of some kind. One night he stopped by the home of a wolf. "*Hai-yah!*" said that one; "what is my brother doing so far from home?"

"Ah!" replied Scarface, "I seek the place where the Sun lives; I am sent to speak with him."

"I have travelled far," said the wolf. "I know all the prairies, the valleys, and the mountains, but I have never seen the Sun's home. Wait; I know one who is very wise. Ask the bear. He may tell you."

The next day the man travelled on again, stopping now and then to pick a few berries, and when night came he arrived at the bear's lodge.

"Where is your home?" asked the bear. "Why are you travelling alone, my brother?"

"Help me! Pity me!" replied the young man; "because of her words† I seek the Sun. I go to ask him for her."

"I know not where he stops," replied the bear. "I have travelled by many rivers, and I know the mountains, yet I have never seen his lodge. There is some one beyond, that striped-face, who is very smart. Go and ask him."

The badger was in his hole. Stooping over, the young man shouted: "Oh, cunning striped-face! Oh, generous animal! I wish to speak with you."

"What do you want?" said the badger, poking his head out of the hole.

"I want to find the Sun's home," replied Scarface. "I want to speak with him."

"I do not know where he lives," replied the badger. "I never travel very far. Over there in the timber is a wolverine. He is always travelling around, and is of much knowledge. Maybe he can tell you."

Then Scarface went to the woods and looked all around for the wolverine, but could not find him. So he sat down to rest. "*Hai'-yu! Hai'-yu!*" he cried. "Wolverine, take pity on me. My food is gone, my moccasins worn out. Now I must die."

"What is it, my brother?" he heard, and looking around, he saw the animal sitting near.

"She whom I would marry," said Scarface, "belongs to the Sun; I am trying to find where he lives, to ask him for her."

"Ah!" said the wolverine. "I know where he lives. Wait; it is nearly night. To-morrow I will show you the trail to the big water. He lives on the other side of it."

Early in the morning, the wolverine showed him the trail, and Scarface followed it until he came to the water's edge. He looked out over it, and his heart almost stopped. Never before had any one seen such a big water. The other side could not be seen, and there was no end to it. Scarface sat down on the shore. His food was all gone, his moccasins worn out. His heart was sick. "I cannot cross this big water," he said. "I cannot return to the people. Here, by this water, I shall die."

Not so. His Helpers were there. Two swans came swimming up to the shore. "Why have you come here?" they asked him. "What are you doing? It is very far to the place where your people live."

†A Blackfoot often talks of what this or that person said, without mentioning names.

"I am here," replied Scarface, "to die. Far away, in my country, is a beautiful girl. I want to marry her, but she belongs to the Sun. So I started to find him and ask for her. I have travelled many days. My food is gone. I cannot go back. I cannot cross this big water, so I am going to die."

"No," said the swans; "it shall not be so. Across this water is the home of that Above Person. Get on our backs, and we will take you there."

Scarface quickly arose. He felt strong again. He waded out into the water and lay down on the swans' backs, and they started off. Very deep and black is that fearful water. Strange people live there, mighty animals which often seize and drown a person. The swans carried him safely, and took him to the other side. Here was a broad hard trail leading back from the water's edge.

"*Kyi*," said the swans. "You are now close to the Sun's lodge. Follow that trail, and you will soon see it."

III

Scarface started up the trail, and pretty soon he came to some beautiful things, lying in it. There was a war shirt, a shield, and a bow and arrows. He had never seen such pretty weapons; but he did not touch them. He walked carefully around them, and travelled on. A little way further on, he met a young man, the handsomest person he had ever seen. His hair was very long, and he wore clothing made of strange skins. His moccasins were sewn with bright colored feathers. The young man said to him, "Did you see some weapons lying on the trail?"

"Yes," replied Scarface; "I saw them."

"But did you not touch them?" asked the young man.

"No; I thought some one had left them there, so I did not take them."

"You are not a thief," said the young man. "What is your name?"

"Scarface."

"Where are you going?"

"To the Sun."

"My name," said the young man, "is A-pi-su'-ahts.[†] The Sun is my father; come, I will take you to our lodge. My father is not now at home, but he will come in at night."

Soon they came to the lodge. It was very large and handsome; strange medicine animals were painted on it. Behind, on a tripod, were strange weapons and beautiful clothes – the Sun's. Scarface was

[†]Early Riser, i.e., the Morning Star.

ashamed to go in, but Morning Star said, "Do not be afraid, my friend; we are glad you have come."

They entered. One person was sitting there, Ko-ko-mik'-e-is,[†] the Sun's wife, Morning Star's mother. She spoke to Scarface kindly, and gave him something to eat. "Why have you come so far from your people?" she asked.

Then Scarface told her about the beautiful girl he wanted to marry. "She belongs to the Sun," he said. "I have come to ask him for her."

When it was time for the Sun to come home, the Moon hid Scarface under a pile of robes. As soon as the Sun got to the doorway, he stopped, and said, "I smell a person."

"Yes, father," said Morning Star; "a good young man has come to see you. I know he is good, for he found some of my things on the trail and did not touch them."

Then Scarface came out from under the robes, and the Sun entered and sat down. "I am glad you have come to our lodge," he said. "Stay with us as long as you think best. My son is lonesome sometimes; be his friend."

The next day the Moon called Scarface out of the lodge, and said to him: "Go with Morning Star where you please, but never hunt near that big water; do not let him go there. It is the home of great birds which have long sharp bills; they kill people. I have had many sons, but these birds have killed them all. Morning Star is the only one left."

So Scarface stayed there a long time and hunted with Morning Star. One day they came near the water, and saw the big birds.

"Come," said Morning Star; "let us go and kill those birds."

"No, no!" replied Scarface; "we must not go there. Those are very terrible birds; they will kill us."

Morning Star would not listen. He ran towards the water, and Scarface followed. He knew that he must kill the birds and save the boy. If not, the Sun would be angry and might kill him. He ran ahead and met the birds, which were coming towards him to fight, and killed every one of them with his spear: not one was left. Then the young men cut off their heads, and carried them home. Morning Star's mother was glad when they told her what they had done, and showed her the birds' heads. She cried, and called Scarface "my son." When the Sun came home at night, she told him about it, and he too was glad. "My son," he

[†]Night Red Light, the Moon.

said to Scarface, "I will not forget what you have this day done for me. Tell me now, what can I do for you?"

"*Hai'-yu,*" replied Scarface. "*Hai'-yu,* pity me. I am here to ask you for that girl. I want to marry her. I asked her, and she was glad; but she says you own her, that you told her not to marry."

"What you say is true," said the Sun. "I have watched the days, so I know it. Now, then, I give her to you; she is yours. I am glad she has been wise. I know she has never done wrong. The Sun pities good women. They shall live a long time. So shall their husbands and children. Now you will soon go home. Let me tell you something. Be wise and listen: I am the only chief. Everything is mine. I made the earth, the mountains, prairies, rivers, and forests. I made the people and all the animals. This is why I say I alone am the chief. I can never die. True, the winter makes me old and weak, but every summer I grow young again."

Then said the Sun: "What one of all animals is smartest? The raven is, for he always finds food. He is never hungry. Which one of all the animals is most *Nat-o'-ye?*† The buffalo is. Of all animals, I like him best. He is for the people. He is your food and your shelter. What part of his body is sacred? The tongue is. That is mine. What else is sacred? Berries are. They are mine too. Come with me and see the world." He took Scarface to the edge of the sky, and they looked down and saw it. It is round and flat, and all around the edge is the jumping-off place [or walls straight down]. Then said the Sun: "When any man is sick or in danger, his wife may promise to build me a lodge, if he recovers. If the woman is pure and true, then I will be pleased and help the man. But if she is bad, if she lies, then I will be angry. You shall build the lodge like the world, round, with walls, but first you must build a sweathouse of a hundred sticks. It shall be like the sky [a hemisphere], and half of it shall be painted red. That is me. The other half you will paint black. That is the night."

Further said the Sun: "Which is the best, the heart or the brain? The brain is. The heart often lies, the brain never." Then he told Scarface everything about making the Medicine Lodge, and when he had finished, he rubbed a powerful medicine on his face, and the scar disappeared. Then he gave him two raven feathers, saying: "These are the

†This word may be translated as "of the Sun," "having Sun power," or more properly, something sacred. Cf. the end of the following narrative. – KK

sign for the girl, that I give her to you. They must always be worn by the husband of the woman who builds a Medicine Lodge."

The young man was now ready to return home. Morning Star and the Sun gave him many beautiful presents. The Moon cried and kissed him, and called him "my son." Then the Sun showed him the short trail. It was the Wolf Road (Milky Way). He followed it, and soon reached the ground.

IV

It was a very hot day. All the lodge skins were raised, and the people sat in the shade. There was a chief, a very generous man, and all day long people kept coming to his lodge to feast and smoke with him. Early in the morning this chief saw a person sitting out on a butte near by, close wrapped in his robe. The chief's friends came and went, the sun reached the middle, and passed on, down towards the mountains. Still this person did not move. When it was almost night, the chief said: "Why does that person sit there so long? The heat has been strong, but he has never eaten nor drunk. He may be a stranger; go and ask him in."

So some young men went up to him, and said: "Why do you sit here in the great heat all day? Come to the shade of the lodges. The chief asks you to feast with him."

Then the person arose and threw off his robe, and they were surprised. He wore beautiful clothes. His bow, shield, and other weapons were of strange make. But they knew his face, although the scar was gone, and they ran ahead, shouting, "The scarface poor young man has come. He is poor no longer. The scar on his face is gone."

All the people rushed out to see him. "Where have you been?" they asked. "Where did you get all these pretty things?" He did not answer. There in the crowd stood that young woman; and taking the two raven feathers from his head, he gave them to her, and said: "The trail was very long, and I nearly died, but by those Helpers, I found his lodge. He is glad. He sends these feathers to you. They are the sign."

Great was her gladness then. They were married, and made the first Medicine Lodge, as the Sun had said. The Sun was glad. He gave them great age. They were never sick. When they were very old, one morning, their children said: "Awake! Rise and eat." They did not move. In the night, in sleep, without pain, their shadows had departed for the Sand Hills.

Blackfoot

Legend of Star Boy (Later, Poïa, Scarface)

BRINGS-DOWN-THE-SUN

"There are two bright stars," Brings-Down-the-Sun said, "that sometimes rise together, just before the sun comes up, Morning Star and Young Morning Star or Star Boy (referring to the conjunction of the planets Venus and Jupiter before daybreak). I will tell you the story of these two Morning Stars, as it was related to my by my father, having been handed down to him through many generations.

"We know not when the Sun-dance had its origin. It was long ago, when the Blackfeet used dogs for beasts of burden instead of horses; when they stretched the legs and bodies of their dogs on sticks to make them large, and when they used stones instead of wooden pegs to hold down their lodges. In those days, during the moon of flowers (early summer), our people were camped near the mountains. It was a cloudless night and a warm wind blew over the prairie. Two young girls were sleeping in the long grass outside the lodge. Before daybreak, the eldest sister, So-at-sa-ki (Feather Woman), awoke. The Morning Star was just rising from the prairie. He was very beautiful, shining through the clear air of early morning. She lay gazing at this wonderful star, until he seemed very close to her, and she imagined that he was her lover. Finally she awoke her sister, exclaiming, 'Look at the Morning Star! He is beautiful and must be very wise. Many of the young men have wanted to marry me, but I love only the Morning Star.' When the leaves were turning yellow (autumn), So-at-sa-ki became very unhappy, finding herself with child. She was a pure maiden, although not knowing the father of her child. When the people discovered her secret, they taunted and ridiculed her, until she wanted to die. One day while the geese were flying southward, So-at-sa-ki went along to the river for water. As she was returning home, she beheld a young man standing before her in the trail. She modestly turned aside to pass, but he put forth

Walter McClintock, *The Old North Trail* (London: Macmillan, 1910), 491–503.

his hand, as if to detain her, and she said angrily, 'Stand aside! None of the young men have ever before dared to stop me.' He replied, 'I am the Morning Star. One night, during the moon of flowers, I beheld you sleeping in the open and loved you. I have now come to ask you to return with me to the sky, to the lodge of my father, the Sun, where we will live together, and you will have no more trouble.'

"Then So-at-sa-ki remembered the night in spring, when she slept outside the lodge, and now realised that Morning Star was her husband. She saw in his hair a yellow plume, and in his hand a juniper branch with a spider web hanging from one end. He was tall and straight and his hair was long and shining. His beautiful clothes were of soft-tanned skins, and from them came a fragrance of pine and sweet grass. So-at-sa-ki replied hesitatingly, 'I must first say farewell to my father and mother.' But Morning Star allowed her to speak to no one. Fastening the feather in her hair and giving her the juniper branch to hold, he directed her to shut her eyes. She held the upper strand of the spider web in her hand and placed her feet upon the lower one. When he told her to open her eyes, she was in the sky. They were standing together before a large lodge. Morning Star said, 'This is the home of my father and mother, the Sun and the Moon,' and bade her enter. It was day-time and the Sun was away on his long journey, but the Moon was at home. Morning Star addressed his mother saying, 'One night I beheld this girl sleeping on the prairie. I loved her and she is now my wife.' The Moon welcomed So-at-sa-ki to their home. In the evening, when the Sun Chief came home, he also gladly received her. The Moon clothed So-at-sa-ki in a soft-tanned buckskin dress, trimmed with elk-teeth. She also presented her with wristlets of elk-teeth and an elk-skin robe, decorated with the sacred paint, saying, 'I give you these because you have married our son.' So-at-sa-ki lived happily in the sky with Morning Star, and learned many wonderful things. When her child was born, they called him Star Boy. The Moon then gave So-at-sa-ki a root digger, saying, 'This should be used only by pure women. You can dig all kinds of roots with it, but I warn you not to dig up the large turnip growing near the home of the Spider Man. You have now a child and it would bring unhappiness to us all.'

"Everywhere So-at-sa-ki went, she carried her baby and the root digger. She often saw the large turnip, but was afraid to touch it. One day, while passing the wonderful turnip, she thought of the mysterious warning of the Moon, and became curious to see what might be underneath. Laying her baby on the ground, she dug until her root digger stuck fast. Two large cranes came flying from the east. So-at-sa-ki besought them to help her. Thrice she called in vain, but upon the fourth call, they circled and lighted beside her. The chief crane sat upon one side of the turnip and his wife on the other. He took hold of the turnip with his long sharp bill, and moved it backwards and forwards, singing the medicine song,

'This root is sacred. Wherever I dig, my roots are sacred.'

"He repeated this song to the north, south, east and west. After the fourth song he pulled up the turnip. So-at-sa-ki looked through the hole and beheld the earth. Although she had not known it, the turnip had filled the same hole, through which Morning Star had brought her into the sky. Looking down, she saw the camp of the Blackfeet, where she had lived. She sat for a long while gazing at the old familiar scenes. The young men were playing games. The women were tanning hides and making lodges, gathering berries on the hills, and crossing the meadows to the river for water. When she turned to go home, she was crying, for she felt lonely, and longed to be back again upon the green prairies with her own people. When So-at-sa-ki arrived at the lodge, Morning Star and his mother were waiting. As soon as Morning Star looked at his wife, he exclaimed, 'You have dug up the sacred turnip!' When she did not reply, the Moon said, 'I warned you not to dig up the turnip, because I love Star Boy and do not wish to part with him.' Nothing more was said, because it was day-time and the great Sun Chief was still away on his long journey. In the evening, when he entered the lodge, he exclaimed, 'What is the matter with my daughter? She looks sad and must be in trouble.' So-at-sa-ki replied, 'Yes, I am homesick, because I have to-day looked down upon my people.' Then the Sun Chief was angry and said to Morning Star, 'If she has disobeyed, you must send her home.' The Moon interceded for So-at-sa-ki, but the Sun answered, 'She can no longer be happy with us. It is better for her to return to her own people.' Morning Star led So-at-sa-ki to the home of the Spider Man, whose web had drawn her up to the sky. He placed on her head the sacred Medicine Bonnet, which is worn only by pure women. He laid Star Boy on her breast, and wrapping them both in the elk-skin robe, bade her farewell, saying, 'We will let you down into the centre of the Indian camp and the people will behold you as you come from the sky.' The Spider Man then carefully let them down through the hole to the earth.

"It was an evening in midsummer, during the moon when the berries are ripe, when So-at-sa-ki was let down from the sky. Many of the people were outside their lodges, when suddenly they beheld a bright light in the northern sky. They saw it pass across the heavens and watched, until it sank to the ground. When the Indians reached the place, where the star had fallen, they saw a strange looking bundle. When the elk-skin cover was opened, they found a woman and her child. So-at-sa-ki was recognized by her parents. She returned to their lodge and lived with them, but never was happy. She used to go with Star Boy to the summit of a high ridge, where she sat and mourned for her husband. One night she remained alone upon the ridge. Before daybreak, when Morning Star arose from the plains, she begged him to take her back. Then he spoke to her, 'You disobeyed and therefore cannot return to the sky. Your sin is the cause of your sorrow and has brought trouble to you and your people.'

"Before So-at-sa-ki died, she told all these things to her father and mother, just as I now tell them to you. Star Boy's grandparents also died. Although born in the home of the Sun, he was very poor. He had no clothes, not even moccasins to wear. He was so timid and shy that he never played with other children. When the Blackfeet moved camp, he always followed barefoot, far behind the rest of the tribe. He feared to travel with the other people, because the other boys stoned and abused him. On his face was a mysterious scar, which became more marked as he grew older. He was ridiculed by everyone and in derision was called Poïa (Scarface).

"When Poïa became a young man, he loved a maiden of his own tribe. She was very beautiful and the daughter of a leading chief. Many of the young men wanted to marry her, but she refused them all. Poïa sent this maiden a present, with the message that he wanted to marry her, but she was proud and disdained his love. She scornfully told him, she would not accept him as her lover, until he would remove the scar from his face. Scarface was deeply grieved by the reply. He consulted with an old medicine woman, his only friend. She revealed to him, that the scar had been placed on his face by the Sun God, and that only the Sun himself could remove it. Poïa resolved to go to the home of the Sun God. The medicine woman made moccasins for him and gave him a supply of pemmican.

"Poïa journeyed alone across the plains and through the mountains, enduring many hardships and great dangers. Finally he came to the Big Water (Pacific Ocean). For three days and three nights he lay upon the shore, fasting and praying to the Sun God. On the evening of the fourth day, he beheld a bright trail leading across the water. He travelled this path until he drew near the home of the Sun, when he hid himself and waited. In the morning, the great Sun Chief came from his lodge, ready for his daily journey. He did not recognise Poïa. Angered at beholding a creature from the earth, he said to the Moon, his wife, 'I will kill him, for he comes from a good-for-nothing-race,' but she interceded and saved his life. Morning Star, their only son, a young man with a handsome face and beautifully dressed, came forth from the lodge. He brought with him dried sweet grass, which he burned as incense. He first placed Poïa in the sacred smoke, and then led him into the presence of his father and mother, the Sun and Moon. Poïa related the story of his long journey, because of his rejection by the girl he loved. Morning Star then saw how sad and worn he looked. He felt sorry for him and promised to help him.

"Poïa lived in the lodge of the Sun and Moon with Morning Star. Once, when they were hunting together, Poïa killed seven enormous birds, which had threatened the life of Morning Star. He presented four of the dead birds to the Sun and three to the Moon. The Sun rejoiced, when he knew that the dangerous birds were killed, and the Moon felt so grateful, that she besought her husband to repay him. On the intercession of Morning Star, the Sun God consented to remove the scar. He also appointed Poïa as his messenger to the Blackfeet, promising, if they would give a festival (Sun-dance) in his honor, once every year, he would restore their sick to health. He taught Poïa the secrets of the Sun-dance, and instructed him in the prayers and songs to be used. He gave him two raven feathers to wear as a sign that he came from the Sun, and a robe of soft-tanned elk-skin, with the warning that it must be worn only by a virtuous woman. She can then give the Sun-dance and the sick will recover. Morning Star gave him a magic flute and a wonderful song, with which he would be able to charm the heart of the girl he loved.

"Poïa returned to the earth and the Blackfeet camp by the Wolf Trail (Milky Way), the short path to the earth. When he had fully instructed his people concerning the Sun-dance, the Sun God took him back to the sky with the girl he loved. When Poïa returned to the home of the

Sun, the Sun God made him bright and beautiful, just like his father, Morning Star. In those days Morning Star and his son could be seen together in the east. Because Poïa appears first in the sky, the Blackfeet often mistake him for his father, and he is therefore sometimes called Poks-o-piks-o-aks, Mistake Morning Star.

"I remember," continued Brings-Down-the-Sun, "when I was a young man, seeing these two bright stars rising, one after the other, before the Sun. Then, if we were going on a war, or hunting expedition, my father would awake me, saying, 'My son, I see Morning Star and Young Morning Star in the sky above the prairie. Day will soon break and it is time we were started.' For many years these stars have travelled apart. I have also seen them together in the evening sky. They went down after the sun. This summer, Morning Star and Poïa are again travelling together. I see them in the eastern sky, rising together over the prairie before dawn. Poïa comes up first. His father, Morning Star, rises soon afterwards, and then his grandfather, the Sun.

"Morning Star was given to us as a sign to herald the coming of the Sun. When he appears above the horizon, we know a new day is about to dawn. Many medicine men have dreamed of the Sun, and of the Moon, but I have never yet heard of one so powerful as to dream of Morning Star, because he shows himself in the sky for such a short time.

"The 'Star that stands still' (North Star) is different from other stars, because it never moves. All the other stars walk around it. It is a hole in the sky, the same hole through which So-at-sa-ki was first drawn up to the sky and then let down again to earth. It is the hole, through which she gazed upon the earth, after digging up the forbidden turnip. Its light is the radiance from the home of the Sun God shining through. The half circle of stars to the east (Northern Crown) is the lodge of the Spider Man, and the five bright stars just beyond (in the constellation of Hercules) are his five fingers, with which he spun the web, upon which So-at-sa-ki was let down from the sky. Whenever you see the half-buried and overgrown circles, or clusters of stones on the plains, marking the sites of Blackfeet camps in the ancient days, when they used stones to hold down the sides of their lodges, you will know why the half-circle of stars was called by our fathers, 'The Lodge of the Spider Man.'

"When So-at-sa-ki came back to earth from the lodge of the Sun, she brought with her the sacred Medicine Bonnet and dress trimmed with elk-teeth, the Turnip Digger, Sweet Grass (incense), and the Prongs for lifting hot coals from the fire. Ever since those days, these sacred articles have been used in the Sun-dance by the woman who makes the vow. The Turnip Digger is always tied to the Medicine Case, containing the Medicine Bonnet, and it now hangs from the tripod behind my lodge."

Brings-Down-the-Sun then arose saying, "The Last Brother is now pointing towards the horizon. Day will soon dawn and it is time for us to sleep." As we turned to gaze at the constellation of the Great Bear, a ball of fire suddenly appeared high in the northern sky. It flashed across the heavens, leaving in its wake a beautiful light, and burst into a shower of sparks, as it vanished in the southern sky. The Indians were filled with awe and broke out in exclamations of wonder and of fear. Some said it was a Dusty Star (Meteor), others that it was too large for a Dusty Star, which is always small and looks like a star changing its place in the sky. Those, who were filled with dread, spoke of it in subdued whispers as Is-tsi, – "The Fire"; and said it was an omen of bad luck.

Brings-Down-the-Sun had been silent. When I asked his explanation of the strange sign, he said, "The Sun God is all powerful, he watches over every one and sees everything. The Great Mystery may have sent this wonderful star as a warning, that there will be much sickness during the coming winter, or, it may be a sign that a great chief has just died. By a great chief I mean a man who had a good heart and has lived a straight life." When Brings-Down-the-Sun had finished speaking, the North Piegans quietly withdrew to their lodges.

When I lay down on my blankets, beneath the big cottonwood, the moon had risen over Lookout Butte, and was shining upon my bed, through an opening in the trees. My mind was filled with thoughts of the poetical beauty of the legends I had just heard from Brings-Down-the-Sun; of the wonderful imagination of the ancient Blackfeet medicine men who originated them; of the brilliant beauty of the night skies, which had inspired them, and of the scrupulous care with which they had been handed down from father to son.

These inspiring thoughts about the heavens were rudely interrupted by my old enemy, Kops-ksis-e, the North Piegan watch dog. He came prowling through the trees, as if in search of lurking enemies. But he was really on a thieving expedition to our camp for food, creeping stealthily along, like a moving shadow in the moonlight. When he came very suddenly and unexpectedly on my bed, covered with white canvas, he was at first startled, and stood with half-suppressed growls, but when he discovered that it belonged to the white man, whom he had, from the first, hated and distrusted, his fear quickly changed to anger. With fierce barks and bristling hair, he advanced to drive me out. Fortunately, I understood the ways of Indian dogs. If I had shown any sign of fear, he would have attacked me with a sudden rush. But I seized a big stick, and went so quickly into action, that the thoroughly frightened Kops-ksis-e gave a series of frightened yelps and fled into the forest.

Returning to my blankets, I had no sooner fallen into a light sleep, than I was again aroused, by the sound of an Indian riding furiously down the steep embankment from the plain. When I heard him enter the woods, the thought at once flashed through my mind, that it was Bull Plume, the defeated medicine man, coming to make me the victim of some vindictive purpose, before I could leave his country.† My bed was near a small path, a short cut from the main trail, which ran around our camp. I heard the rider coming down the trail, until he had turned into the side path, which would bring him directly to my bed. Jumping from my blankets, I hid in the thick underbrush. When his horse came to my canvas, shining in the moonlight, it reared and with a snort plunged to one side. For a moment, the rider lost his balance and swayed, as if to fall, but, quickly recovering himself, he tried to force his horse across my bed. But the frightened animal went crashing aside into the underbrush and, to my great relief, disappeared in the forest, his rider singing a Wolf song until lost in the distance.

When the moon was high, I fell asleep. It seemed but a brief interval, until I was aroused, before daybreak, by Menake and Nitana preparing our morning meal. I rolled from my warm blankets into the chill air, with a "tired feeling." I was soon refreshed by a cold bath in the river and by the fresh air of the woods in the early dawn. Taking my lariat, I hurried past the silent white lodges of the north Piegans to the hills, where our horses were feeding. Passing from the shadows of the big trees to the open prairie, I was met by a gentle breeze, coming from the mountains, fragrant with the sweet odour of wild flowers and growing grass. I climbed Lookout Butte and, from its summit, saw the shadowy forms of our horses in a meadow nearby. On the eastern horizon I beheld the two magnificent planets, Venus and Jupiter, now in conjunction. Jupiter had risen first, and I realised that he was Poïa (Scarface), and that the other planet was his father, Morning Star.

†Bull Plume was a Piegan chief jealous of McClintock's friendship with Brings-Down-the-Sun because of the latter's superior prestige and knowledge of Blackfoot traditions. – KK

While driving the horses back to camp, I heard the distant cries of wolves and coyotes. The Rockies were beginning to flush with a soft rosy light, reflected from the eastern sky. Then the higher summits were touched by the first direct rays of the sun. The red glow crept slowly down, lighting up in turn the dark timbered slopes below, until, at length, the sun rose majestically above the plains, and the whole landscape was flooded with the brilliant and glorious light of a new day. Directly, there burst forth, on all sides, a bird chorus of wonderful harmony and gladness, as if all nature joined in welcoming the Sun God's coming.[†]

†This reference to the Sun God is meant to recall McClintock's earlier report of the speech of Blackfoot Mad Wolf at the conclusion of a Sun Dance (*The Old North Trail*), 322. – KK

Blackfoot

Excerpt from *Fools Crow*

JAMES WELCH

The woman knelt in a clearing beyond the alder grove. Her white dress was as bright as new snow in the blue light. She sat back on her heels and lifted her arms to the horizon on the eastern edge of the bowl. Beside her lay the bulging sack and before her, at her knees, lay the digging stick. She had fastened in her hair a yellow feather. In one hand she clutched a juniper bough. A spider's web was woven among the shiny fingers of the bough.

Fools Crow squatted at the edge of the clearing behind her, his back resting against an alder trunk. It was quiet in the bowl and he became aware, once again, of the absence of bird and animal. But as he thought this, he felt a presence behind him, a slow breathing. He turned his head quickly and saw the woman's dog, three paces behind and slightly to the side. The dog was sitting patiently, as though he had witnessed this scene in this clearing many times. Fools Crow looked into the dark eyes and the dog glanced at him, then returned his gaze to the woman.

"Sa-sak-si," whispered Fools Crow. "Come, Freckle-face."

The dog did not hesitate. He walked the few paces, then sat down beside Fools Crow.

"Tell me what your mistress is doing."

But the dog did not look at him.

Just then the woman began to sing. She sang softly, but her music filled the bowl; it was as though it were made to hold her song. The words echoed round and round, and Fools Crow was filled with awe.

James Welch, *Fools Crow* (New York: Viking, 1986). The excerpt begins on page 336 (chapter 31); after the space break, which marks the omission of chapter 32 (pages 339–48), a chapter that interrupts Fools Crow's visionary experience with accounts of his family's daily life, the quotation resumes at the beginning of chapter 33, including pages 349–59.

"There is my son, and there is Morning Star,
Together they ride forever, across the morning sky.
Many have wanted to marry me,
I love only Morning Star."

Three times she sang this, then three times more, and when Fools Crow looked up at the horizon before her, he saw Morning Star and his son, Poia, against the deep blue of the false dawn. The woman began to wail, and her wailing filled the bowl with the voices of a thousand geese, and Fools Crow closed his eyes and clapped his hands over his ears, but the sound was once again in him and he was outside of himself, a child again, staring at the wintry lake and the flashing wings.

And then the wailing stopped. Fools Crow opened his eyes, and Early Riser and Poia were gone. The horizon was streaked with the pale yellow of dawn. There was the sound of a drum, and the sky turned lighter and lighter, and then Sun Chief himself entered the bowl, casting his brilliant light down to the small clearing, and the clean night smells gave way to the dusty odors of the moon of the burnt grass.

The woman sat with her back bent and her head down. Her arms were at her sides, and although she still held the juniper bough, it lay on the grass, dusty and limp. Fools Crow wanted to go away, to shrink back into the trees, but he could not bear to leave her this way. He walked quietly into the clearing, and when he reached her he touched her shoulder. He squatted beside her and looked into her face. The tears had dried, but something in the face told Fools Crow of a grief so deep it would always be there and no words from him could help. She opened her eyes and looked at him without seeing. Her eyes were the blue of the light in her lodge that Fools Crow had seen earlier, the light that created no shadows. Just then, Freckle-face, who had never left the edge of the clearing, barked and the woman blinked, and when she looked up the sun filled her eyes.

"Are you well?" said Fools Crow.

The woman slowly moved her head, taking in the clearing as though she were seeing it for the first time. "I was digging turnips," she said. "I must have lost my way." She heaved herself up from the ground, tired and heavy, like an old cow. She sighed and picked up her sack and digging stick. When she straightened up, she looked at Fools Crow and smiled and the youthful look returned. "Look, I have a whole bagful."

Fools Crow looked off to the eastern horizon. The mountain was a dusty green. Near the top, beneath the granite face, he could see a small pocket of yellow snow. On the other side of the peak, it would be winter, and his people would be there, waiting for a direction or a sign. Would they wait forever? Fools Crow turned back to the woman.

"Who do you mourn?" He was surprised by the anger in his voice. "Who are you?" . . .

"Who do you mourn?" he said.

They were sitting across the cold fire pit from each other. She had spent the day painting a design on the yellow skin. Fools Crow had watched her mix her paints and he had watched her dab the paint on the skin, but when he looked at the skin he could not see her design. The paints vanished and yet she painted on, as though she could see some image emerging. After a time, Fools Crow had given up and gone for a walk. Then he returned to the lodge and smoked and thought about the woman's strange mourning in the clearing, but he could make no sense of it. Afterward she had walked down to the river and stripped off her dress and moccasins and bathed. He had watched her as she submerged herself, then came up, sputtering, tossing her short hair, wiping her face with her hands. She splashed water on her breasts and arms. She looked at him and smiled, and he realized that she was the first woman, other than Red Paint, that he had seen naked since becoming a man. And he felt no shame.

Now, as he looked into the pale blue eyes, he noticed that something about her had changed. Her eyes had changed. He saw age in them, the watery flat eyes of an old one. He thought again of her splashing water on her breasts and how he had marveled at their firmness, and the flatness of her belly.

"It is finished," she said. She rolled up the yellow skin and laid it aside. She wiped her fingers with a strip of skin, then looked across at Fools Crow. "I am So-at-sa-ki."

At first Fools Crow didn't make the connection. He had become used to the waiting, and the way she said the name seemed as timeless as everything else in her world. Then he felt the small prickles of sweat sting his forehead, and when he opened his mouth the words came out harshly: "Feather Woman!"

She smiled faintly.

"But you died – you died in mourning!"

"It is true that I mourned the loss of my husband, and it is true that I died. There was much sorrow in me and I did not care to live. And so I left your world, a pitiful creature whom no one missed or mourned. But I did not go to the Sand Hills to join my beloved relatives. I came here – Sun brought me here – to live in mourning. Now he sends my husband and son here each dawn to remind me of my transgression."

"Morning Star and Star Boy," murmured Fools Crow.

"Yes, they come every morning, and every morning I beg them to take me back, but they do not listen to an old woman." Feather Woman's voice had lost the vigor that Fools Crow had come to enjoy. She spoke in a grave, flat rhythm. "You saw me in the clearing. You saw the yellow feather and the juniper bough with the spider's web. These things were given to me that long-ago night Morning Star took me to live with him in Sun's house. The web is the ladder I climbed. Spider Man built the ladder to the sky, and I entered my husband's dwelling place and was embraced by his father and mother, Sun Chief and Night Red Light. We were very happy, all of us, and even happier when I gave birth to Star Boy, the one your people now call Poia. Sun and Moon beamed with pleasure each time they looked upon their grandson. Morning Star walked with great pride, and I – I was the happiest of all, for I was indeed blessed in that sacred lodge."

Feather Woman closed her eyes and smiled, as though she were reliving those happy times when she had lived with the Above Ones. Fools Crow sat in silence, for he was still stunned by her revelation. And he was suddenly frightened to be in the presence of one who had been sacred to his people and who had fallen so low that no one mourned her when she died. Yet when he looked into her eyes he saw only kindness and warmth.

"One morning I went out to dig turnips. I had been warned by my mother-in-law not to dig the large turnip in the middle of the field, for it was a sacred turnip. I thanked her and told her I had no intention of doing so. All morning I dug, all the time coming nearer to the sacred turnip. The closer I came the more fascinated I became. I seemed to be drawn to it and then I was upon it. It was large and it frightened me and I ran away. I dug more turnips and soon I was near it again. Oh, I was frightened, but I had no control over myself. I dropped to my knees and started to dig. I dug deeper and deeper but to no avail. Finally, with all my strength I thrust my stick deep into the earth. I thought I would push back on the stick and pop the turnip out, but neither stick nor turnip would move. I had wedged the stick too tightly. Oh, I pushed and pulled, and then I became frantic because I was afraid Moon would find me doing what she had warned me against. I worked with all my strength to free my stick, but soon I became exhausted and lay down to rest and weep. Then I spotted two cranes flying overhead. I called out to them to help me, and after several circles they landed. They began to sing sacred songs, one to each of the four directions, and after the fourth song Crane Chief took the stick in his bill and started to move it. Before long, the turnip popped out and left a hole in the sky. I thanked the cranes and they flew on. It was then that I looked down into the hole and saw my people. I saw my mother and father, my sister, our lodge. I saw my village, and the people were busy and happy. Women were working on hides, children were playing in the river, men were making arrows and racing their horses. It was so lovely and peaceful that I became homesick. I wanted to be with them. I wanted to tease my sister, to hug my mother and to braid my father's hair. But I was so far away I could never be with them again. I cried and cried and soon Star Boy, who was an infant on my back, began to cry. After a while I overcame my sorrow and gathered up my sack of turnips and digging stick and returned to Sun's lodge. Morning Star, my dear husband, looked into my eyes and knew what I had done. Moon exlaimed, 'You foolish girl, you have done the one thing you were not to do.' Soon Sun arrived home and Moon told him of my sin. He became very angry and told me I must leave his house, for I would never be happy there again. I would always miss my people. He gave me the sacred medicine bonnet and my digging stick. Then he wrapped Star Boy and me in an elkskin and sent us back to our people's world."

Fools Crow had been looking at Feather Woman's hands, the very hands that had dug the sacred turnip, but in the silence he stole a glance outside the entrance. Freckle-face sat alertly, looking in at the woman. He did not seem to be aware of Fools Crow's presence.

"Storytellers say that Spider Man let you down and you became a bright fire in the sky. The people thought it was a feeding star, and when they found the spot it landed, there were you and Star Boy. They say you were never happy again, that you rejected your people, that each dawn you would beg Morning Star to take you back."

"It is so even now. One dawn, in the long-ago, he spoke to me. He said, 'You have brought upon yourself your own misery – and misery to your people.' And it is true. Now you see sickness and hunger, Napikwans [whites] and war. It is no wonder the people didn't mourn me when I left their world." A small joyless smile crossed her lips.

Fools Crow looked out at Freckle-face. He remembered the wailing of a thousand geese in the bowl that morning. He saw the great water birds' flashing wings and he saw Feather Woman with her arms outstretched, beseeching Morning Star and her son to allow her to fly with them across the sky He couldn't understand – all these winters, these summers, why did she continue? It was so hopeless. Then he heard her voice and he realized with shame that she had read his thoughts.

"One day I will rejoin my husband and son. I will return with them to their lodge and there we will be happy again – and your people will suffer no more." Now her eyes were bright again, the eyes of a young one.

The spell had been broken and Fools Crow was again aware of light and shadows, of warmth and the odor of dusty summer pines. Freckle-face had entered the lodge and now sat beside Feather Woman, a look of contentment and loyalty on his face. He has been her only companion all these winters forever, thought Fools Crow, and he suddenly loved them both and was glad he had come to their world.

"You should be proud of giving birth to Poia," he said, "for he has given the Pikunis their sacred summer ceremony. Long ago he taught the Pikunis the ways of the Sun Dance, and they honor Sun Chief exactly as he instructed. In this way you make Sun Chief to smile on his children and to provide for them."

Fools Crow was puzzled by the look of alarm on Feather Woman's face. Had he not spoken truly? Had she misunderstood him? For a short time she seemed hesitant, even timid. She had not been this way before. Even her wailing and crying had been strong, her grief full of resolve.

She picked up the yellow skin and unrolled it. She laid it on the white bighead robe and smoothed it out with her long brown fingers. Then she stood and left the tipi. Freckle-face followed her. At the entrance she looked back briefly, then was gone.

Fools Crow sat for a moment and looked out at the blue river. Somehow he knew that the point of his journey had been finally reached. He was in no hurry as he crept around the fire pit and knelt and looked down at the yellow skin. It was a well-tanned skin, creaseless, without thin spots or cracks.

At first he didn't see the designs. He rubbed his eyes and blinked and leaned closer – and he saw the first one. The pigments were not strong and he had a hard time seeing it in its entirety. The yellow light within the tipi was strong and almost washed the colors away. Then he saw a circle and, within the circle, the familiar triangular shapes of painted lodges. There were many lodges. In the middle were the lodges of the bear, elk, beaver and otter. Outside the circle many horses, bridled and painted, stood in a white background. Fools Crow was confused by the proximity of the sacred lodges surrounded by whiteness. These lodges belonged to different bands and came together only during the Sun Dance ceremonies; yet, in the design, the white represented the snow of winter moons. As he looked at the representation he thought at first that it was only a poorly done winter count or war history. But then the horses began to move; almost imperceptibly, the horses came alive. One switched its tail, another took a step, another pawed at the snow. Then he noticed a wisp of smoke coming from one of the lodges, and he saw a dog sit up and scratch his ear with a hind leg.

Fools Crow shrank back from the skin with a small cry. He trembled and he wanted to run away, to leave that place and the strange woman, to return to Red Paint and his family. He was no longer eager to complete his journey, to learn the fate of his people. Nitsokan [his spirit guide]. Why had Nitsokan chosen him? Why did he have to see this thing? He tried to stand, to leave, but his legs wouldn't move. He was rooted to that spot and he couldn't stop looking into the yellow skin. He was powerless to keep from seeing, and so he saw inside the lodges and he saw the agony of the sick ones, the grief of the mothers and fathers, the children, the old ones. And he saw the bundled bodies of the dead, slung across the painted horses being led from camp. He saw inside the lodges of all the Pikunis and he saw suffering and crying and wailing. He saw mothers mutilate themselves, men rush from lodge to lodge, clutching their young ones, the elders sending up their futile prayers.

Through his tears, Fools Crow felt his eyes wander over the design. He recognized people from the Hard Topknots, the Never Laughs, the Grease Melters, the Many Chiefs, but only after he had searched all the lodges did he know what he was looking for – his own lodge and that of his mother and father. They were not in the village. Nor were the lodges of most of the Lone Eaters. He let out his breath in a sigh, but a lodge on the edge of the encampment caught his eye. It was the painted ermine lodge of Three Bears. Outside, Three Bears' sits-beside-him wife knelt in the snow with her head down. There were two other lodges from the Lone Eaters band.

The white-scabs disease has reached us, thought Fools Crow. We did not act quickly enough. We did not go north to the land of the Siksikas.

It will be only a matter of time before all the Lone Eaters join this village of sickness.

Then the village was gone and Fools Crow saw only the yellow skin. He sighed deeply, and his heart was heavy in his chest. He closed his eyes, and in his weariness he could think of nothing, could feel nothing but a mild gratitude that Red Paint had not yet moved their lodge to that village of death.

Fools Crow had seen enough, but when he opened his eyes he saw a faint design, as indistinct as a shadow. He bent forward and the shadow became a red wash across the skin. Then the red wash became a column of horses. Stick figures rode the horses and their heads were colored yellow. Small black curly marks turned into buffalo coats and one of the yellow-heads moved, turned around and looked at the other yellow-heads. And then the red horses were moving through a snowy valley. Fools Crow heard the squeak of leather and the bark of a dog. He looked back to the sound of the bark and saw the seizers' fort on Pile-of-rocks River. A small knot of men and women were watching the seizers ride off.

It was bitter cold and the seizers rode with their collars up and wool scarves tied over their caps and ears. Their horses lifted their legs high and snorted white smoke in the cold air. As Fools Crow swept the column, from rear to front, the number of seizers grew until he could see hundreds of them, each with a long-gun in his scabbard. At the head rode a seizer chief that Fools Crow had never seen before. But beside him, his broad yellow face partially hidden in the collar of his buffalo coat, rode the scout, Joe Kipp.

When the seizers reached the edge of the valley they rode up a wide gully and up to the short-grass prairie. Fools Crow put his hand to his mouth to muffle the cry that had begun in his throat. He recognized that gully. It was the one he had just ridden down on his black buffalo-runner. The seizers were traveling north to the country of the Pikunis. . . .

Then the design faded but its image lingered in Fools Crow's mind. He wanted to call it back, to learn of the hairy faces' destination. All of the bands were camped in that direction, along the Two Medicine and Bear rivers. The seizers' journey in such weather most certainly had an object, a mission. Were they after Mountain Chief? Who would they make cry?

Fools Crow looked at the skin again for a trace of the design. Instead, it had become all-over yellow with wandering dark lines and splotches of blackness like fresh blackhorn dung. Gradually he began to see the features of the design, and it was the Pikuni country with its creeks and rivers and small mountain ranges. He noticed the Two Medicine River, but the winter camp of the Lone Eaters was not there. He could see so far he thought he must be on a cloud high above. He recognized the Bear River, the Sweet Grass Hills, the Bear Paws and the Little Mountains. To the south he saw the Big River and, farther south, the Yellow Mountains. Off to the west, he saw the upsweep of the Backbone, its forested darkness giving way to gray spires that rent the yellow sky. His eyes were filled with wonder at the grand sweep of prairie, the ground-of-many-gifts that had favored his people. After the other designs, this one filled him with peace and humility and his spirits rose up. The moon of the yellow grass meant good hunting, abundance for all. Fools Crow began to look for those places which the blackhorn herds favored this time of the year. He searched around the Sweet Grass Hills, the Yellow River, the Shield-floated-away River, Snake Butte and Round Butte. But he did not find the blackhorns. He looked along the breaks north of the Big River, and he looked to the country of the Hard Gooseneck and the White Grass Butte, the Meat Strings [mountains]. But there were no blackhorns. And there were no long legs and no bighorns. There were no wags-his-tails or prairie runners.

It was as if the earth had swallowed up the animals. Where once there were rivers of dark blackhorns, now there were none. To see such a vast, empty prairie made Fools Crow uneasy. Perhaps the magic of the yellow skin had chosen to hide the blackhorns from him. Perhaps they were there but he was not meant to see them. As he thought these things, his eyes were focusing on something that seemed not to fit in the landscape. He looked closer. It was a square dwelling place like the Four Horns agency on the Milk River. But this one was farther north, on Badger Creek, in the heart of the Pikuni country. Then he saw the lodges pitched around the square compound and there was snow on the ground. He saw people standing around the tipis and the buildings. They were huddled in worn blankets. Some had scarves tied around their heads. Many had scraps of cloth tied around their feet. They were a pitiful people, and Fools Crow did not recognize them.

Near the entrance to the compound he saw a large-wheeled wagon and a team of large gray horses. There were three long boxes in the back. The horses started and they pulled the wagon across the flat and up the incline to the south. At the top of the ridge the wagon stopped and the four men who had been riding in back unloaded the boxes near a pile of other long boxes. As Fools Crow watched the wagon return to the compound, he felt something dark pass through his heart and he knew that the boxes contained dead ones. But what did they die of? There were more boxes on the ridge than he could count. Was it the white-scabs? And why didn't the people bury their dead in the proper way?

Once again he searched the yellow skin for an answer. But the yellow land told him nothing. Then he saw a woman carrying something from the compound. It was a metal bucket and it was filled halfway with guts. As he watched her hurry along, he recognized something about her. The gaunt hollow-cheeked face, the eyes that stared at nothing as she walked – they hid somebody that Fools Crow had known.

Three women who had been sitting beside their lodges got to their feet and began to approach the woman. They had their hands out and their voices were weak and piteous. The woman tried to walk by them but they blocked her path. As two of the women distracted her with their weak pawing, the third reached into the bucket and came up with a handful of intestines. She began to run away, followed by the other two. Fools Crow looked again into the familiar woman's face; in its gaunt hardness, he saw the girl his mother had wanted him to marry in happier days. Little Bird Woman, daughter of Crow Foot, hugged the bucket to her breast and hurried on.

Fools Crow began to frantically search the drab village. He saw many other familiar faces, but he did not take the time to identify them. Many were marked by the pocks of the white-scabs; many were too hollow to be recognizable. He saw four men carrying a burden in a blanket. As it passed beneath his eyes he saw it was the body of a boy, not much older than ten or twelve winters. One of the men holding a corner of the blanket looked up and Fools Crow looked into the face of Eagle Ribs, the horse-taker, the brave who had scouted on Fools Crow's first raid against the Crows. He shouted to Eagle Ribs but the man did not look up again. It was all he could do to carry his share of the burden.

The scene began to fade into the design, and that too faded, until there was nothing but the yellow skin. This time Fools Crow did not attempt to call it back. He had seen the end of the blackhorns and the starvation of the Pikunis. He had been brought here, to the strange woman's lodge in this strange world, to see the fate of his people. And he was powerless to change it, for he knew the yellow skin spoke a truth far greater than his meager powers, then the power of all his people.

As he sat in his hopeless resignation, he heard the sound of children laughing and he recognized it as the sound he had heard since entering this world. The laughter and chatter mocked him, but he was weary deep in his bones and he had no spirit to despise it. It took him a long time to realize that he was looking at another design on the skin. In the middle of the design was a long white building with four of the Napikwan square ice-shields on each of the long sides. The building was not far from a grove of big-leaf trees that marked the course of the Milk River as it spilled out from the Backbone. Fools Crow could see Ear Mountain and Danger Butte with its war lodge. The lodge was caved in, its poles and logs scattered in the long grass. He looked back to the white building and saw faces through the ice-shields, and they were young and open with laughter. Outside, there were other children, running and playing, laughing. The girls wore long dresses and high-topped shoes. They held hands and danced around and around in a circle. The boys, in white shirts and short pants, chased each other. But a small group of children stood at the edge, near the white building. They were dark-skinned, and they watched the other children. The two dark boys wore clothing like the other boys and their hair was cut short. The three girls wore cloth dresses and they stood timidly a short distance from a large white woman who held a brass bell. Around the building and the ground the children played on stood a fence made of twisted wire and pointed barbs. Beyond the fence there was nothing but the rolling prairie.

COMMENTARY

Since the largest body of traditional Native American discourse that has been preserved consists of myths, it is unfortunate that nobody agrees on what myths are, or what their functions may be. For nearly 150 years, since Friedrich Max Müller began promulgating his "solar myth" theory, polemical debates about what myth is and what it does have been as unremitting as indecisive. The fiercest combats, involving folklorists, anthropologists, philosophers, psychologists, linguists, literary critics, and a wide spectrum of eccentrics (the categories frequently overlapping), have centered on claims – a new one about every twenty years – for a "science" of mythology. This darkling plain where corpses of theories are piled high (displaying how strong is our compulsion to fabricate "scientific" validity for a mode of discourse alien to modern culture) exposes a major fantasy underlying much contemporary critical discourse. "Sciences" of myth seem analogous to what after the Civil War was called the experience of "the phantom limb," a feeling by mutilated veterans of sensations in arms or legs long since amputated. Avoiding such hallucinations, I propose a hypothesis not as to what myth is but as to what may be central features of mythic imagining.[3]

An overview of the past 150 years' controversies suggests one positive tendency: an increasing inclination to emphasize that all myths are stories. Standard dictionaries today, for example, almost universally define myth as a form of narrative. Understanding how narrative functions, therefore, is indispensable to understanding how myths function. Myth narrative, of course, possesses its own attributes, which distinguish it, for instance, from novelistic narrative. Primary is the feature dramatized by Bronislaw Malinowski's insistence that mythic story is also always more than story. Malinowski's linking of mythic narrative to "ritual" should not distract us (as it is all too likely to do) from the essence of his argument, which is that myths are mutilated if torn from their sociocultural context, their embeddedness in the ongoing practices of a particular way of life. We should not allow fascination with mythic story in itself to distract us from the manner in which it is integral to the daily experience of its tellers and listeners.[4] Ethnographic evidence overwhelmingly supports Malinowski's contention, which explains why all attempts to treat mythic narratives as "literature" must be unsatisfactory. What *we* refer to as literature is "aesthetic" discourse: that is to say, discourse distinguishable from other, nonaesthetic, "practical" discourses. Our aesthetic discourse may have some practical effects, but it is by definition differentiated from the daily practices of our sociocultural life – special and valuable to us *because* thus distinct. Genuine myths cannot be so detached. Myth arises out of and remains totally enmeshed in practical aspects of the life of myth tellers and myth listeners. Myth is practice. Myth tellings are enactments.[5]

Although we create confusion when we call myths "literature," they indubitably can be shaped with potent artistry. They can be carried out with economic grace, elegant elaboration, cogency, vividness; their pleasing formal relations can be intensely evocative. All stories can be well told or badly told, and the excellence of their telling, the skill of their making, is a crucial feature of myths. Among peoples such as American Indians who are active in enacting myths, superior telling is esteemed – just as skill in the practice of making arrows, tanning hides, or speaking in council is admired.

Acknowledgment that Indian myth enactments (however skillfully or unskillfully performed) are enmeshed within the web of other interactions of social life allows us to distinguish productively between the artistry of Native American myths and the artistry of our literature. The distinction permits us to appreciate the oral character of Indian mythology. Failure to address the fact that these stories originated in nonliterate societies has vitiated many analyses. We read traditional American Indian myths in distorting translations, not merely of the original language but also of transient oral events transposed into enduring printed objects.

Admitting how deaf we print-oriented readers are to the constraints and potentialities of oral artistry should focus attention on audiences. The audience of any written work is necessarily fictional: writers must imagine their audiences.[6] The audience of oral discourse is visibly and audibly present, *here imagining*, rather than *elsewhere imagined*. The myth audience's shaping physical presence assures that this discourse is always a practical social transaction. That the transaction depends on imagining permits us to be intellectually stimulated and emotionally moved even by distorting translations of powerful myths. We should not mistakenly identify mythic art with that which makes our own written literature analogously evocative. The excellences are of course related – Indian myths and our literature are both artifacts created by human beings – but the functioning of imagination in the two modes differs radically.

The core of my hypothesis, then, is that myths are imaginative acts of a kind with which we have become unfamiliar. My hypothesis assumes (to eliminate at once a bugaboo of some mythographers) an individual as the immediate source of every myth enactment, because only individuals imagine; to speak of "communal imagination" is to invoke a metaphor of dubious value. Yet every individual mind exists within and is constituted by (influenced yet reciprocally influencing) its specific sociocultural circumstances, which in an oral society are significantly determined by repeated mind-shaping recitations of myths. This obvious point needs emphasis, because myths are most often focally expressive of individualistic and communal forces interacting. These relations in nonliterate communities may be imagined in fashions surprising, even baffling, to us.

I find that the most useful definitions of imagination are those in common usage, in which "to imagine" ordinarily means two different but related processes linked by a conception of "fantasy." When someone says, "Ah, you're just imagining that," you are accused of "fantasizing" in its most usual sense: inventing mentally what has never existed and presumably never can, or willfully ignoring physical actualities for psychically engendered "unrealities." When, however, you are urged to "use your imagination, stupid," there is a positive appeal to fantasy: a demand that you employ your psychic capacities to reach beyond what is immediately present here and now and beyond routinized rational patterns toward some novel possibility. The injunction to "use your imagination" urges you to allow your mind to move toward something not yet realized but realizable. Imagination in this sense underlies every kind of planning, every purposeful human accomplishment; it is in fact the primary power that *constitutes* culture.

Contemporary psychologists and philosophers seem fearful of talking about imagination (a phobia probably related to compulsions to rationalize mythologies), so I turn back to a cultural analysis of fantasy by the English romantic poet Percy Shelley. Shelley defined the services that imagination renders humanity through a counterattack on an essay by his friend Thomas Love Peacock. Peacock argued with astringent humor that the imagining which produces poetry (poetry for him as for Shelley being representative of all aesthetic accomplishment) had become useless in contemporary, rationalized, technologically sophisticated cultures. Shelley perceived that Peacock's view would become a dominant presupposition in Western society (as indeed it has) unless it could be refuted by a demonstration that imagination is the *generative* force of *all* cultural accomplishments. Shelley, therefore, distinguished imagination from reason. He identified the latter as the capacity of the human psyche to organize already existing ideas and perceptions, the former as the power to achieve new perceptions and novel thoughts, to arouse consciousness of hitherto "unapprehended relations."[7]

The power to improve upon what already exists, what has been given to us, undergirds humankind's manipulations of natural phenomena to create cultures. Shelley recognized, however, that culturally formed practices, patterns of thinking and patterns of perceiving, become routinized and worse than useless. He regarded successful culture as necessarily always self-reconstituting through acts of imagination. This is why he emphasized defamiliarization, the concept later developed by Russian formalists. They identified defamiliarizing as a major function of Western art, which strips away the veiling film of familiarity that blinds us to the ever changing reality of relationships to which we have become too accustomed – like the painting we so carefully place on a living room wall and within months never notice.

Shelley differed from the Russian formalists, however, in concentrating upon defamiliarization not as a feature of personal psychology but as a cultural phenomenon. He was especially concerned with the renewal of communal constructs and social systems, which he called "forms of opinion." Unless these are consistently reconstituted, they become mechanical routines, hindrances to further development of both individuals and communities. Unless a people's imaginings continuously rework received systems, they rigidify, constricting and deforming the life they had originally enhanced. Probably because he was a poet, Shelley saw a deadly symptom of this reifying in routinization of language. The appearance of cliché is primary evidence that we are no longer vitally imagining what we talk or write about.

Cliché is the exact opposite of formalized language, wherein a word or phrase is deliberately repeated even though (or because) it is recognized as archaic, perhaps even so archaic that its meaning is doubtful. Formally archaic language compels listeners to think about the strangeness of language's powers (as well as its historical character) and is thus a technique of defamiliarizing because it disables us from taking our language for granted. Myths frequently play an analogous role in refreshing the self-consciousness of social systems and "forms of opinion" by deliberately employing archaic language, archaic stories, and archaic modes of enactment.

Although unusual in our intellectual tradition, Shelley's idea that culture persists vitally *only* through continual self-renovations is analogous to an enormous number of Indian beliefs and practices that ethnologists refer to under the rubric of "world renewal." The term points to ceremonies combining speech and behavior, which are intended to assure revitalization of a sustaining interplay between a particular culture and its natural environment. Shelley was a progressive, even a revolutionary, trying to break free of the feudal mind-set epitomized by the term *ancien régime,* so he regularly emphasized that imagination enables what is "new" and "novel" to break up reified conventions. But his stress on defamiliarization affirmed continually reawakened awareness of the conditions of our existence, both natural and cultural, as essential to a healthy society. American Indian ideas of "renewal" as restoration of traditional ways are misunderstood if regarded as mere exercises in repetition. Indian imaginings that revitalize their culture and its relation to their environment never exclude the possibility (even the desirability) of transformation through reassessment of tradition.

The foundation of my hypothesis about mythmaking, then, is that human beings, by continually reimagining their cultures through myths, can change as well as preserve those cultures. Myths help to affirm a special way of living by defamiliarizing it. Every culture is a creation that begins in human imagining. Shelley is the first of a small group of modern thinkers (notable among whom is José Ortega y Gasset) who perceive the danger that technological, print-based culture encourages people to take it for granted. Most of us do not actively, participatively, continually reimagine our culture; thus, unwittingly, we alienate ourselves from it even while we think we are supporting it fervently. One does not contribute to sustaining a way of life when one takes it for granted, discoursing about it only in clichés.

Among American Indians, whose traditional societies were without writing, continual reimagining of culture was an imperative. Their cultures continued to exist only through being acted out, conversed about, realized in speech and behavior. If a preliterate people stops talking self-consciously about its culture, that culture vanishes. This may even help to explain the importance of dreams to many Native American peoples; were they to stop dreaming their culture, it would disappear.

Contrarily, the reward for constantly reimagining one's culture both in dreaming and in myth enacting is immediate and powerful: the satisfaction of participating in renovating one's nurturing way of life. The force of social interdependence is thus experienced directly by each imagining individual. Every least thing appears intensely charged with social meaning; even trivial matters are, one might say, culturally overdetermined. Individual behavior in such societies tends toward the ceremonious rather than, as with us, the casual and spontaneous. Indian decorations illustrate the point. The tiny beaded caret on a moccasin is simultaneously decorative and "symbolic" (meaning imaginatively stimulating) of how its wearer can race over mountains. The jagged streak of white painted on a pony's side evokes the brilliant swiftness of the lightning flash with which the rider has been blessed in his dream of grandfathers bestowing on him warrior power. Indian cultures exist through the fashion in which every part of their world is both the object and the inspiration of continual imagining and reimagining.

If we think of myths as imaginative reenactments in the circumstances just sketched, we may study their artistry without converting them into "oral literature," deforming them to fit our conception of the aesthetic. Examination of specific tellings then allows us to recognize something like a "mythic style" of narration, although this will not lead to definitions of universal mythic form. It will lead to more nuanced appreciation of the particularities of what Clifford Geertz calls "local knowledge," and of relationships along the line of what Ludwig Wittgenstein called "family resemblances." To illustrate, albeit crudely, the "nonliterary" artistry of mythic narrative I contrast the Blackfoot myth "The Sand Hills" that opens this chapter with a famous parable about Death from our tradition.

A man who was walking in the market of Damascus came face to face with Death. He noticed an expression of surprise on the spectre's horrid countenance, but they passed one another without speaking. The fellow was frightened, and went to a wise man to ask what should be done. The wise man told him that Death had probably come to Damascus to fetch him away next morning. The poor man was terrified at this, and asked how he could escape. The only way they could think of between them was that the victim should ride all night to Aleppo. So the man did ride to Aleppo – it was a terrible ride which had never been done before – and when he was there he walked in the market place, congratulating himself on having eluded Death. Just then Death came up to him and tapped him on the shoulder. "Excuse me," he said, "but I have come for you." "Why," exclaimed the terrified man, "I thought I met you in Damascus yesterday!" "Exactly," said Death. "That was why I looked surprised – for I had been told to meet you today, in Aleppo."[8]

I cite this celebrated tale, which has been ceaselessly repeated throughout Western culture since its appearance in the Middle East twenty-five hundred years ago, in the version of T. H. White's popular reworking of Thomas Malory's *Morte d'Arthur* as *The Once and Future King*. White identifies the tale not inaptly as a "gruesome chestnut." Like John O'Hara, in his contemporaneous reference to the tale in *Appointment in Samarra* (1934), White represents the story as epitomizing belief in an inescapable destiny. Commentators have suggested that the irony structuring the parable parallels the irony characteristic of Greek tragedy, as when Oedipus blindly brings destruction on himself. The *absence* of such dramatic clarity in the Blackfoot "Sand Hills" is what causes us the most interpretive difficulty.

Against the Western tale ordered by fated inevitability, the Blackfoot narrative exploits a mode of uncertainty that diffuses, rather than focuses, irony. The myth concludes without absolute symmetry. The hunter dies, but for causes not certain; death's inevitability here is background, not a dramatized figure. We are left with diverse possibilities to wonder about. Why did the hunter take sick and die? Because he lied to the dead man? By chance (as he had chanced on the buffalo), without any influence from his meeting the dead man? Or was what killed him primarily his fear of death? Some orientation might be given could we hear the tone in which the dead man addresses the returned hunter – plaintively or threateningly. Thus to seek answers in the *manner* of oral enactment, however, is to perceive that the Blackfoot narrative is constructed to encourage variability of interpretation, not finality of meaning. Two tellers might differ radically in the intonation they bestow upon the dead man's speech. This story deals not with the absoluteness of death but with the contingencies of a dead buffalo and a dead man. Blackfoot narrative logic here opens out rather than focusing in, because it speaks to the complexities of death's ongoing intermingling with life: the man returns for arrow points needed to [illegible] one can live. The listener is oriented toward speculation, precluding that formalistic closure which in our tradition is a manifestation of "aesthetic" order.

I do not claim complete representativeness for this arbitrary contrast, but it alerts us to the circumstance that Native American traditional myths often conclude in a manner preventing the kinds of formal completeness we associate with aesthetic success. One cause is obvious: myths in a preliterate society are told *in order to be retold*, retellings being what keep a particular culture alive. Oral myths are structured as transmissive enactments fostering reinterpretations. The ironic finality of "Death in Aleppo" allows it, one might say, to be repeated but not retold, because it has already achieved perfected form.[9] The Blackfoot myth, to the contrary, is arranged to facilitate the transformationalism implicit in interpretive retellings. Each new teller offers a version (deriving from what he or she *has made* of the story when listening to it being told, whether once or many times) and expects listeners to make their own reinterpretations of what they hear.

Two outstanding, if antithetical, characteristics of Indian myths are extreme brevity and extreme length. I postpone consideration of very long myths, although we have ignored to our disadvantage problems posed by narratives told over a period of many hours, sometimes days. Mythic brevity, although more commented on, has not been adequately studied either, even though the extraordinary succinctness of many myths immediately baffles many modern readers. Oral narratives, of course, can be short because they are part of a familiar corpus of interconnected stories and ongoing practices. Indians have frequently explained mythic brevity in such terms as "Our stories are short because we know a lot." Even a few words can evoke an almost complete cultural context in a relatively small, highly self-aware society. Stylistic implications of this situation appear when we contrast "The Captive," a characteristic short-short story of Jorge Luis Borges, against what might be an Indian version of his narrative.

> They tell this story in Junin or in Tapalque. A boy disappeared after an Indian raid; he was said to have been carried off by the Indians. His parents made a futile search for him. After long years a soldier who came from the interior told them of an Indian with sky-blue eyes, who might very well be their son. At last they found this man (the chronicle loses track of the exact circumstances and I don't want to invent what I don't know) and thought they recognized

him. The man, formed by the lonely life of the wilds, no longer understood the words of his native language, but let himself be led, indifferent and docile, up to their house. There he stopped, perhaps because the others stopped. He looked at the door, but without understanding. Suddenly he lowered his head, let out a shout, went down the entrance hall and the two long patios at a run, and burst into the kitchen. Without hesitation he plunged his arm up the blackened fireplace chimney and pulled out a little horn-handled knife he had hidden there as a boy. His eyes shone with joy and his parents wept because they had found their son.

Perhaps other recollections followed this one, but the Indian was not able to live within walls, and one day he went off to look for his wilderness. I wonder what he felt in that vertiginous moment when the past and present were confused; I would like to know if the lost son was reborn and died in that moment of rapture, or if he managed to recognize, like an infant or a dog at least, his parents and his home.[10]

An Indian version of the story might read thus:

A boy disappeared after an Indian raid. Years later a man from the interior told his parents of an Indian who might be their son. They found this man, who didn't understand their words, but let himself be led to their house. He looked at the door. Then he shouted, rushed into the kitchen, thrust his arm up the fireplace chimney, and pulled out a little knife. He laughed and his parents wept.

One day he went off again.

This artificial juxtaposition illustrates how brevity in oral storytelling may be evocative by concentrating on actions as actions, by excluding description, motive analysis, philosophizing, even figures of speech. What seems a formal "poverty" of many oral tales in fact testifies to the intensity of social transactiveness embodied in their exclusive attention to *events*. We are likely to be most surprised by omission of comment on causes, especially the absence of remark on motive. Such elisions result when the oral narrator's subjectivity is dissolved into the narrative totality: the teller's interpretation is the shape given by the enactment as a whole. Myth tellers regard themselves as transmitting a story existing before – and persisting after – their version. This is why what we misperceive as trivial variations in myth tellings are often for native listeners significant; small changes in representation of actions may signal a major revision in the total meaning of a familiar story.

Our judgment that myths lack complexity and suffer from inadequate articulation of details arises from a failure to understand the oral enactment situation. We tend to forget that because oral tellers are physically with the audience, their task is to make that subjective presence meaningful through *this* socially effective enactment of what is probably a traditional story. Frequently, as I illustrate in several of my commentaries, Indian tellers – by concentrating solely on events constituting a narrative, especially by avoiding comment on motivations – deliberately provoke their listeners to speculate on possible causes for the characters' behavior. I have come to believe that many native peoples regard psychic motivations as more complicated and multifaceted than most of today's readers do.

In the small, intensely interactive, and technologically simple societies characteristic of most Native American peoples, individuals and individual behavior, as Pierre Bourdieu and Ernest Gellner have observed, are "many stranded" (to use Gellner's terminology) as opposed to the "single-strandedness" of contemporary, highly rationalized, print-dominated, technological societies. Gellner exemplifies the difference thus: "A man buying something from a village neighbor in a tribal community is dealing not only with a seller [as when we make a purchase at a shopping mall] but also with a kinsman, collaborator, ally or rival, potential supplier of a bride for his son, fellow juryman, ritual participant, fellow defender of the village, fellow council member."[11] In oral stories, representations of motivation at work in such situations usually avoid both reductive simplification to a single dominating motive and elaborate description of the complicated tangle of motives at work; through a starkly "objective" narrative of specific actions they evoke in their listeners an imagining of the complex of considerations creating particular behavior. Such a rhetorical mode is especially appropriate in the retelling of familiar tales. Again, we must be alert to what we assume to be simplifications or omissions in myth tellings, recognizing them as in fact possible signals for audience imagining to which we are unaccustomed.[12]

This brings us back to the meaning of versions. Mythographers' reluctance to admit that myths may be *essentially* variable arises from a misconception (nurtured by our submergence in print culture) that myths in preliterate societies serve as coercive social controls and only preserve the past. In fact, however, myths keep preliterate societies alive, and what cannot change is dead. Myths facilitate sociocultural adaptations to shifting circumstances (physical or historical, external or internal) by sustaining continuity through modification. The ideal of perfected form in Western literary artistry fosters aspiration for the unique, the fully "original," which modification can only deface. Our works of art exist, as it were, distinct from their culture, like boulders in a stream.[13] Myth enactments in nonliterate societies tend toward creation of transmissively reinterpretable forms, toward differentiations not aiming for permanent existence as autonomous artifacts but, instead, seeking to assure the continuing vitality of cultural practices upon which depend the production of any artifacts.

Oral myths are transmissive. Transmissiveness is often sustained by variations in tellings. There are, to be sure, examples of oral enactments separated by many years which are almost verbatim verbal repetitions. "Oral memory" on occasion can be incredibly precise. But such extraordinary repetitions occur, I suggest, because a teller has decided that an occasion calls for as exact a repetition as possible; deliberate variations or attempts at perfect nonvariation are equally purposeful. Native American mythic retellings do not normally strive to be identical with earlier enactments because they nurture processes of continual social self-renewal. These processes are unfamiliar to contemporary readers. Writing, especially print, seems to release culture from the imperative awareness of need for constant self-reconstituting. Yet all life forms survive only by adapting, adjusting to new circumstances. Myths are means by which cultures adapt. Contrary to current misconceptions of oral myths as mere repositories of tradition, these narratives are a discursive practice by which preliterate societies modify as well as reaffirm their cultural systems. Myths so operate because they articulate – thereby presenting for renewed scrutiny and possible reassessment – the shifting forces that *generate* specific cultural practices.

This crucial function is difficult to illustrate briefly, but I am making the attempt by juxtaposing four versions of a Yurok blood-money myth. Even this method is problematic, since we usually assume that different versions result from a mistake or ill-advised editorial work. We possess no critical tools for investigating deliberate mythic variations. Indeed, our predominant methods of myth study, still usually forms of structuralism, are principally directed to explaining away differences in myth tellings, classifying them as manifestations of concealed ("deep") patterns of regularity.

The Yurok blood-money myths presented above were all told to my father during his early visits to the Yurok almost a century ago. All the tellers were in the same situation, accommodating an inquiring young anthropologist. There are many other Yurok stories about their "money" or dentalium, an imported seashell. One might better call the dentalium shells "treasure," since the Yurok saved up strings of dentalia more often than they used them for exchange. It would be difficult, however, to find a society that was more concerned with its "money" than the Yurok, and many of their myths focus on dentalia and other forms of wealth, such as woodpecker crests. Dentalium, we learn from the third of these myths, belongs among the *woge*, supernatural "people" who lived along the Klamath River before the Yurok came there. The chief Yurok hero who kills dangerous monsters and puts the world to rights was Pulekukwerek, the protagonist of the first and fourth versions. Wohpekumeu, a founder of Yurok culture, often appears as more shifty and sensuously distractable than the morally austere Pulekukwerek.

The teller of the first version of the institution of money in compensation for murder was Kate of Wahsek, a middle-aged woman with a well-educated daughter, Julia Wilson, who was fluent in English. Kate was married to another full-blood Yurok uncontaminated by white influence. Kate's stories, my father judged, were of the kind that Yuroks would customarily tell to children and strangers; they provide a rapid but accurate summary of basic Yurok philosophy and cosmology and the roles of central figures of Yurok mythology. One notices in Kate's version that the origin of blood money is directly linked to the physical condition of the present earth and sky, and that the tradition of payment for killing is founded in actions by the Thunders, great natural/supernatural powers that can be confronted only by a hero as potent as Pulekukwerek.

The second telling is by Jack of Murek, a wealthy man who belonged to a family of consequence, particularly notable for its doctors (who among the Yuroks are women). Although he is clearly a traditionalist, Jack's version concentrates on the psychology of the custom: the originating acts in Kate's version are summarized by Jack in two sentences. Thunder's instructions explain why the custom works: the Yurok money is emotionally equivalent to kin feeling. One observes that it is when the survivor looks at his hidden treasure (like our stereotypical miser examining his hoard) that he will remember and feel sorrow for his kinsman – not the other way around. This is unsentimental, yet

Jack's psychology seems sound: if wealth were not very highly valued, the blood-money system could not function.

The third version is by William Johnson, who came from a good family but had been crippled so that his legs were useless. He had become a skilled craftsman with his hands, especially at making the woodpecker-crest headbands highly prized by the Yurok, in 1900 selling for as much as twenty-five dollars. This is the only myth told by Johnson that my father recorded, which is unfortunate, since it is a small masterpiece. The insight into why money is so valued by the Yuroks is brilliant – and more attractive than Freudian explanations. Dentalium is the only one of the *woge* that has stayed with the Yuroks. Money may be small, but it is powerful because it is the sole superhuman force remaining with humans, on their persons, in their purses. William Johnson in a sense reverses the causality of the first two versions: Dentalium remains *so that* there can be a blood-money system. Johnson (like Jack of Murek) uses his story to explore how and why the custom operates as it does, although his focus (unlike Jack's) is the basic psychology of money rather than of compensation.

The last version is by Lame Billy of Weitspus, also from a good Yurok family but crippled, although before his disability he had been an active hunter, fisherman, and boatman. The last occupation is especially significant, because Yurok life is centered on the Klamath River – Yurok major directions, for example, are upriver and downriver – and a good boatman would probably have experienced most aspects of traditional Yurok life. My father thought Lame Billy the best teller of his many informants,

> equally at ease in narrating a story of the folktale type, of the hero order, a myth of the origin of institutions, or one of the conventional Yurok creator-rectifier-trickster traditions. The subject mattered very little, provided it allowed treatment in his concrete and expansive manner. A bald incident he developed into a definite plot. . . . His personages command sympathy because they are quickly worked into people. . . . Billy's heroes and their friends and opponents maintain an invariable dignity of character.[14]

Billy's skills as a storyteller are vivid even in this myth (one of the shortest of his narratives recorded by my father), especially his capacity to create an intriguing plot swiftly. Here he makes us first observe with Wohpekumeu a man who "looks like Pulekukwerek" – but why would *he* kill a man? This is not mere plot for the sake of plot. Notably absent from Billy's version is any reference to Thunder or the *woge*. Billy dramatizes the way a "reasonable" system of justice is established by a random killing – and it is difficult not to think that he thus illuminates something about all cultural creations, their originative arbitrariness.

The final segment raises other interesting possibilities, besides being the first to describe sanctions if the custom is violated. Perhaps a modern reader would go too far in seeing Pulekukwerek's nearly falling off the tree as symbolic: the moral or emotional price of instituting the blood-money practice is high, and even a hero almost loses his power in establishing the institution. There can be no doubt, however, that Billy's version evokes some of the anguish resulting from the harsh reality that makes a blood-money convention necessary. Yurok life is violent; Pulekukwerek claims no more than that "now they will not kill often."

Each of these versions not only tells of the origin of an important Yurok institution from a different perspective but also unfolds an individual imagining of how this cultural formation might have taken shape so as to accommodate common personal feelings and recognized social imperatives. The different versions bring to awareness diverse social and psychological pressures upon which the institution must draw for its communal efficacy. The versions therefore may fairly be described as exploratory rather than as simply doctrinal. Each offers the listener an opportunity to think about a different aspect of what gives rise to an accepted custom, rather than describing its practice or affirming its appropriateness. Each "confirms" the custom only by individualistically imagining the psychosocial tensions that the blood-money system aims to (but does not always) resolve: "if they don't pay . . ."

It is all too easy for us to forget that myths in oral societies were always told by particular individuals to particular audiences and were therefore always potential vehicles for imaginings that did not conform perfectly to "standard" or traditional attitudes. Perhaps among these Yurok enactments a personal style is fully visible for us only in Lame Billy's skill in constructing a gripping narrative, although it seems to me that a wry thoughtfulness distinguishes William Johnson's version. My point, however, is that we should try not to deduce the personality of the tellers from their tellings but to recognize that oral myths come into being through individual imaginings of the cultural conditions of the imaginers, and that myths frequently serve as means to investigate whatever pressures produced the subject of the myth. Careful examination of mythic forms – if we can free ourselves from disabling preconceptions induced by our dependence on printed texts – supports the view that Native American myths often function in such a consciously evaluative fashion through their articulation of psychosocial forces that generate cultural institutions.

My application of Claude Lévi-Strauss's dictum that a myth consists of all its versions is more rigorous than his own. In my view, the dictum implies that there can be no definitive system for defining the forms and uses of myths, either in themselves or in relation to one another. Any such system is a disguised return of the Western-fabricated concept of an archetypal, "original" ur-myth of which all versions are mere variants – a fantasy which in its obvious form Lévi-Strauss deserves credit for helping to debunk. My proposal is that we perceive each "version" as an individual enactment that is to a degree distorted if explained in terms of *any* universal system of myth classification.

Lévi-Strauss's structuralism in fact would be impossible to practice were one to adhere rigorously to his fundamental principle that *a* myth always consists of *all* its versions – most simply, because one can never be sure when somebody is going to retell the myth once more. Lévi-Strauss claims to meet this objection by asserting that his method works only for a "substantial" body of versions – his proof being an analysis of six versions of the Zuni "emergence myth." That myth has been told thousands of times, and told with at least as many variations as those we have observed in the four brief Yurok blood-money myths. Structuralism as thus practiced can only pretend respect for mythic forms while in actuality denying mythic artistry and eliminating its dynamically exploratory potencies. Structuralism thereby obscures myth's practical adaptive utility for human cultures. Cultures have enabled humans to compete successfully with other creatures in our evolutionary world by permitting swift and complex innovative adaptations, some of which are facilitated by myth enactments.

This proposition will trouble many people, because it welcomes something like a chaotic view of mythology. In "The Structural Study of Myth" Lévi-Strauss specifically recommends his method as substituting "order" for "chaos" in understanding myths. Yet one could not from the first three Yurok blood-money myths predict the fourth, nor do the four enable one to predict the next. Such openness testifies to the practicality of self-conscious human imagining and is in accord with many Indians' descriptions of their mythology as transmissive discourse.

Lévi-Straussian structuralism, like other "scientific theories" of discourse, applies to cultural phenomena preconceptions drawn from physical science of an antiquated kind.[15] Discourse critics cling to what may be called the "semiotic paradigm," which originated in the linguistics of Ferdinand Saussure before World War I. What has made Mikhail Bakhtin's ideas so upsettingly exciting is that in almost classical Kuhnian fashion they shift the paradigm on which structuralist and poststructuralist theorizing about discourse is founded. Paul de Man expresses the bewilderment felt by victims of such a shift when he wonders how Bakhtin's dialogic approach "can be so enthusiastically received by theoreticians of very diverse persuasions and made to appear as a valid way out of many of the quandaries that have plagued us for so long."[16]

Briefly, Bakhtin subsumes Saussure's *langue/parole* dialectic under the concept of *utterance*, forcing us to reconceive how sign and signifier (as well as *langue* and *parole*) are related, while revising assumptions about what constitutes individuality and socialization, since these are phenomena inseparable from language use.[17] Comprehending language through the concept of utterance enforces recognition of the importance of "speech genres." My approach is meant to suggest the value of perceiving myth as something like a major Bakhtinian speech genre in nonliterate Native American societies.

Understanding discourse through speech genres overturns the Western tendency to define "individual" and "social" as binary opposites, a definition that American anthropologists have increasingly found inapplicable to traditional Native American societies. If the "social" is opposed to the "individual," the psychic tends to be regarded as purely private and the ideological as purely social. To Bakhtin:

> Notions of that sort are fundamentally false. . . . If the content of the individual psyche is just as social as is ideology, then, on the other hand, ideological phenomena are just as individual (in the ideological meaning of the word) as are psychological phenomena. Every ideological product bears the imprint of the individuality of its creator or creators, but even this imprint is just as social as are all the other properties and attributes of ideological phenomena.[18]

From this perspective the Saussurean *langue/parole* opposition (which leads to the signifier/signified opposition) dissolves into the continual construction and reconstruction of the processes of ideology in the speech practices that form the living social relationships we abstractly term "society" – as if it were a static entity distinct from the specific interactions constituting it. Ideology for Bakhtin is the ongoing conflictual interactivity by which individuals through their utterances relate to one another, simultaneously producing and becoming products of the social practices they thus bring into existence. Although, as Michael Holquist says, the individual "responds to social stimuli by authoring its own responses," these carry within them the uses and interpretations of the language employed by previous speakers in earlier social engagements.[19] Language practice therefore is the supreme mediator between conventionality and creativity. This power of language derives from its combining of "immediate" with "historical" complexities: every utterance not only confronts the answering utterance of someone else *present* but is also constructed out of utterances that have preceded it, that are "other" in a "historical" fashion. As Susan Stewart observes, because language always encounters (and always has encountered) others, and is mutable, reversible, and contaminable, it possesses the power to be continually regenerative.[20]

I suggest that the intricacies of these Bakhtinian conceptions are clarified when one looks at the evidence from traditional Indian societies. Mythic enactments demonstrate that individualized utterance can be created only out of previous utterances by others. Formalized retellings display how conventionality produces reassessive innovations dependent upon the tradition being verbally evoked. Myth, in short, would seem to illustrate exactly what Bakhtin calls a complex speech genre.[21] Speech genres are constituted by utterance, units of speech communication (not, like sentences, units of language) whose boundaries are determined by a change in speakers: "The speaker ends his utterance in order to relinquish the floor to the other or to make room for the other's active responsive understanding. The utterance is not a conventional unit but a real unit" (71).

Speech genres are also distinguished by finalization of the utterance: the change in speaker can take place only "because the speaker has said . . . *everything* he wishes to say at a particular moment or under particular circumstances. . . . The first and foremost criterion for the finalization of the utterance is *the possibility of responding to it*, or more precisely and broadly, of assuming a responsive attitude toward it" (76). This appears to define the usual circumstances of myth enactments: one teller concludes in a manner precluding perfected closure because the enactment's finalization, "the indicator of the *wholeness* of the utterance" (76), facilitates responsiveness in listeners – often in the form of a retelling, the purpose of telling myths being to facilitate their retelling.

No less applicable to Indian myth enunciations is Bakhtin's insistence on the expressive aspect of speech genres. "There can be no such thing as an absolutely neutral utterance. The speaker's evaluative attitude toward the subject of his speech (regardless of what his subject may be) also determines the choice of lexical, grammatical, and compositional means of the utterance" (84). This defines the subject of ethnopoetics, which seeks to describe the formal properties of myth enactments. Ethnopoetic analysis of Native American storytelling, spearheaded by Dell Hymes, Dennis Tedlock, and Barre Toelken (followed by a large number of American anthropologists and linguists), has highlighted the crux of mythic form as the conjunction of personal variations-in-telling with conventionalized rhythmic and lexical vocal patternings.[22] This is exactly the nexus Bakhtin finds determinative of complex speech genres: "Expressive intonation is a constitutive marker of utterance. It does not exist in the system of language as such, that is, outside the utterance. . . . expression does not inhere in the word itself. It originates at the point of contact between the word and actual reality, under the conditions of that real situation articulated by the individual utterance" (85, 88).

By distinguishing utterance from language Bakhtin (inadvertently) provides a definition of how in the mythic retelling process the traditional is continuously made anew. The process "can be characterized as the process of *assimilation* – more or less creative – of others' words (and not the words of a language)" (89). Words that are "others'" and not of "language" are the recognized substance of Indian myth enactments. They are not artistically shaped by the metrical or other abstractly formal patterns that constitute the foundation of Western literary aesthetics. The living mythic tradition requires fluidity in its measuredness and openness in particularizing its conventionality, because such telling "is filled with others' words, varying degrees of otherness or varying degrees of 'our-own-ness,' varying degrees of awareness and detachment. These words of others carry with them their own expression, their own evaluative tone, which we assimilate, rework, and reaccentuate" (89). This view enables us to keep attention on the blindingly obvious (yet, by print-oriented critics, usually forgotten) fact that in oral cultures myths can exist only as they are imagined and uttered by one person to another or others, so the forms of their telling must be dominated by what Bakhtin calls *addressivity*: "the quality of turning to someone" which is a "constitutive feature of the utterance; without it the utterance does not and cannot exist" (99).

In Bakhtin's view human solitude is a fiction; human existence can be no other than social existence, evidence for which is that even our names are given to us by others. Language for him, therefore, is not (as it is for poststructuralists) a duplicitous, self-enclosed, self-undermining process into which cultured beings "fall" helplessly from some strange prelinguistic state of Rousseauian immaculate innocence. For Bakhtin, language is the only means by which the complete humanness of humankind can be realized; it is enriched and fulfilled through social interactivity – above all, through people talking to one another. For him, a "single consciousness is a contradiction in terms," the product of misunderstandings (encouraged in print cultures) about the human condition: "I am conscious of myself and become myself only while revealing myself for another, through another, and with the help of another. . . . Not that which takes place within, but that which takes place on the *boundary* between one's own and someone else's consciousness, on the *threshold*. . . . *To be* means *to communicate*. . . . To be means to be for another, and through the other, for oneself."[23] In preliterate societies a cultured individual is one continuously engaged in communicating, manifesting consciousness through reciprocal utterances with others. This helps to explain certain features of oral myth: for example, the omission of private, unexpressed, purely personal motivations and emotions. As more than one Western anthropologist has observed, such "unperformed sentiments" have little value in oral societies, can even be said scarcely to occur there, since "persons" exist through the fashion in which they interact.

Studying Dostoyevsky, Bakhtin observes that an idea is not a subjective, individual-psychological formulation; rather, "the idea is interindividual and intersubjective. The sphere of its existence is not the individual consciousness, but the dialogical intercourse *between* consciousnesses. The idea is a *living event* which is played out at the point where two or more consciousnesses meet dialogically. . . . Like the word, the idea wants to be heard, understood, and 'answered' by other voices from other positions."[24] The truth of that observation is displayed in any community without writing. Within such a community, ideas and ideological determinations can be realized only through speech exchanges among individuals. In these circumstances, what I call the exploratory quality of myths (in Bakhtinian terms, narratives existing only within situations of formalized "answerability" and "addressivity") appears virtually inevitable, and manifestly practical.

Some recent ethnological research points in the Bakhtinian direction I am articulating, even though it begins from different premises. Because it does not deal with a Native American culture, the work of Roy Wagner among the Daribi of New Guinea, for example, is interesting in this perspective. Wagner insists as strongly as I that we must distinguish myths from "literature."[25] Emphasizing that myths are "events" which impinge on conventionalized relations *dislocatively* (253–57), he demonstrates that Daribi myths need to be understood in terms of the conventions upon which they innovate, with the result that each mythic telling "is a novel expression that intentionally 'deconventionalizes' the conventional (and unintentionally conventionalizes the unconventional): a new meaning has been formed (and an old meaning extended). The novel expression both amplifies and controverts the significance of the convention upon which it innovates" (28). For Wagner, such mythic enactments are the core of a preliterate society's vitality, since in them is manifested "the continual invention and reinvention of culture out of itself" (24).

A paradigm shift does not invalidate all the research and thinking it redirects; it offers a reflexive position from which one may productively reevaluate that thinking and research. I have singled out Lévi-Strauss as exemplary of the deficiencies in virtually all "discourse analysis" of recent generations, in part because some of his contributions to the study of myth deserve salvaging. His principle that myth consists of all its versions is, if taken literally, of inestimable value. His method of analysis, moreover, has forced all commentators to recognize that mythic coherence more often than not utilizes principles of parallelism, contrast, and inversion (principles, one notes, of "answerability"), rather than the linear, sequential connectivity favored in our monologic discourse. He thus opens the way toward appreciation of oral artistries alien to print-culture aesthetics. His proposal that myths be read like a musical score, in two directions simultaneously, is usefully provocative, as is his observation that myths comprise layerings of "bundles of relations." The limitations in his approach derive mainly from his aping old scientific methods that manifest the Eurocentric, elitist bias of virtually all Saussurean-dependent culture studies.[26]

The classicist G. S. Kirk seems right to identify this bias as the core of modernist theorizing about myth, which is distinguished by a fanatic determination to universalize. Kirk, whom I cite because his focus on classical mythology locates him about as far from Native American myths as one can get, founds his strictures on the principle that there is a manifest variety of different *uses* (what I have called purposes of telling) for myth, and different uses "presuppose different interests, methods and kinds of imagination on the part of the tellers of tales, and different kinds of reaction on the part of their audiences; a variation of interplay between individual and collective emotions, and between deliberate and spontaneous invention." Kirk therefore believes that "traditional oral tale is the only safe basis for a broad definition of myth" and that a primary task for a contemporary student of mythology is to keep focused on the "narrative force that cannot be infringed" in order always to analyze in a manner "both flexible and multiform," responsive to the diverse singularities of myth tellings.[27]

This attitude we must train ourselves to accept if we wish to understand Native American myths, recognizing above all that variation of versions is not a phenomenon to be explained away by imposed classificatory systems.[28] We should assume that variant versions are normal, not in need of rectification, and that myth tellings assist tellers and listeners in evaluating forces (both personal and social) that *generate* traditional doctrines or practices. These presuppositions seem to me congruent with undogmatic structuralist approaches, which have no need to confine themselves within an antihistorical perspective. Such structuralism, in fact, adapts readily to a hypothesis that myths articulate imaginings of productive transformations in cultural practices.

The applicability of my hypothesis can be illustrated by brief comments on three versions of a major Blackfoot-Piegan myth. The story of Feather Woman and Scarface has been much studied as an instance of what has been classified as the "Star Husband" myth type.[29] The three versions reproduced here were chosen because each embodies a self-conscious effort to make accessible to a non-Indian audience something of the myth's socioreligious significance for the Blackfeet – as well as its remarkable emotional power. Taken together, I hope they may help nonspecialists learn how to respond rewardingly to the individuality of mythic enactments.

The first version, "Scarface," is only one segment of the "Feather Woman" myth. Oral narratives are built of "modular" units, separable episodes that can be combined in different ways or told as independent stories.[30] No doubt sometimes "Scarface" was (as here) recounted independently of the larger myth of which it is a conclusion (Tom Peters's recitation of "The Girl Who Married the Bear," discussed in the next chapter, offers a striking instance of this kind of "truncated" performance). The meaning of a story, of course, is altered when it is detached from another narrative element, whether or not it is fitted into another story unit. Thus "Scarface" by itself appears as a kind of romance with a happy ending, barely hinting at the pervasive sorrow that marks "Feather Woman" as a whole.

George Bird Grinnell's purpose in presenting "Scarface" is clear:

> The white person who gives his idea of a story of Indian life inevitably looks at things from the civilized point of view, and assigns to the Indian such motives and feelings as govern the civilized man. But often the feelings which lead an Indian to perform a particular action are not those which would induce a white man to do the same thing, or if they are, the train of reasoning which led up to the Indian's motive is not the reasoning of the white man.
>
> In a volume about the Pawnees, I endeavored to show how Indians think and feel by letting some of them tell their own stories in their own fashion, and thus explain in their own way how they look at the every-day occurrences of their life, what motives govern them, and how they reason.[31]

Although writing in the condescending language of a century ago, Grinnell wants to let the Indians speak for themselves, because he had come to admire them and to appreciate many virtues in their traditional ways of life. The idealism, the purity, even the erotic romanticism of "Scarface," not to mention the loving skill with which this version is unfolded, made it appropriate for what he thought of as a celebration of the Blackfoot people. In presenting this part of the myth alone, however, Grinnell does not adequately alert readers to Scarface's connection with his people's most important religious ceremony, the Sun Dance – even though his subtitle points to the intense spiritual significance with which this myth is invested for a Blackfoot.

Yet given his aims and the audience Grinnell believed he was addressing, his choice of version is reasonable. And one could say that the uniqueness of each myth enactment is illustrated by his selectivity – albeit transferred to a cross-cultural and print-dominated situation. There are gains and losses in all selectings. The loss of religious significance may for Grinnell's readers be compensated for by the beautiful tact with which romantic features are managed in this telling, features celebrating the moral worth of elemental human desires. Exemplary of that tact is the transformation of the more usual scornfulness of Scarface's inamorata into sympathetic encouragement of him, so that the conclusion is a fulfillment for both hero and heroine. A function of the Sun Dance is to sustain the combination of personal integrity with generous sympathy displayed by these protagonists, because these qualities enable individuals by realizing their deepest personal desires to sanctify the life of their community. The romantic features of this story are the reverse of idle escapism; they are the very stuff from which is shaped the religious and cultural aspirations of the Blackfoot people.

Walter McClintock gives us a version of the "complete" myth, which enables us to understand why folklorists classify it in the category "Star Husband." But McClintock foregrounds an element invariably disregarded by classifiers: its carefully constructed "frame"; we encounter the myth embedded in the story of the narrator hearing it told. This provides an analogue to the framing of many myth enactments. Oral recitations, after all, always occur at a particular occasion with particular listeners, and tellings are fitted to such situational specifics. McClintock's embedding also emphasizes another element that classifiers excise: the emotional impact upon an audience. He tries to make us feel through a representation of his feelings as listener how potently this myth dramatizes the opposition of cosmic yearnings to domestically familiar attachments, a source of perhaps humankind's most familiar heartsickness. To oversimplify, McClintock's admiration for the sky above him when he beds down after hearing the story reminds us of the girl's yearning toward the bright star. The framing possesses special appropriateness because of the detail of the *two* girls: the "superfluous" character allows us to recognize the heroine's longing as not mere personal idiosyncrasy but intensification of a "common" feeling, evinced by McClintock's looking at the stars.

Connectedness carries strong affect in this myth because it is created out of dramatizations of the pains of separation, appearing first in the girl's seemingly vain yearning. Fulfillment of her desire, however, leads finally to a permanent separation from her husband and the wonderful radiance of their marriage. In the "complete" myth we evaluate Scarface's happiness in relation to Feather Woman's sorrow, so there is poignant irony in his return to the sky (from which she is excluded) after having educated his people in the rites of the Sun Dance. The ambivalence so evoked (which becomes a key to James Welch's retelling) illustrates how myths articulate the desires and fears motivating the establishment of cultural practices. The action here turns on the contradictory longings of Feather Woman, first for the celestial beauty of Morning Star and then for the remembered terrestrial family life of her people. The Sun Dance's ritualizing of physical self-torture and spiritual aspiration into ceremonial evocations of celestial support for domestic life address exactly that emotional antinomy.

McClintock's embedded telling is also evocative of less specific sources of Blackfoot religiosity. The linkage of the past (a generations-old story) to the very concrete present (especially when McClintock's recollection of the telling he has just heard is disrupted by the pesky dog and then by the recently angered Bull Plume's attempt to trample him) confirms the relevance of the story not just to ritualized behavior but also to ordinary, often unpleasant, actualities of daily – and nightly – life. That relevance is accentuated when McClintock tells of awakening early and going after the horses, a description that cannot but appeal to anyone who has camped in the Rockies. He then sees the conjunction of planets which is the inspiration of the myth, and that sight in the context of the enchanting dawn repeats experientially what the myth told of: the mysterious loveliness of the celestial objects coexisting with, though entirely different from, lovely qualities of the familiar earthly scene. The scene can be described as familiar because McClintock's "framing" dramatizes for us the physical habitat of the Blackfeet out of which the myth has emerged. In thus linking story and sensory surroundings, without pretending to become a Blackfoot, McClintock can speak unabashedly of the "Sun God's" coming. He has been enabled to experience the interdependence of natural with supernatural, an interdependence fraught with the emotions through which Blackfoot myth sanctifies without sentimentalizing the daily life of a people's culture.

The myth's lack of sentimentality animates James Welch's retelling, near the end of his powerful historical novel *Fools Crow*, which narrates in Western literary form the destruction by whites of Welch's people a century earlier. Because Welch's retelling comes as a climactic conclusion to a carefully structured novel, I cannot do justice to all its functions and the variety of its resonances. But it is noteworthy that he fictionalizes the emotions central to all tellings of the Feather Woman story – the yearning of a desperate homesickness, the pain of enduring irrevocable loss of what one passionately loves – in a way that enables us today to feel the personal sufferings of which the historical tragedy of Blackfoot communal experience is constituted.

In adding to the Feather Woman story her depiction on a deerskin of the terrible future of the Pikuni (Blackfoot) people, Welch (refracting the tradition of her peering down at Blackfoot life through the turnip hole) extends to the community the personal sadness of Feather Woman's fate and foregrounds the qualities of shame, fear, and loss as inseparable from the myth's celebration of celestial blessings and natural harmony. In so doing, Welch adheres to the mythic method, even though fictionalizing it. He thrusts into his presentation of the myth the historical narrative of the Blackfeet caught within the nonmythic realm of decimating disease and United States aggression, so that the suffering and homesickness of the traditional story resonate communally in a new fashion within the "frame" of his particular telling.

Thus Feather Woman's bringing of lifelong sorrow upon herself by digging up the forbidden turnip, as experienced by Fools Crow, now prefigures the mystery of the historical disaster that has stricken his people. Why do they suffer? Welch's telling provides no answer, for it reproduces the myth's insistence that Scarface's apotheosis does not include his mother, making his happiness accentuate her anguish. In their moment of cultural despair the Blackfeet can perhaps for the first time fully empathize with her suffering. Welch makes us feel that the myth was shaped to prepare his people for such unimaginable pain. In this way he gathers into his fiction something of myth's power to evoke the intersecting of individual and social forces that make problematic an institution or historical situation which is its subject.

Through the Feather Woman myth Welch asks for the Pikunis: what failure in their practices, or what failure in their system of belief, can be responsible for what has befallen them? The grim response the myth dramatizes is that there is always the possibility of enduring sorrow for individuals and societies alike, poignantly epitomized here by the seemingly trivial detail of Indian children excluded from play at the white school. It is appropriate that Welch turns to one of his people's central myths at the climactic nadir of his novel, because such a myth is shaped out of many imaginings of personal and communal crises. Western commentators on myth from Max Müller to Lévi-Strauss have been unwilling to recognize that myths are invented and adapted through diverse enactments to provide practical assistance for people in confronting actual problems, even unexampled social catastrophes. By refusing to admit that "primitive" people in fact live lives as "historical" as our own, Western experts have denied to those they pretend to admire the terrible honor of tragic experience and the imaginative strength to face boldly the realities of defeat and irreparable loss.

NOTES

1. The name Blackfoot has been applied to the confederacy called by the Crees *Siksika* (meaning "blackfooted people," referring to their black moccasins), consisting of the Blackfoot, the Blood (or Kainah), and the Piegan (Pikuni) peoples, populous Algonquian-speaking tribes that traditionally ranged throughout Montana and Alberta, Canada. Dividing into autonomous bands that in winter lived separately, these people reunited in summer for the Sun Dance (which among the Blackfoot was sponsored and organized by a "medicine woman" in expression of gratitude for some favor) and to hunt buffalo. The bands were subdivided into military, religious, and dance associations – the last two groups containing both men and women, and each having its own regalia and ceremonial practices. Medicine bundles were a focus of religious observances. Skin tipis, owned by women, were often pictorially decorated by men, as were various skin containers. The Blackfoot were primarily hunters, especially of buffalo after obtaining horses in the early eighteenth century, and they were frequently at war with the Nez Percé, Assiniboin, Cree, and Crow tribes. By the end of the eighteenth century, however, the Blackfoot also became successful fur traders. Ravaged by epidemics of smallpox and measles, and further weakened by the destruction of the buffalo and diminishment of other game, they reluctantly took up reservation life at the end of the nineteenth century. Despite the hardships of trying to survive in barren territory, their population has begun again to grow, and they have been able to preserve significant elements of their cultural and religious heritage.

Besides *Fools Crow*, excerpted here, James Welch has published three powerful novels that brilliantly – if grimly – dramatize contemporary Blackfoot life on and near the reservation in northern Montana: *Winter in the Blood* (1974), *The Death of Jim Loney* (1979), and *The Indian Lawyer* (1990). Supplementing the excellent but more personal accounts in Grinnell, *Blackfoot Lodge Tales*, and McClintock, *The Old North Trail*, is a good general history by John C. Ewers, *The Blackfeet: Raiders on the Northwestern Plains* (Norman: University of Oklahoma

Press, 1958). Wissler and Duvall, *Mythology of the Blackfoot Indians*, from which "The Sand Hills" is cited, is perhaps the fullest collection available.

2. The Yurok people lived principally along the lower Klamath River in California and the adjoining coast around the river's mouth. Village leadership was usually that of the wealthiest family, for the Yuroks highly valued "money," consisting principally of dentalia, seashells imported from outside their territory. The Yuroks were quite class conscious, with strong regard for individual property rights, the upper classes speaking with elaborate ceremoniousness and esteeming extremely refined manners. Yurok houses were built of redwood planks with gabled roofs. Healing was carried out by carefully trained women doctors. Intensely religious, Yurok men spent much time in purifying themselves in sweathouses. The chief social functions were dances, among which the most important were the Brush Dances, Jumping Dance, and Deerskin Dance, often performed in spectacularly decorated regalia. As they were essentially a river people, the core of the Yurok diet was fish, obtained from the river and ocean by men fishing from dugout boats. See A. L. Kroeber, "The Yurok," in his *Handbook of California Indians*, Bureau of American Ethnology Bulletin 78 (Washington DC, 1925), 1–97; Robert Spott and A. L. Kroeber, "Yurok Narratives," *University of California Publications in American Archaeology and Ethnology* 35 (1943): 143–256; R. H. Robins, *The Yurok Language: Grammar, Texts, Lexicon*, University of California Publications in Linguistics, 15 (Berkeley CA, 1958).

3. Pierre Bourdieu has articulated probably the most sophisticated critiques of "scientific" approaches to myth and culture. In his early *The Logic of Practice: Outline of a Theory of Practice*, trans. Richard Nice (Cambridge: Cambridge University Press, 1972), Bourdieu insists that a "science of myth . . . destroys the truth it makes available to apprehension, because it has been won and built up against the experience it enables one to name" (117). This critique is founded on Bourdieu's challenge to all "objectivist" description, "which grasps practices from the outside . . . instead of constructing their generative principle by situating itself within the very movement of their accomplishment" (3). The consequence of this view is his demand that ethnological understanding must depend upon comprehension of a people's "habitus," the "durably installed generative principle of unregulated improvisations" (78). The convergence of my thought with Bourdieu's on several issues should be apparent; my argument that myths of nonliterate peoples focus on the forces generating practices, for example, helps to explain how, as he recognizes, myths offer special insight into a "habitus."

4. See Bronislaw Malinowski, *Magic, Science, and Religion and Other Essays* (Garden City NY: Doubleday, 1954); the key essay is "Myth in Primitive Psychol-

ogy," a reworking of Malinowski's first articulation of his view of myth as originally enunciated in a 1925 lecture honoring Sir James Frazer.

5. "Enactment" (rather than "performance") emphasizes that myth tellings are social transactions of intensity and complexity, as is admirably explained by Roger D. Abrahams, "Toward Enactment-Centered Theory of Folklore," in *Frontiers of Folklore*, ed. William R. Bascom, American Association for the Advancement of Science, Selected Symposia, Series 5 (Boulder CO: Westview, 1977), 79–120.

6. See Walter J. Ong, *Interfaces of the Word: Studies in the Evolution of Consciousness and Culture* (Ithaca NY: Cornell University Press, 1977). Among Ong's other relevant works (whose importance to discourse theorizing and cultural studies is still undervalued) is *Orality and Literacy* (London: Methuen, 1982). Stephen A. Tyler, "The Vision Quest in the West, or What the Mind's Eye Sees," *Journal of Anthropological Research* 40 (1984): 23–40, acutely dissects (in a fashion complementing Ong's philological researches) the "hegemony of the visual" in Western thought from antiquity through Jacques Derrida, defining a profound bias in our culture toward conceiving of thinking processes in visual terms – which renders oral forms of structuring difficult for us to comprehend.

7. A well-edited text of "The Defense of Poetry" is to be found in *Shelley's Poetry and Prose*, ed. Donald H. Reiman and Sharon B. Powers (New York: Norton, 1977), 480–508, from which my quotations are drawn.

8. T. H. White, *The Once and Future King* (London: Collins, 1939), 295.

9. O'Hara's certainty that the meaning of his allusion to the parable will be understood appears in the wording of his novel's title. Oral stories, incidentally, do not possess in our sense "titles." They are, however, very often "framed," introduced formally, or recited in ritualized circumstances – a point discussed in relation to "The Girl Who Married the Bear" (chapter 3). Our leading scholar on oral retellings as reinterpretations is Dennis Tedlock, many of whose most valuable essays are gathered in his indispensable *The Spoken Word and the Work of Interpretation* (Philadelphia: University of Pennsylvania Press, 1983).

10. Jorge Luis Borges, "The Captive," trans. Elaine Kerrigan, in *A Personal Anthology* (New York: Grove Press, 1967), 175. © 1967, Grove/Atlantic, Inc.

11. Ernest Gellner, *Plough, Sword, and Book* (Chicago: University of Chicago Press, 1988), 44. The relation of such social situations to linguistic practice has been one of Bourdieu's most consistent concerns, underlying his critiques of Saussurean and Chomskian assumptions (whether applied to aboriginal or contemporary societies) from his earliest publications to such recent work as appears in the collection of essays *The Field of Cultural Production: Essays on Art and Literature*, ed. Randall Johnson (Cambridge: Polity Press, 1993). As John-

son summarizes Bourdieu's view of *appropriateness* in the analysis of sociolinguistic circumstances, "The kind of competence that *actual* speakers possess is not a capacity to generate an unlimited sequence of grammatically well-formed sentences, but rather a capacity to produce expressions which are appropriate for particular situations" (7). In "many-stranded" societies, in my view, inevitably complicated mixtures of motives are most appropriately represented in oral narratives not by enumeration or by emphasis upon a restricted selection but by an appeal to imagine the complex mixture through omission of everything but narration of action-behavior. Such evocation-by-omission is especially appropriate in the telling of familiar stories that have been much thought about and interpreted.

12. Unfamiliarity with alien modes of imagining extends into many sociological dimensions; there is, for example, irony in Borges's story being about a false Indian, since the Argentines genocidally obliterated all real native peoples in their nation. More directly relevant to different styles of imaginative response is Borges's second paragraph, in which the narrator's private speculations preclude *ours*. Borges's "art" lies in presenting us with a finished artifact, a story not only about the dead but itself "dead": that is, an aesthetic object, not, like an Indian myth, a dynamic contribution to a transmissive process by which a people continues to reimagine its culture,

13. Edward Said has drawn attention to the importance of this phenomenon: for example, "It has been the essence of experience in the West at least since the late eighteenth century . . . to divide the realms of culture and experience into apparently separate spheres" (*Culture and Imperialism* [New York: Knopf, 1993], 58).

14. A. L. Kroeber, *Yurok Myths*, 16–17.

15. In fairness to Lévi-Strauss it should be noted that his attempts to reduce mythic discourse to mathematical formula – he claims that $F_x(a) : F_y(b) \simeq F_x(b) : F_{a-1}(y)$ defines *every* myth's aggregation of its variants – have been deliberate and sustained with consistency. The formula just cited was first published in "The Structural Study of Myth," *Journal of American Folklore* 78 (1955): 428–44 (among a rich collection of essays on myth, including pieces by David Bidney, Stanley Edgar Hyman, and Philip Wheelwright, brought together by Richard Dorson) – the source from which all my quotations of Lévi-Strauss are taken. I find no significant deviation from the fundamental principles there enunciated even in his publications of recent years, such as *The Story of Lynx* (Chicago: University of Chicago Press, 1995). Most contemporary literary critics, unlike Lévi-Strauss, seem unaware of the dependence of their theories on quite antiquated scientific ideas.

16. Paul de Man, "Dialogue and Dialogism,' *Poetics Today* 4, no.1 (1983): 99.

17. Bakhtin deliberately founded his views in opposition to Saussurean principles, fully aware that doing so implied commitment to a sociology and psychology antagonistic to Western thinking: hence his book attacking Freud and the congruence of his ideas with those of the Russian psychologist Lev Vygotsky. Vygotsky, incidentally, also attacked Jean Piaget, whom Lévi-Strauss cites (along with Saussure) as among his primary intellectual influences. Bakhtin (who says little about preliterate societies) does not privilege speech over writing or vice versa; his fundamental concept of "utterance" is equally applicable to what is written or spoken.

18. Mikhail Bakhtin, *Marxism and the Philosophy of Language*, trans. Ladislaw Matjecka and I. R. Titunic (New York: Studies in Language, 1973), 34, cited by Gary Saul Morson, "Dialog, Monolog, and the Social," in his excellent collection *Bakhtin: Essays and Dialogues on his Works* (Chicago: University of Chicago Press, 1986), 86.

19. Michael Holquist, *Bakhtin and His World* (London: Routledge, 1990), esp. the chapter "Novelness as Dialogue," and his comments on "preadaptation," 128–29.

20. Susan Stewart, "Shouts on the Street: Bakhtin's Anti-Linguistics," in Morson, *Bakhtin*, 41–58.

21. Mikhail Bakhtin, "The Problem of Speech Genres," in *Speech Genres and Other Late Essays*, trans. Vern W. McGee, ed. Caryl Emerson and Michael Holquist (Austin: University of Texas Press, 1986), 60–102. Page references are to this text.

22. The translation by Toelken of "Coyote and the Prairie Dogs," reproduced in chapter 4, illustrates precisely the congruence of Bakhtinian theory and American ethnopoetic practice. For the indispensable work of Dell Hymes, see *"In Vain I Tried to Tell You": Essays in Native American Ethnopoetics* (Philadelphia: University of Pennsylvania Press, 1981); and for Tedlock, *The Spoken Word and the Work of Interpretation.*

23. Translated and quoted by Caryl Emerson (in her essay "The Outer Word and Inner Speech: Bakhtin, Vygotsky, and the Internalization of Language," in Morson, *Bakhtin*, 33) from Bakhtin's 1961 notes "Toward a Reworking of the Dostoyevsky Book." Emerson has translated and edited these notes in *Mikhail Bakhtin's Problems of Dostoyevsky's Poetics* (Minneapolis: University of Minnesota Press, 1984), 283–302. Interestingly, Bakhtin's conception of individual consciousness is entirely in accord with some of the latest neurological studies of brain function as developed by the Nobel Prize winner Gerald M. Edelman, discussed in Karl Kroeber, *Ecological Literary Criticism* (New York: Columbia University Press, 1994). The congruence may not be entirely accidental, because in St. Petersburg Bakhtin was

closely associated with some outstanding Russian biologists, from one of whom in fact he took the idea of the chronotope.

24. Mikhail Bakhtin, *Problems of Dostoyevsky's Poetics*, trans. R. W. Rostel (Ann Arbor: University of Michigan Press, 1978), 38.

25. Roy Wagner, *Lethal Speech: Daribi Myth as Symbolic Obviation* (Ithaca NY: Cornell University Press, 1978), 35. Subsequent page numbers refer to this volume.

26. Robert Stam, *Subversive Pleasures: Bakhtin, Cultural Criticism, and Film* (Baltimore: Johns Hopkins University Press, 1986), 30, is one among several recent critics who have pointed out Saussure's preoccupation with maintaining the linguistic hegemony of conservative Francophone traditions, and the coincidence of his principal work with systematic efforts of French educators to obliterate dialects and class usages.

27. G. S. Kirk, "On Defining Myths," *Phronesis: A Journal for Ancient Philosophy* 1 (1973): 65, 67, 68. Kirk's later *Myth: Its Meaning and Functions in Ancient and Other Cultures* (Cambridge: Cambridge University Press, 1978) develops this approach and devotes the second chapter to an analysis of Lévi-Strauss's theories and practice.

28. The flexibility of myth was perhaps first significantly emphasized by Raymond Firth, "The Plasticity of Myth: Cases from Tikopia," *Ethnologica* 2 (1960): 181–88. Firth's presentation helped to stimulate the Dutch scholar Theodore van Baaren's essay "The Flexibility of Myth," *Studies in the History of Religions* 22 (1972): 199–206, the first account I know to identify mutability as a defining characteristic of myth. Resistance to the idea of myth's plasticity remains powerful, despite the evidence brought forward by ethnographers such as Tedlock and the emphatic clarity of scholars such as Victor Turner on the essential variability of performance in oral cultures: for example, his assertion "that no performance of a given cult ritual ever precisely resembles another" (*"Chihamba, The White Spirit": A Ritual Drama of the Ndemba* [Manchester: Manchester University Press, 1969], 3).

29. Stith Thompson's exhaustive multicultural commentary on the "Star Husband" has formed the basis for most subsequent analyses; see "The Star Husband Tale," *Studia Septenrionalia* 4 (1953): 93–163, reprinted in *The Study of Folklore*, ed. Alan Dundes (Englewood Cliffs NJ: Prentice-Hall, 1964), 414–74.

30. I have examined the modular or segmented structure of narrative in Karl Kroeber, *Retelling/Rereading: The Fate of Storytelling in Modern Times* (New Brunswick NJ: Rutgers University Press, 1992), esp. 73–80; see also chapters 3 and 4 below.

31. Grinnell, *Blackfoot Lodge Tales*, xii–xiii.

3
Human Cultures, Animal Cultures

Tlingit[1]

The Woman Who Married the Bear

TOM PETERS

[PART ONE]

There were two women, sisters.
They went for meat
to the place where animals were killed,
to the place where moose were killed.
When they were returning home
the meat was all
packed out.
That's when the two sisters
came on the berries,
they came on the berries.

Well, when they came on them just then
the people left them behind.
Then the younger sister
said, "Hurry now" to her older sister.
She walked behind her.
She went quickly and
along where people had walked.

Then from there
the older sister
walked right through

Haa Shuká, Our Ancestors: Tlingit Oral Narratives, trans. and ed. Nora Marks Dauenhauer and Richard Dauenhauer (Seattle: University of Washington Press, 1987), 167–94. Lines in the translation represent the way the story was told: each slight pause is indicated by a line ending; where the pause is longer, a comma, semicolon, or period reflects its length; spaces between lines indicate very long pauses. Indentations merely indicate a line (speech without pause) too long for the width of the page.

right where
a brown bear
had defecated; she stepped on it.
That was what she slipped on, it's said.
And those berries of hers all spilled from her hands,
What was it she said then
to the Brown Bear? She insulted it.
But her sister had already left her.
That's when

that's when the man appeared in front of her.
Nice!
Where was this man from?
A young man.
As soon as he came by her he said to her
"Come with me,
come with me," he said to her.
"No!
My parents
will miss me."
"We will go there.
Just come, come with me forever,
come home with me,
come home with me
to the place where my home is."
At first she didn't want to go.
Maybe he did something to her mind.
Then she went with him.
They hadn't gone very far
when a log
was lying there.
They went over it.
They hadn't been going far
when another log was lying there.
They walked
for three days.
Here they were really mountains.
That's what seemed like logs to the woman.
Then, while they were walking along then

they came on people.
They were surely human beings; that's just how they seemed to her.

That's when
the one she had gone with said to her,
"Don't look up.
At dawn,
don't look among the people."
But then
at what point was it?
"I wonder why he's saying this to me," she thought.
Weren't they the woman's people?
Weren't they
her father
her mother?
"I wonder why he's saying this to me," she thought.
Then, when she woke up
at dawn
that's when
she pushed the blanket-like thing down from her face.
So many animals were asleep inside there,
brown bears.

From here
they separated from the people.
But from then on, the brown bear would hunt just around there.
There were salmon.
Things were drying
on the mountain –
ground squirrel
ground hog.

It was exactly
one year.
She had been gone with him
more than a year,
one spring and one winter.

When winter began coming

they had settled in.
She didn't know he was something else either, but thought he was a human being.
"We will live up there," he said.
How she liked it!
It seemed to her
like a house made of branches.
Nice!
It was very nice.
It was the way a house should be.
That's when
he told her
"Bring down some
branches
from up there for our bed."
The woman immediately went up there.
Then she knew what he was, that he was a brown bear who had captured her.
"Don't break the branches from up there.
Pick them from the ground."

Just then,
when she broke the branches, she broke them from above.
Then she brought them.
"Let me see.
Did you break them from up there?
Yes.
Let me see!"
That's when she gave them to him.
"Drat!
I told you 'Pick them from the ground.'
Now you've marked where we live."

It was known
to her father
and to her mother
and others
where the den was.
They could see from her footprints that she had gone

with him.
Then they moved to a different place.
Then they stayed there, they stayed there.
She was with him long enough to have two children.
They were just
like people.
They moved to a different place.
They settled there.
How the people of our village are
that's how they were.
Everything,
there was nothing that they needed,
at home.

But that time
there were five of them
the brothers of hers.
That was when they tried.
They could see their sister's footprints, they could see
that she had gone
with that thing.
He knew immediately that his life was in their hands.
When spring returned, when spring finally returned,
the brothers of hers
all five of them,
picked medicine leaves.
They did it just to get him, just to get the bear.
It is truly sensitive
people say. Do you know what is called "leaves"?
That's the first Tlingit you didn't know.
[*Nora Dauenhauer:* Is it made to acquire something?]
Yeah! Yeah!
It is known here that they were imported from over there.
This was told to us.
I never wanted to try those things.
It is really strictly handled, they say.
They are the ones,
they are the ones
that were made for things like money.

And those too were made correctly.
Maybe it was something that made you crazy, they say.
They made medicine,
from then on, medicine was made.
Eight days,
for eight days
in the morning
no
food was eaten
and no water
water,
no water was drunk.
Then spring really returned,
spring time
April.
Now they tried.
Then there used to be
dogs
trained with medicine.
"Chewing Ribs"
was the name
of the dog.
Those brothers
didn't go searching just once.
Today
this morning
the eldest
would go
to the hill.
Then the next one
then the next one.
Ah, ha!
At one point it was the turn of the youngest
of the women's brothers.
When spring
returned
she would go outside, groping her way, like this.
Ah, ha!
Spring finally returned.

That's when
the animal,
the brown bear,
had a vision
of his brothers-in-law.
"Your brothers
are making medicine against me.
Oh, oh.
Oh, oh.
It seems like it's the youngest who will get me.
Be brave."
That's what he told her, what the one with her
told the woman
and her children too,
both of them.
"Be brave.
When I fall into their hands, be brave,
when I fall into your brothers' hands."
At that time the woman would beg the animal with all she could.
"Have pity on my brothers.
Don't do anything to them,"
she would say to it.
"The younger one
your youngest brother will be the one."
From then
he already knew what the woman
was going to do.
There were two
stones this size.
Each time they ate
she'd roll them secretly
in his food.
When they finished doing that,
"There!"
But it seemed to him as if she had done it openly.
Surely the bear was an animal of the forest.
"There he is!
Your brother is coming here.
Be brave."

Just as soon,
as soon as it became dawn
his thoughts shot in,
his thoughts.
Here,
when they shot inside
they were just like a beam of light,
maybe they were just like a flashlight.
That is how they shot
through the house.
He caught the beams right there.
He snapped them back outside.
These were people's thoughts, it's said.
Because of that the black bear
and the brown bear
can see people.
They're pretty hard to find.
That's why he couldn't find it,
because of his thoughts.
When a man's thoughts
are shot inside its den,
he snaps them back toward the entrance.
That's why they can't find it.
Heh.
Ah, ha.
When she heard this from him,
when he told her these things,
that's when
the woman finally went out to the entrance of the den.

Here
she put those stones
between her legs,
those stones
she had,
then, toward the beach,
on the side of the mountain,
on the frozen
crust she rolled them down

and he found one.

He walked along the side of the mountain.

That dog of his
knew right then,
that dog of his that hunted with him.
Heh!
While it was going along
it acted
as if it got a scent of something on the snow.
It ran around sniffing.
Here it was where the stone had rolled down, wasn't it?
Up that way
he followed it.
The people of today
are not like the ones of long ago.
They were tough.
If they went from here no matter
  how many miles they had to go
  they'd make it in a day.
And now. . . .
What are they?
"Ah, hah!
Ah, ha! your brother's getting close,"
he told her, it is said.
Then like when
spears
are hung from rafters
is how his teeth looked to the woman.
He pulled them out
from there.
That is when she really
begged of him,
"Pity my brother," she said.

He was approaching up there.
Heh.
Then

suddenly the bear heard the dog barking
from the topside.
It wasn't like a dog of today.
They were as smart as humans
long ago.
Well, probably they were the same on the coast, too,
those dogs.

Over there
it is always done like this when the entrance of a den is approached.
From the upper side.
You can't go straight up.
Only from the upper side.
Whatever, even a piece of clothing, was tossed in.
That is what he did.
He tossed his mitten
into the entrance.
He could only see the paw
inside
then sweeping behind.

"Be brave,
I will go out
to him.
I will play with your brother,"
he said to her, it's said.

The bear lured him
into coming down.
That's when he instructed her.
"When your brother finishes with me
don't be careless with my skin.
You tell them right away.
You tell him.
Drape my skin
with the head
toward the setting sun."
That's why it's still done now.
From this very story.

It is never tossed away carelessly.
A pole is placed under it thus.
It is hung and pointed
towards the sunset, from his words.

He came right to the entrance there.
He stood facing it.
Ah hah!
But even at that
his dog didn't tire from barking.
He had already killed the bear.
He went up to it.
What else was there in the den?
Someone spoke from inside.

"Your mouth will get tired,
Chewing Ribs?"

He just stood there.
What's more, his sister came out of there,
the one who had been gone
so long.
He got here.
The children also, the two of them.
"From there
this skin of mine
you will always keep with you,"
is what he had said to her.
That's when he taught her
this song of his.
"You will sing this
when you hang my skin,"
he said to her.

Song 1

I went through every one of those young people
and the last brother,
I know he did the right thing.

Song 2

I dreamed about it
that they were going after him [me?].

[PART TWO]

It was
the brown bear
that I was telling about.
Then
things were settled.
She became accustomed to her village people.
Then
she lived the way
she had as long ago.
It was then she had her husband's
former skin
the way he had told her to do.
Yes. "When you go out
you will put this skin of mine
on your back."
Yes; this is what he once told her.
From then her children
had reached her size.
Then
she would leave them
when people would hunt ground squirrels.
she would only go a short way.
How did she get the squirrels?
Only the mound of her pack would be seen moving along to her house.
Oly when she was ready to go
Would she pull on
the skin that was her husband's.
Yes.
At times it would be going after berries,
when she was going to get berries.
Just as she was leaving home, as she started out, she would pull it on.
She would become
a real bear.
Her children too.

Up there where last year's berries grew
in the berry patch.
She would come out on the mountain.
Her children with her too.
After doing this so many times,
the brothers of hers
asked their mother
"Mother!
will you tell my sister
we want to just play a game with her?"
That was when she told her mother
"No!
No!
It is not right
for them to do this to me.
Yes. I am not the same anymore as I used to be.
When
I pull on
my husband's
skin
I don't think my old thoughts any more.
This is why. No!
Let me be.
Let me live among you as long as possible."
But still the brothers asked her
"Mother! please ask
our sister
to let us play with her."
How many times
they must have asked this.
Finally she said to them
"Well, okay, let's go!
Let's go!
Let them play with me."
After she said this to her mother
she left.
As soon as she left home she pulled on
the skin of her husband.
She looked just like a brown bear.

Her children too
the two of them
went alongside of her.
It was up there
above everyone on the face of the mountain
among the berries.
This is when she came out there.
Maybe they didn't believe she would.
The blades
of the arrows
were
pieces of bark.
Pieces of bark were placed on the tip.

Except the blade of the one who found her,
her brother, the youngest one.
It was he,
there were two arrows of his.
They each had
a real arrowhead.
There was
what is called
a quiver.
Arrows
are kept in it.
It's worn around the neck.
He put the arrows inside it.
He didn't do to his sister what his older brothers did, it's said.
He only watched.
From then his older brothers
stalked her.
The way an animal
is struck with arrows
is how they did it.
When the first one's arrow,
when the first one's arrow
struck her
was when her cry was heard.
"From behind you."

Here's when she turned on them.
How many of them were there? They were helpless against her.
And her children too.
When they were dead is when the younger brother,
the one with the two arrowheads,
drew them out.
  (Slap!
  Slap!)
He killed her,
that sister of his.
Now that is the end.

Beaver[2]

The Girl and Her Younger Brother

ANTOINE HUNTER

One time there was a young girl
who started her period first time.
They put her in a sideways hole in the ground,
"her house over there."
Great big, so she could sew and things.
They put her younger brother in the hole too,
so he would be a good hunter and get all kinds of game.
He would always have good luck.
The animals would never run away from him.
That boy would grow up to be a famous hunter.
He would be a good hunter and get all kinds of game.

They put two strings out of the hole.
When they wanted meat, they pulled one string,
and they drew in meat from the boy and drymeat for the girl.
When they wanted water, they pulled the other string,
and they got water.
They were going to stay in there ten days.

That girl had a sister who was married to a grizzly bear.
She had gone off in the bush with her grizzly bear husband
a long time ago.
That girl also had some brothers,

Trans. Robin Ridington, in *Coming to Light: Contemporary Translation of Native Literatures of North America*, ed. Brian Swann (New York: Random House, 1994), 186–89. The annotation is Ridington's.

and they went out in the bush to hunt.
Those two brothers came across a grizzly bear's hole.
Then they went and cut green sticks and peeled off the bark.
With those white sticks they started poking in the hole.
The grizzly told his wife –
"Tell my *klase* you are in there."†
But she wouldn't.
So the grizzly ran out to kill the brothers.
Before he could strike at them, they shot him and killed him.
They killed their grizzly brother-in-law.
They made a mistake.
They didn't mean to do that,
but their sister didn't speak, so they didn't know.

After the grizzly was dead,
the brothers told their sister to come out.
But she wouldn't.
They told her all kinds of things,
but she wouldn't come out.
Finally they told her
she was going to pack her husband's head and hide and backbone.
Then she came out, and she was really happy.
They made a pack for her
with the hide and backbone and head,
and they started off.

The two brothers walked in front,
and their sister followed a little ways behind.
Every time she was behind a little hill –
every time there was a little hill
between her and her brothers,
the dogs would start to bark.
"Why are the dogs barking like that?"
her brothers asked.
"They are afraid of your brother-in-law," she said.
One of his paws was dangling from the pack,
its claws swinging as she walked along the trail.

†*Klase* = brother-in-law.

Finally they got back home.
The grizzly man's wife didn't come back close.
She made her camp a little ways from her brothers' camp.
All night long the dogs barked at her camp,
but the brothers didn't bother to see what was the matter.

The next morning
the girl in the hole and her brother
pulled the string for water.
But nobody came to them.
They called and called,
but nobody came.
The older sister said to her brother –
"I'm going to lift up the tarp on top of us,
and you look out and see if you can see anybody."

The boy crawled out of the hole and looked around.
He didn't see anybody.
He went to his mother's camp.
His mother was sleeping there with her neck chewed off.
His brothers too.
Their necks were chewed from their bodies,
and they were lying where they were sleeping.
The little boy went to his oldest sister's camp –
the one who was married to the grizzly bear.
She was sitting there by a big, big fire
with her legs spread apart.
Her younger brother remembered her.

He went back to his sister in the hole.
He told her everything that had happened.
He was worried about how they were going to live after that.
He was afraid they would starve.

His older sister said –
"I'll make you a bow and arrows.
You see if you can get something."
"All right," the boy said.
"You go and see if you can kill our older sister," she said.

So she made him a bow and arrows,
and she came out of the hole too.
They went to their older sister's camp.
They talked to her.
"Why did you kill our mother and our brothers?
"What did you do that for?" they said.

"I'm a grizzly bear now. I'm not their sister.
Those aren't any relations of mine.
Besides – they killed my husband."
"Where's your heart?" they asked –
and their sister opened her hand,
and there was her heart pulsating away.

The boy shot through her other hand.
She fell on the fire,
and they put more wood on her
to make sure she wouldn't come alive again.
The woman and her brother ran outside.
They were worried about how they were going to live.
"We're the only people alive in this world,"
she told her brother.
"We may as well get married and have some children."
But her younger brother didn't want to –
it was his own sister.

He cried and cried.
So his sister said –
"I know! You run around the hill on this side,
and I'll run around the hill on the other side,
and if we meet in the middle, we'll get married."
So the younger brother ran around one side,
and his older sister ran around the hill on the other side,
and they met halfway around on the other side.

The woman put her arms around the boy.
"All right, we're going to get married.
You be my husband," she said.
But the boy still didn't want it.

He cried and cried.
"I have an idea," the woman thought.
"I'll paint around your eyes."
She got something, and she painted circles around his eyes.
That was for hunting.

That boy was too young to kill animals with a bow and arrow.
He didn't know how to make the arrowheads.
But every time he looked at an animal –
moose, bear, caribou, chicken –
it just dropped dead.

That woman must have been a medicine woman.
She must have known something about eyes.

And that boy didn't even touch that girl,
and she had a baby every year.
Every year till they had a big bunch of kids.
Then the brothers married the sisters,
and their children married each other,
and so on.

And that's how all the people in this world were made.
That's the end.

Cherokee[3]

Bear Man

AYŪNINI

A man went hunting in the mountains and came across a black bear, which he wounded with an arrow. The bear turned and started to run the other way, and the hunter followed, shooting one arrow after another into it without bringing it down. Now, this was a medicine bear, and could talk or read the thoughts of people without their saying a word. At last he stopped and pulled the arrows out of his side and gave them to the man, saying, "It is of no use for you to shoot at me, for you cannot kill me. Come to my house and let us live together." The hunter thought to himself, "He may kill me," but the bear read his thoughts and said, "No, I won't hurt you." The man thought again, "How can I get anything to eat?" But the bear knew his thoughts, and said, "There shall be plenty." So the hunter went with the bear.

They went on together until they came to a hole in the side of the mountain, and the bear said, "This is not where I live, but there is going to a council here and we will see what they do." They went in, and the hole widened as they went, until they came to a large cave like a townhouse. It was full of bears – old bears, young bears, and cubs, white bears, black bears, and brown bears – and a large white bear was the chief. They sat down in a corner, but soon the bears scented the hunter and began to ask, "What is it that smells bad?" The chief said, "Don't talk so; it is only a stranger come to see us. Let him alone." Food was getting scarce in the mountains, and the council was to decide what to do about it. They had sent out messengers all over, and while they were talking two bears came in and reported that they had found a country in the low grounds where there were so many chestnuts and acorns that mast was knee deep. Then they were all pleased, and got ready for a dance, and the dance leader was the one the Indians call Kalâs′-gûn-

Trans. James Mooney, *Myths of the Cherokees*, Annual Report of the Bureau of American Ethnology 19 (Washington DC, 1908), 327–29.

ăhi'ta, "Long Hams," a great black bear that is always lean. After the dance the bears noticed the hunter's bow and arrows, and one said, "This is what men use to kill us. Let us see if we can manage them, and maybe we can fight man with his own weapons." So they took the bow and arrows from the hunter to try them. They fitted the arrow and drew back the string, but when they let go it caught in their long claws and the arrows dropped to the ground. They saw that they could not use the bow and arrows and gave them back to the man. When the dance and the council were over, they began to go home, excepting the White Bear chief, who lived there, and at last the hunter and the bear went out together.

They went on until they came to another hole in the side of the mountain, when the bear said, "This is where I live," and they went in. By this time the hunter was very hungry and was wondering how he could get something to eat. The ohter knew his thoughts, and sitting up on his hind legs he rubbed his stomach with his forepaws – *so* – and at once he had both paws full of chestnuts and gave them to the man. He rubbed his stomach again – *so* – and had his paws full of huckleberries, and gave them to the man. He rubbed again – *so* – and gave the man both paws full of blackberries. He rubbed again – *so* – and had his paws full of acorns, but the man said that he could not eat them, and that he had enough already.

The hunter lived in the cave with the bear all winter, until long hair like that of a bear began to grow all over his body and he began to act like a bear; but he still walked like a man. One day in early spring the bear said to him, "Your people down in the settlement are getting ready for a grand hunt in these mountains, and they will come to this cave and kill me and take these clothes from me" – he meant his skin – "but they will not hurt you and will take you home with them." The bear knew what the people were doing down in the settlement just as he always knew what the man was thinking about. Some days passed and the bear said again, "This is the day when the Topknots will come to kill me, but the Split-noses will come first and find us. When they have killed me they will drag me outside the cave and take off my clothes and cut me in pieces. You must cover the blood with leaves, and when they are taking you away look back after you have gone a piece and you will see something."

Soon they heard the hunters coming up the mountain, and then the dogs found the cave and began to bark. The hunters came and looked inside and saw the bear and killed him with their arrows. Then they dragged him outside the cave and skinned the body and cut it in quarters to carry home. The dogs kept on barking until the hunters thought there must be another bear in the cave. They looked in again and saw the man away at the farther end. At first they thought it was another bear on account of his long hair, but they soon saw it was the hunter who had been lost the year before, so they went in and brought him out. Then each hunter took a load of the bear meat and they started home again, bringing the man and the skin with them. Before they left the man piled leaves over the spot where they had cut up the bear, and when they had gone a little way he looked behind and saw the bear rise up out of the leaves, shake himself, and go back into the woods.

When they came near the settlement the man told the hunters that he must be shut up where no one could see him, without anything to eat or drink for seven days and nights, until the bear nature had left him and he became like a man again. So they shut him up alone in a house and tried to keep very still about it, but the news got out and his wife heard of it. She came for her husband, but the people would not let her near him; but she came every day and begged so hard that at last after four or five days they let her have him. She took him home with her, but in a short time he died, because he still had a bear's nature and could not live like a man. If they had kept him shut up and fasting until the end of the seven days he would have become a man again and would have lived.

Kiowa[4]

Star Girl

KABA

There was a camp and in this camp there was a young woman who was married. She had one sister and six brothers. This woman used to go after wood to carry on her back. Her husband loved her. He would paint her face every day before she went for wood. One day in the woods this young wife met a bear with whom she fell in love. The bear did not like the paint on her face and would lick it off. Her husband wondered why, although he always painted her face, when she returned with wood the paint was off. He realized that his paint had been washed off by some one in the woods. He thought he would paint her once again and follow her and see who it was who washed off the paint. As usual the woman went to the woods. He followed until he saw her met by a bear who licked her and hugged her. So he said to himself that now he knew who it was who rubbed the paint off his wife's face. Meanwhile the two parted, the bear took off for the tall brush and the woman gathered her wood. The young husband returned to camp at once and waited for his wife. He asked her why she rubbed the paint off her face. He said that he had painted her to show his love for her, that she might look beautiful. She answered that it was sweat that washed off her paint. But he knew better, he knew how the paint had been rubbed off. He called together all the men and told them there was a bear in the woods, they were to round him up and kill him. So the men went out with their bows and arrows and rounded up the bear and killed him. His wife told him that if he killed the bear to bring back a piece of hide for her to tan and make something of. So her husband brought her a piece of hide and watched to see what she would do with it. He found her weeping as she examined the hide. Her husband asked her why she

Trans. Elsie Clews Parsons, *Kiowa Tales*, Memoirs of the American Folklore Society 22 (Philadephia, 1929), 9–11.

was weeping. She answered, "I have something in my eye that makes the tears run."

This young woman and her sister and a band of girls went down to the creek. After they got there, her sister proposed that they play a game of bear, one to act as bear and the others to go near the den and pick berries, and the bear would chase them until he caught one of them (*setyayum*, bear play). The woman with the bear hide played the part of bear. She told her little sister to run back to the camp and hide where there were a bitch and her pups. Upon the first run in the game, her sister ran as she was told. The young woman placed the bearskin on her back in order to become a real bear. On the second and third trial of the skin on her back, she turned part bear. On the fourth trial she was all bear. She ran after the girls and caught them and killed them. She went into the camp and attacked the people. The men tried to kill her, but failed. The bear killed all in the camp. She went to where the dog and the pups were to find her sister. She took her sister with her to where they had lived and had her do the work that was to be done. She was trying to find a way whereby she might kill her little sister. This Bear Woman ordered her little sister to take a digging stick to kill for her meal a jack rabbit and not to come back until she had killed one; if she did [not], she would kill her. So she took the stick and went where she thought she might find a jack rabbit. She was unable to kill one, and she cried as she went along. Meanwhile the brothers who had been away from home hunting were returning and heard someone crying. One of the boys, Tâphįki (Hear-quick man, Sharp Ear) hear someone cry. Bǫǫki (see-quick man, Sharp Eye) saw her and recognized in her their little sister. they all went up to their little sister and asked her why she was crying. She said their sister had turned to bear and had killed everybody but her and had ordered her to go out and kill a jack rabbit. So one of the brothers, T'ǫguki (Good-aim man), took the stick and scared up a jack rabbit. The rabbit ran away and stopped to look back and Good-aim man motioned at the rabbit four times with his stick, which he let go. It turned over once and killed the rabbit. He said, "Now, sister, take this rabbit to our sister. It she asks you how you killed it, lay it down, motion towards it four times and throw the stick and hit it as I did." She took the rabbit and went back. Her sister asked her how she had killed it. She said she would show her how she killed it. Bear Woman told her to try it, if she missed her mark she would kill her.

Bear Woman would send out her little sister to gather wood. She would lie in the entrance of the tipi and would tell her little sister not to touch her feet lest she kill her. Her brother, G'uuki (Smart man), had told her to go around the camp and gather up what bone needles she could find and stick them in the floor, but to leave a space for her to get away by. "Get a heavy stick and as she sleeps hit her across the shin. Sharp Ear will be listening for you and Sharp Eye will be on the watch for you." She did as they told her. She made her get-away to where her brothers were. After Bear Woman was struck, she raised up on her hind legs and then fell over on to the bone needles. While she was pulling them out, the girl ran to her brothers. After she reached her brothers, Bear Woman began to trail her. They all started to run. About the time they were getting tired out, Fast Runner (Sâyiki) gave his magic power to make them run faster. Bear Woman had more power than Fast Runner, so they were overtaken. The closer Bear Woman came, the more they cried for help. Suddenly they heard someone saying to them to come near him. At first they could not make out from what direction the voice came. On hearing it the second time, they ran in the direction of the voice. Bear Woman was near them. But the rock they had heard told them to run around it four times (clockwise) and then stand upon it. They stood upon the rock and the rock raised up. Bear Woman arrived and made a leap, but could not reach them. His sister told Sharp Shooter (Guaki) there was but one place Bear Woman could be killed, between the toes. Turned-to-Bear struggled against the rock, scratching it, until she moved it to an angle, before they were able to kill her. The rock rose up into the sky; they stayed up there, and the rock came down. They stayed up there until they turned into stars, Tamatọdâ, Star Girls. The rock still stands leaning over as the Bear Woman left it and with the scratches of Turned-to-Bear upon it.

Chinook-Clackamas[5]

Grizzly Woman Killed People

VICTORIA HOWARD

ONE: GRIZZLY WOMAN DECEIVES AND KILLS WOMEN

Preface They lived on and on in their village;
their headman's house was in the center.

I. [Grizzly Woman becomes a headman's wife]

A Soon now,
a woman reached him;
they said,
"Some woman has reached our headman";
now they lived on there.

B In spring,
she went I don't know where,
she came back at evening:
Oh dear! she brought back camas;
now she began to share it about.

C They told her,
"Where did you gather them?"
She told them,
"Well, I reached a burned-over place,
it's just camas there,
the camas stand thick."

D They told her,
"Goodness, whenever you go again,
we'll follow you."
"Very well,"

Trans. Melville Jacobs, retrans. Dell Hymes in Hymes, *"In Vain I Tried to Tell You": Essays in Native American Ethnopoetics* (Philadelphia: University of Pennsylvania Press, 1981), 342–81. To emphasize the formal symmetry of the story, Hymes uses large roman numerals to indicate what he takes to be the "acts" of the narrative drama and small roman numbers to demarcate "scenes"; capital letters indicate "stanzaic" units. Indentation patterns, he believes, reflect the original form.

she told them,
"Perhaps tomorrow."
E "Indeed. We will follow you too."
"All right,"
she told them.

II. [Grizzly Woman takes women for camas(1)]
A In the morning,
now they go,
I don't know how many canoes went,
they arrived,
they went ashore,
they dug.
B It became evening,
now they camped;
they said,
"Later tomorrow, then . . ."
They lay down to sleep the night.
C At daybreak,
she took her arrow-spear,
she went among them,
she pierced their hearts,
she killed them *all*.
D Now it was day,
now she carried them off;
she laid them down,
she hid their paddles;
she thought,
"Now I will go,
I will go home."
E She brought those very camas, the people's;
She arrived at the village,
she told them,
"They sent these to you."
She went to another house,
she told them,
"Later tomorrow,
then I will go fetch them."
They told her,

"We will follow you too."
"To be sure,"
she told them.

III. [Grizzly Woman takes women for camas (2)]
A In the morning,
now they get ready,
now they go, three canoes;
they went,
they arrived;
Their (predecessors') canoes are tied,
they tied their canoes too,
they went ashore.
She told them,
"Oh *dear*, perhaps they are over yonder.
There there are even lots more camas.
Stay here first.
Later tomorrow.
then we'll go in that direction."
"Indeed,"
they told her;
they dug.
B It became evening,
they (the camas) were brought up,
they started fires.
Soon,
now Grizzly Woman arrived on the run,
she told them,
"Oh dear . . . , now they have lots of camas;
they tell me,
'Perhaps we will cook them right here."
"Indeed,"
they told her.
C Now they began to eat,
they ceased:
no Grizzly Woman.
Soon they heard singing;
they said,
"Oh dear! they are singing!

Listen to them!"
They listened.
Soon she arrived on the run,
she told them,
"Why are you silent?
Yonder those folks are singing."
"To be sure!"
they told her,
"We hear them";
they said,
"Let us sing too."
Now they began to sing.
They ceased.
They lay down to sleep.
D At daybreak,
now again she went among them,
she numbed them (with her spirit-power).
Now again she took her arrow-spear,
she pierced their hearts,
she killed them all.
In the morning,
now again she carried them off,
she laid them all
where she had put away the first ones.
E She gathered up their camas,
she put it in (her bag);
Now she went home,
she arrived;
now again she informed them the same way:
"They won't come (today).
After a while,
Then they will come,"
she told them.
"Indeed,"
they told her.
Now others said,
"We will go too."

IV. [Grizzly Woman takes women for camas (3)]

i A In the morning,
now they got ready,
they went;
again she took them,
they arrived,
they went ashore.

B They became somehow (disturbed).
She told them,
"Right here they kept working.
Perhaps they moved off a little yonder,
there are even lots more camas."
"Indeed,"
they told her;
they dug.

C One said,
"What do you think?
Seems a long long time since these (were) digging places."
"Surely,"
they told her,
"We noticed (that about) them."
They ceased.

ii A In the evening,
they camped there;
they said,
"It's not as it should be,
Something somehow (is wrong)."

B Soon,
now Grizzly arrived on the run,
she told them,
"Why are you so silent?
Those yonder,
they are singing,
they are giggling,
they are laughing –
those who came first –
now they have baked their camas there."

"Ind*ee*d,"
they told her,
"It's just (that) we became somehow (disturbed)."
"G*oo*dness!"
she told them,
"What for?
Soon,
again they will begin dancing.
Suppose I run,
I go to see them again."
She ran.

C Soon,
as they stayed there,
they heard singing.
They said,
"Truly it is so;
Now they sing,
listen."
"Surely,"
they said;
they stayed there.

iii A Now again she got back to them,
she told them,
"You start to sing too!"
"To be sure,"
they told her;
they started to sing in vain,
no,
they ceased.
They lay down to sleep;
Grizzly also lay down;
they slept.

iv Now Grizzly Woman arose,
she numbed them (with her spirit-power),
she got her arrow-spear.
Now again she went among them,
she pierced their hearts,
she killed them all.
In the morning,

now again she carried them
where she had put down those first ones;
all done;
she ceased.

v A Now she put their camas in (her bag);
Now she went back,
she arrived;
Now again she told them the same way,
"They sent those to you."

B "Indeed,"
they told her;
"The first ones who went,
now they are baking them."

C "Oh dear! Let us go tomorrow too!"
"Yes,"
she told them.

V. [Grizzly Woman takes women for camas (4)]

i A In the morning,
now they get ready,
they go;
they arrived,
they went ashore;
they arrived
where their (predecessors') fire was.

B One burst out crying.
She was told,
"Why are you making a bad omen for yourself?"
She told them,
"No.
Somehow something (is wrong).
It happens to our people
where you are looking."
"No::::::!
A long long time (since) their fire,
now it is gone there,"
they told her.
"Never mind! She keeps saying nothing at all!" (said Grizzly).

C They went to dig,
they dug;
that one tries in vain,
she will become silent,
now again she will cry.

ii A They ceased at evening,
they went to their camp,
they sat;
they said,
"We will not build a fire."

B Soon,
now again Grizzly arrived on the run,
she told them,
"Why have you become this (way)?"
They told her,
"This one has become ill."
"Indeed. Soon she will cease (to be)."

C Now again they lay down to sleep.
She arrived on the run,
she told them,
"Oh *dear*! Have you lain down to sleep there?"
They told her,
"Yes . . . Later tomorrow morning,
we will dig."
"Indeed,"
she told them,
"I will go inform them."
They pay no attention to her.
She ran.
Soon,
they heard:
"Oh *dear*! they are singing."
They said,
"Listen! they are singing."
One said,
she said,
"Do you really think it is true?"
They became silent.

iii Now again she hurried to them,
she told them,
"They were going to come;
I told them,
'*Long* ago they lay down to sleep.
Nevermind.'
Now I will lie down too."
Now she lay down.
They slept.

iv Now again she numbed them (with her spirit-power).
Now she arose,
she got her arrow-spear;
now again she went among them,
she pierced their hearts.
In the morning,
now again she carried them.
All done . . .
she ceased.

v A She put their camas in (her bag),
a very few.
Now she went back,
she arrived,
she shared their camas around.

B She told them,
"They became lazy,
they dug a few,
they said,
'Later tomorrow morning, then,'"
"Indeed,"
they told her.

C Now some again said,
"We too will go in the morning."
Her sister-in-law also said,
"I also will go in the morning."
Right away her little younger sister said,
"I also will go, older sister!"

D She (Grizzly) said,
"Already you also!
Why should you go along?"

She (Water Bug) said,
  "I will just go along with my older sister."
E "*No*!"
  she told her,
    "You will not go."
She said,
  "I will go!"
She told her,
  "No."
"I will go."
Her older sister told her (Grizzly),
  "She is just saying that to you.
    We two (you and I) will go in the morning.

TWO. WATER BUG OVERCOMES GRIZZLY WOMAN

VI. [Grizzly Woman discovered]
A In the morning,
  now they got ready,
    the very first is Water Bug;
      she went,
        she hid in the canoe.
They went to the river,
  they got in their canoe,
    they went.
Grizzly turned and looked,
  she saw her,
    she said,
      "Dear oh dear! I told you not to come."
She pays *no* attention to her there.
They went,
  they arrived,
    they went ashore.
B Grizzly Woman forgot (about her);
  she forgot,
    she did not take her older sister's paddles.
Water Bug took them,
  she went,
    she hid them;
She ran about,

she got *all* those paddles (previously hidden by Grizzly),
she moved them away.
C Now she went ashore,
she reached her older sister,
she told her,
"Those here are *all* dead.
Let us go."
Now the two went,
they reached them,
Dear oh dear . . . there are corpses.
The two sat,
they wept;
she told her older sister,
"Wash your face;
She will become suspicious."

VII. [Grizzly Woman disclosed]
A The two arrived,
they informed them;
they wept;
they ceased,
they washed their faces.
Water Bug told them,
"Say nothing at all.
When she will tell us,
'You should sing,'
you should do that.
Be very careful!"
Soon,
now she hurried to them;
she nudged her older sister,
she nudged her;
she said,
"Now she will tell us!"
B She told them,
"Why are you so *still*?
You are lying to the people about something, Water Bug!"
She pays *no* attention to her.
She told them,

"Oh *dear*! Now they are drying their cooked camas."
She nudged her older sister.
She (Grizzly) ceased,
now she left them.

C Again now the two informed them, Water Bug (and her sister).
She said,
"Be careful!"
"Yes indeed,"
they told her.
"You are not to be first,
her plan is to kill me first";
she informed them of everything,
she told them,
"When she falls asleep,
now we will leave here."
"Indeed,"
they told her.
She ran to the river,
she picked up shells,
she brought them to her older sister.

VIII. [Grizzly Woman foiled]

i Now it *became* night,
they had lain down to sleep;
she got to them.
"Surely,"
she said,
"now you lied about something to them."
She paid no attention,
she said nothing whatever;
they had lain down to sleep.

ii A Grizzly Woman said,
"Now I too,
Now I lie down."
Water Bug picked up a lot of wood.

B She (Grizzly) told her,
"Why will you make a fire all night?
So that is why you came – (to be a nuisance) –
you're thinking,

Maybe some young man will get to your sister!"
She paid no attention.
C "Sleep acts on them,
in the morning they will get up,
they will dig."
She paid no attention,
she lay down to sleep,
she put those shells on her eyes.
iii A Soon,
they fire went down a little;
Grizzly Woman arose slowly, silently.
She saw her,
she nudged her older sister,
the two see her.
She went up to them,
she looked at Water Bug:
she is watching her.
B "Oh, goodness!"
she told her,
"Aren't you going to go to sleep?
Youths are going about."
"Oooo,"
she went,
Water Bug went (feigning sudden fright at being awakened).
C She got up,
she fixed the fire,
she put large pieces of wood on the fire.
"Ahh,"
she told her,
"Why indeed are you going to make a fire all night?"
She told her nothing whatever,
she lay down again.
iv A Soon,
the fire went down.
Now again Grizzly Woman got up.
she approached sl*ow*ly, silently;
She (Water Bug) heard,
"T'áLmu t'áLmu."

B "Ooooo!"
went Water Bug
"Oh *dear*! Aren't you going to go to sleep?"
"Oooo I was dreaming,
I saw a bloody arrow-spear."
"Goodness! Now she will lie to them;
Leave them alone,
they are sleeping."
Now again she lay down to sleep.

C Water Bug got up,
again she put more wood on the fire.
She told her,
"So that is why you came!
You might wake people all night."
Water Bug lay down to sleep.

v Now it was close to dawn,
now Grizzly Woman became sleepy,
she would nod off to sleep.
She would wake up,
she would get up slowly, silently,
she would look at Water Bug:
she is watching her;
now again she lay down.
Soon now it is dawn;
Now Grizzly Woman fell asleep,
Water Bug arose;
Now she cast t'áLmu t'áLmu on her (she numbed her),
She slept.

IX. [Grizzly Woman escaped]

A She told them,
"Quickly! Get up!"
They got up,
they hurried;
they went down to their canoes,
they got on them.

B She ran,
she fetched their paddles,
she put *all* of them in –

her older sister's paddles had holes –
now they went.

C They are going,
they turned to look,
now she is pursuing them there.
She curses Water Bug:
"So that is why you came!
You tell the people lies."
She gets close to them,
she took her snot,
she threw it at them;
their paddles broke.

D She pursued them;
she will get close to them;
she will blow her nose,
she will throw her snot at them;
their paddles will break;
all the paddles they brought,
all became broken.

E Now they have gotten close (to their village);
now she took out her (older sister's paddles;
in vain she threw her snot at them;
there it will go right through them;
they go.

X. [Grizzly Woman destroyed]

A The people said,
"Something (is wrong).
A canoe is coming,
hurrying this way."
They went out,
they said,
"Seems like our chief's wife pursues them."
They got their bows, their arrows.
They arrived,
Water Bug ran,
she told their older brother (the chief):
"She consumes people.
she has taken along a certain number,

She kills them all.
She pursues us."
Now they waited for her.
B Soon,
she came ashore,
now they shot at her.
She would tell them,
"Goodness! Why does Water Bug just lie and lie to you?"
She is *going*,
they shoot at her.
C Her husband sat on top of the house,
he shot at her;
She is close to him there,
now he has only one arrow.
He thought,
"Never mind!"
He threw it at her (shot it despairingly),
he wounded her little finger,
it split,
there she fell,
he had killed her.
In truth there she put her heart,
in her little finger.
D Now they burned her;
he got all of her,
they ground up her bones;
they blew them (ashes) away.
E Now they went,
they went to gather up the corpses,
they arrived.
There they went ashore,
they took Water Bug along,
she showed them the whole place there;
they arrived,
where the first ones (were),
now black,
rotting;
they took them *all* to the canoes.

Now they were taken to their graveyard,
  they buried them *all*,
    they ceased,
      all done.

Story story.

COMMENTARY

The last pages of the preceding chapter present a much revised comparison of versions of the Scarface story which I originally prepared at the request of the distinguished folklorist Richard Dorson. I submitted analyses of two versions of the myth to the critiques of several folklorists and linguists, and analyses and critiques were published together.[6] Dorson wanted this format because he hoped my suggestion that oral artistry contributes to versional variations in myths would advance his efforts to unify the work of literary critics, folklorists, and anthropologists. If myth telling is a self-conscious imaginative act, a focus on the imaginativeness of the act may provide the nexus for the cooperative scholarship Dorson sought and I would like to encourage. I now recognize, however, that our concept of literature is determined by unconscious presuppositions about writing and limited by print-oriented thinking. Claims for the "literary value" of myths (which I have myself made) may seriously, if inadvertently, conceal the authentic artistry in an oral myth. My comments on Native American myths now are intended to help us appreciate the skill of their tellings without defining them as "literature" in our sense of the term.

My purpose makes Catherine McClellan's *The Girl Who Married the Bear* an appropriate, almost an inescapable, focal point.[7] The monograph has been justly praised by many ethnologists but has produced little evaluation of the implications of McClellan's judgments and no systematic development of her analytic procedures. She presents eleven versions of a myth very popular in the Yukon region, comments on some differences between versions, and provides information about the character and circumstances of the different tellers. Her aim is to suggest reasons why the story has been popular, but she also wishes to display its literary value. She complains: "If no effort is made to collect at least five or six versions of a given tale, and if no attempt is made to explain why they vary, I do not know how some of the fundamental patternings of a given body of literature will ever be obtained" (2). Folklorists and anthropologists, though collecting plenty of versions, have usually limited themselves to classifying them formally, thematically, or distributionally. McClellan wants analysis of the variations that will reveal literary qualities, and she is prepared to claim high aesthetic merit for the narrative on which she concentrates: "This particular story attracts the Southern Yukon natives with the same power as does a first-rate psychological drama or novel in our own culture. The themes probably evoke the same intense response in the Indians as those evoked in the Greeks by the great Attic drama" (1).

McClellan focuses on the personal psychology and the biographical circumstances of the different tellers she worked with, but I want to draw attention to more general social purposes discernible in the tellings. This shift of emphasis is facilitated by the appearance in print of other retellings of the myth, notably a later version by one of McClellan's informants, Tom Peters (see the first story in this chapter). This version – unlike the one McClellan had from Peters, which was told to her in English – was recorded in Peters's native Tlingit, as was still another retelling by another McClellan informant. These versions in particular offer new insight into indigenous narrative forms that McClellan discusses.

One may summarize "The Girl Who Married the Bear" as the story of a young girl who is taken away by a bear after she has made insulting remarks about the bear feces over which she leaps or in which she slips while gathering berries. The bear appears to her in the form of a handsome young man, whom she marries and by whom she has two children. She makes it possible, however, for her brothers and their dog to locate the cave in which she lives with the bear, and the brothers there kill the bear, who has given the girl instructions on how his corpse is to be treated. Taken home by the brothers, after a period of self-isolation (because the smell of humans is offensive to her) the girl rejoins her family. Her brothers tease her to put on a bearskin so they can practice hunting with blunted arrows. She at first resists but finally gives in to their requests, turns into a real bear, and kills them.

Diverse tellings of this story (and hundreds are known) pose a number of ethnographic problems, since they offer much self-contradictory evidence to the scholar using them to discover or confirm social practices. McClellan, for example, looking for information on how dead bears were treated, found that the instructions provided by different narratives varied widely. One said the skull should be burned, another that feathers should be burned on top of it; some called for the skull to be placed in a tree, others for it to remain attached to the skin and placed on poles facing west – or north. The stories seemed partly shaped, moreover, by a taboo on cross-sex sibling speech, yet the presentations of the taboo are not entirely consistent. There is even confusion as to what kind of bear marries the girl, brown bear or grizzly, despite sharp distinctions drawn between the species: McClellan's third informant, for instance, claimed that the story explains why grizzlies, unlike brown bears, were never eaten. Some confusions occurred because the story originated in a much earlier time. Although a few of McClellan's informants had themselves killed bears, Indian cultures in the Yukon region in the 1950s (when she was collecting) had lost much of their traditional structure. Illustrative of the psychosocial intricacies created by the passage of time was the explanation by an older informant of the cross-sex speaking taboo: McClellan wouldn't know of the prohibition, he said, because it was no longer operative – although at that moment, by ostentatiously not speaking to a sister present with them, he was himself obeying the taboo.

A powerful and often retold myth, we should recognize, is quite likely to be a source of ethnographic confusions when it more than simply affirms practices or beliefs. If it opens up for examination *sources* – subjective, social, or physical – giving rise to particular beliefs and practices, we should expect enactments to vary in their ways of "reporting" attitudes and practices. Tellers frequently wish to relate a particular myth on a particular occasion for a quite specific reason, often "aiming" at one individual or group in their audience, without attending particularly to ethnographic details.[8]

Variations in purpose for telling in fact reflect the fashion in which myths may respond with sensitivity to variations in the continual play of ongoing social practice. If we take seriously Lévi-Strauss's dictum that all myths exist only through the multiple form of all their versions, we must expect myths adaptable to what I call "exploratory" tendencies to be quite various. At the same time, these myths retain a consistent integrity because they accommodate sociohistorical changes. Their flexible character permits them to remain identifiably the same story even while introducing a variety of new features and sometimes drastically altering descriptions of social behavior and custom. To appreciate the artistry of oral myths we must recognize that flexibility and remember Pierre Bourdieu's admonition that "practice has a logic which is not that of the logician."[9]

However inconsistent in their renderings of ethnographic details, McClellan's informants were all eager to tell a version of "The Girl Who Married the Bear." One informant, rather detached from his traditional cultural heritage, made a revealing remark about a particular incident: "Then this is kind of funny, but it's the story" (47). In an oral culture, after all, story is the primary medium through which the culture sustains itself. Stories therefore must be simultaneously "sturdy" and "steady" enough to transmit continuity while remaining as plastic as the culture itself needs to be. No culture, after all, is a simple artifact like an arrow or bullet indifferent to the air it cleaves. Culture is a living entity continually interacting with its environment and its own internal shiftings; a culture's integrity can be maintained only by openness to the possibility of transformation under the influence of time and shifting circumstances – which is why culture has been such a successful tool for human survival: continuity is preserved by transformation.

Mythic transmission through transformation is exemplified by this story's intense focus on the central ambiguities of social life. "The Girl Who Married the Bear" may deserve the hyperbolic literary comparisons McClellan bestows on it because as mercilessly as Attic tragedy it resists oversimplifying human experience and portrays human life as a tissue of ambivalences inseparable from pain, error, and suffering. The story's potency emanates from the concreteness with which it dramatizes conflicts initiated by competing personal loyalties that constitute a web of communal relations. Such a narrative would be untrue to its fundamental complexity were it to rigidify into exact repetition in retellings.

Differences in the accounts of the story's originating act, for instance, highlight its appeal to something more than confirmation of a conventional prohibition. Some tellers portray the girl as slipping on bear excrement and "naturally" exclaiming her disgust.[10] Others present her as consciously, hubristically, scorning the taboo not to step over bear excrement (sometimes identified as a taboo for women only, other times applicable also to men – another ethnographic uncertainty). These seemingly radical differences, however, do not appear to alter drastically the outcome of the story: the girl destroying her kin. Different causes can produce analogous effects (and different conclusions can arise from similar causes) because the myth does not simply illustrate an inflexible prohibition; it articulates impulses and conditions that give rise to social practices. Variabilities suggest that the myth's appeal to tellers and listeners derives from its capacity to arouse awareness of the underlying potentialities for familial destructiveness lurking within the personal virtue of loyalty and the social virtue of family solidarity.

The artistry of Tom Peters's version, for example, is in depicting with both force and subtlety the contradictions that sociocultural formations try to stabilize through processes of self-adjustment. Primary is the superimposition of the tensions inherent in the relations between blood brothers and brothers-in-law upon the tensions inherent in human relations to natural phenomena within a hunting society. A modern reader, safely insulated from unmediated contact with nature, is likely to undervalue the latter set of tensions. Its effects, however, emerge in the uncertainty created in tellings such as Peters's, not merely as to how the bear will act toward the brothers but, more significantly, as to how in fact he has acted. On first hearing or reading the tale, one may be unsure whether the bear will allow himself to be killed without harming his wife's brothers, as the wife implores him to do. But on rehearing or rereading it, one is likely to become more puzzled as to whether the "noble" bear (as McClellan terms him) gained revenge by allowing himself to be killed. The only certainty is that the girl who urged her husband to sacrifice his life for her brothers ends up killing them herself. Is an unavoidable "natural law" here made hideously manifest? Does conflict set up by a culturally arbitrary distinction/amalgamation of blood kin and marriage kin allow the reemergence of a natural economy of death for death? To interpret adequately the social ambiguities represented so painfully in the myth, one must try to understand their connection to ambiguities of human beings' relationships to other natural (but in our view uncultured) creatures.

Even those who insist that the myth only confirms an established taboo will agree that the prohibition applies to human relations with natural creatures. The tragic peripeteia (whether or not intended by the bear) dramatizes a fundamental tension upon which is founded every sort of human family. The girl favors her blood kin – a favoritism we may sympathize with, since her husband is not human. Yet her favoritism destroys her brothers through the realization in her of a terrible "animalism," whose "naturalness" is implicit in the very idea of "blood kin." It seems no accident that the myth is especially popular in matrilineal societies, where relations of brothers to brothers-in-law are often simultaneously peculiarly important and peculiarly difficult. Yet the myth's deepest power arises from its confrontation of a critical feature of *all* marriage systems. Every human society, in one fashion or another, must struggle with the problem of sexual bondings which threaten the family by introducing into it an "outsider" – whose entry nevertheless sustains by renewing the family.

Today we probably read this myth too personally, thinking of "family" only as a small, nuclear unit. Most of the societies in which the story was popular were divided into what ethnologists call moieties, two parts or clan groups; one normally married only a member of the other moiety. All agemates of the moiety one was born into thus could be regarded as "siblings," older persons as "mothers" and "fathers," and so on. Threats to or strengthenings of "family," therefore, constituted threats to or strengthenings of society as a whole. But even this is probably easier for us to grasp than the superimposition of problems of human life on "bear life," because we no longer live in continual interaction with the natural world.

Many Indian myths, however, build upon a simultaneous consciousness of human strength and weakness relative to other creatures and the natural environment. That double consciousness (conspicuous in Indians' intense pride in their particular culture even while recognizing its utter dependence on natural forces they cannot control) underlies much mythic imagining, finding expression through rhetorical techniques different from those common in our literature. Anthropologists have perceived such dual consciousness in Indians' profound respect toward animals killed for food, respect that often leads (as in our bear myth) to a perception of the animal as freely offering itself to the hunter. Ethnologists have been slower, however, to recognize that this consciousness affects even mythic form.

Myths about bears are particularly helpful for fostering such insight. Bears, which flourished in all parts of North America, were usually the largest and most dangerous animals with which the Indians had to compete, and they are in some ways surprisingly like people. Being omnivores, they may be found fishing or, as in "The Girl Who Married the Bear," in berry patches, and their dens are easily conceivable as habitable caves. Yet their skins are valuable in colder climates, and their fat makes them attractive both as food and as a source of grease. Perhaps more like humans in appearance and manner than any other North

American mammal, even in their powerful dangerousness, bears were often the prey most valued by hunters outside of buffalo country.[11] Bears, therefore, were ideal subjects for representations of interfaces between natural and cultural worlds, perhaps the commonest subject of Indian myths.

The interface frequently is manifested through representations of animals as "people." In "The Girl Who Married the Bear," the bear, which for us is a purely "natural" creature, is depicted as living a "cultured" life. In this story (as in many Indian myths) sexual relations between humans and animals carry no overtones of perversion or bestiality. The absence of these qualities is made possible by the Indians' imagining a fluid analogousness between two kinds of creatures that we imagine only oppositionally. The "otherness" of bears is not to us what the "otherness" of bears is to Indians.[12]

This is a key to our difficulty in responding adequately to the Indians' affective superimposing of problems of human-animal relations on problems of marital relations. For them, there is nothing absolutely perverse in the girl begetting children with the bear, because both girl and bear are both natural and cultured beings. The bear's false appearance to her at the beginning as a handsome young man enacts an "equality" of bear-people and human-people. This kind of narrative enactment, however, involves rhetorical consequences surprising to us. Figures of speech that loom large in our literary art, for instance, are often replaced in Indian myths by what for us is confusing literalness. Thus in Tom Peters's narrative the bear's teeth looked to his wife like bear-hunting spears hung from the rafters when he "pulled them out / from there." In another version the bear removes his teeth and hangs them on the wall, handling his natural attributes exactly as he would "weapons"; in a third version he does the same with his knives (claws). Equivalent are the descriptions of the bear's shamanistic powers. His ability to cloud and confuse the girl's mind is of a piece with his capacity to fend off the thoughts of the brothers seeking him in his lair, a thought duel neatly if anachronistically compared by Tom Peters to combat with flashlights. Without ever ceasing to be entirely a bear, he is represented "literally" as just as "civilized" in his psychic capacities as his human antagonists. This is why it is reasonable to interpret his actions as morally admirable, to regard his deliberate sacrifice of his life as a noble recognition of his responsibilities in marriage.

The myth implies, then (contravening our habitual way of thinking), that "culture" for an Indian is quite "natural." This is not the argument of the myth; it is an assumption that underlies it, animating the contradictoriness of relations that demand articulation through rhetorical forms unfamiliar to us. Animals are like humans not merely through instincts but more importantly through a shared capacity for consciously elaborated social existence. This allows for imagining efficacious (that is, ethically significant) magic, power resulting from the unifying interactivity of "natural" and "cultural" forces. That unity produces what we call "supernatural" effects – that is, impossibilities – but for Indians, "magic" realizes potencies that are inherent in natural processes.[13]

Peters, for instance, emphasizes the magical aspect of the brothers' hunting of the bear, including the preparation of a special leaf infusion, which requires extended fasting and sexual abstinence. He does not reduce the duel between humans and bear to mere physical conflict. Magic (as is the case in many bear myths) allows the bear to yield himself to the hunter without severe physical combat. A contrast revealing our conception of human relations to other creatures as antagonistic (because founded on the concept of culture as antithetical to nature) is provided by William Faulkner's "The Bear." In this celebrated story the hunt climaxes with a detailed depiction of a violent physical struggle between the animal and men. To my knowledge *no* Indian myth about bears employs an equivalent description.

Minimal visualizable descriptive details and few figures of speech permit Indian myths to concentrate on the evocation of psychosocial complexities revealed by the representation of actions purely as actions.[14] The girl is careful, for example, in coming out of the cave after the bear has been killed, to "identify" herself by addressing the brothers' dog by its name. (In another version she sends out the dog with the brothers' arrows neatly tied to its back.) The use of the dog here inverts the act by which she enabled the brothers to locate the den through their dog's recognition of their sister's scent. The dog (the first animal to be domesticated) serves to reinforce the animal-human opposition/equivalence by superimposing it upon gender tensions that the myth simultaneously articulates.[15] McClellan observed several differences that could be linked to whether the teller of this myth was a man or a woman. Women narrators tended, for example, to emphasize with more detail the girl's need for clothing after her husband has been killed, and to expand on her concern for her children/cubs. I have already noted the reference to a cross-sibling speech taboo, which testifies to the undercurrent of incestual fear that shadows this myth.

In observing such features of meaning, however, we need to avoid oversimplifying, not forgetting, for instance, the myth's popularity. Indian "enjoyment" of it requires careful evaluation. Any audience's "enjoyment" of a serious narrative is an ambiguous process. We are "attracted to" or our interest is "piqued by" something that "disturbs" us. Much of a teller's skill, whether an anonymous Indian or Miguel de Cervantes, lies in keeping a balance: stimulating us to attend to some troublesome features of our life while not so arousing our anxieties that we block out the story's deepest meanings or, more simply, refuse to hear or read it.[16]

Besides thinking about the psychology of reception, we need also to inquire into the psychology of telling. Why, we should ask, were so many Indians so eager to tell "The Girl Who Married the Bear?" One reason, however tautological the answer may seem, is that this myth is remarkably "tellable." Almost anyone can successfully tell this story, which lends itself to variations expressive of particular interests and concerns – as McClellan's collection wonderfully demonstrates. "Tellability" is a quality of myth in oral cultures that deserves more examination. It is characteristic of a myth strong enough in basic form to sustain diverse purposes of both personal psychology and social circumstance. That it is "interesting" to tellers means that it allows imaginative narrators to use it productively as they narratively inquire into practices, beliefs, ideas, and emotions shared – although not necessarily comfortably – with their audiences.

The popular character of "The Girl Who Married the Bear" is suggested by the absence in Tlingit versions of the "frames" that Richard Dauenhauer has identified as important to the telling of many Tlingit myths.[17] "The Girl Who Married the Bear" is not religiously central to Tlingit culture, just as it is not the property of, nor even confined in its references to, any particular family or clan, or even tribal group. This "openness" is worth noticing, because Dauenhauer is surely correct to insist that framing devices enhance the transmissibility of narrative. A large number of Native American myths can be fully understood only in terms of "the story of the story" being told: where the narrative comes from, its peculiar relevance to this teller or the immediate telling situation, as we've seen in McClintock's version of the Feather Woman myth. Nevertheless, in many myths throughout North America, like

"The Girl Who Married the Bear," the significance is independent of such framing devices. These stories, one might say, exploit variability: they are popular because so adaptable to a wide range of tellers, audiences, and social circumstances.

We need to be cautious, then, in attributing to such myths Western conceptions of meaning and form, because these conceptions are rooted in admiration for control of the very fluidity that makes the stories appealing to many Indians. Our caution should be increased by the absence from such tales of many formal characteristics that we take as signals of literary art. Besides employing few of our figures of speech, the myths never depend on the rhythmic patternings which for us distinguish poetry. Their patternings (as is suggested by the Dauenhauers' translation of Peters's telling) are thematic, structurings of action rather than sound. No Native American myths, for example, were recounted to the accompaniment of a musical instrument in the manner of the Macedonian "singers of tales" recorded by Albert B. Lord. The difference confirms that the metric and stanzaic regularities so deeply rooted in Western traditions, even Western oral traditions, are not the structuring principles of Indian narratives. These principles are, rather, patterns of *enactment*. The physical telling of the mythic story – the enunciative configuring of actions recounted – constitutes the primary structure of the narrative. If we can attune ourselves to this enactment organizing, we will recognize that metrical regularities, elaborate metaphors and conceits, even detailed descriptions would interfere with the audience's participation in the verbal performance of the actions that constitute the myth – which exists *only* through the act of being retold. Indian myths are not without form, but it is enactment form, accommodating variability in structure that we tend to misperceive, first seeing only formlessness, then overcompensating by imposing regularity according to our ideas about verbal art.

Possibilities of diversification are the "formal essence" of myths such as "The Girl Who Married the Bear." Tellers are drawn to it because, besides being audience-effective, it gives the teller space in the process of telling to develop any number of psychological and social interests. Here we reach an almost unstudied topic, the depth psychology of storytelling. What are the inner rewards and compulsions that impel tellers to narrate as they do? Sometimes there must be a component of what we would call therapeutic need. McClellan, for example, sensed that a couple of the tellings she recorded were partly motivated by the tellers' sense of guilt over the number of animals they had killed. We would be wrong, however, to confine motivations to expiation, to a cleansing of fear, guilt, or anxiety. Curiosity and the desire to test and transgress limits, to seek out sources of power – these too are surely determinative motives in many Indian tellings. We today who seldom tell stories (except to psychoanalysts) are likely to underestimate exploratory motives in emphasizing therapeutic components. Freud was not an Indian.

The more I have studied "The Girl Who Married the Bear," at any rate, the more important motives of inquiry seem to many of its tellings. So I have come to see McClellan's comparison to Attic tragedy as in one way misleading. The "tragic power" in this North American myth does not derive from a perfected singleness of form as does, say, the tragedy that moves us in *Oedipus the King*. A formal openness, even inchoateness, empowers various tellers and various audiences to put the bear tragedy to multiple uses. The artistry giving special formal impressiveness to some tellings of "The Girl Who Married the Bear" is antithetical to the attainment of explicit singularity, which, according to Western critical dogma, is the preeminent feature of "great" works of literature.

It may be useful, therefore, to glance at ethnographic evidence about Indian attitudes toward bears and about the ends to which these may be ceremonially enacted. This will enable us to see more clearly how and why Indian formal structurings, whether in ritual activity or mythic tellings, often contravene our sense of effective form. In descriptions of ceremonial conjoinings of words and acts we may discern the effects of superimposing "internal" psychosocial tensions on "external" hunting tensions, and recognize how such fusions require modes of formalization so unfamiliar as at times to appear virtually formless.

The most extensive study of bear ceremonialism is the impressive essay on the topic by Irving Hallowell.[18] His monograph provides much information on ceremonial and ritual treatment of slain bears, including the practice of setting the corpse upright at a celebratory feast. The essay is also useful for its discussion of the widespread belief that bears "have a language of their own, can understand what human beings say and do, and have forms of social and tribal organization, and lived a life which is parallel in other respects to that of human societies" (77). Hallowell further points out that nothing was to the Indians mere food alone, that the availability of bears (along with other edible animals and plants) was invariably understood as a kind of divine gift to be honored beyond the meeting of physical necessity.

The best specific discussion of social functions connected with bear-woman tales appears in *Under Mount St. Elias,* Frederica de Laguna's careful study of Tlingit ethnology. She describes the Tlingit regard for animals, birds, and fish as powerful beings with souls essentially like those of human beings. She cites the beautiful Tlingit myth that explains these creatures' present bodies as derived from the fur, feather, and scale robes they were wearing at the moment they were frightened from their original dwellings into woods and ocean by Raven's releasing of daylight from the box in which it had been hidden. Her discussion of the treatment of bear corpses and the relevance of their totemic status to hunting practices leads her to a conclusion in keeping with Hallowell's general findings:

> The bear is, of course, the most dangerous of such animals, the one most ardently hunted by adventurous men, and the one most likely to be encountered in the berry bushes by unarmed women. I, therefore, learned more about proper behavior in dealing with bears than about procedures for any other animal except the land otter. It would be wrong, however, to say that the Tlingit had a special Bear Cult, or that they hold the bear in special reverence. Rather the general attitude toward any animal is intensified toward the brown grizzly because the latter is big and powerful, intelligent and manlike in appearance and behavior.[19]

Bears, moreover, are credited with a power to understand what people say. De Laguna quotes a Tlingit as remarking, "Bears are like people, you can talk to them," and Tlingit women as saying that the best way to avoid trouble with a bear met on a berrying expedition is to maintain a quiet demeanor and speak to the bear in gentle tones. The conviction that bears understand speech was, as Hallowell shows, widespread across North America, and among many Indian peoples there was an equivalent to the Tlingit belief that bears also have telepathic powers: not only aware of what people at home, far away, may say and think about them, bears may know even after death how their bodies are treated, physically and verbally.

De Laguna seems correct in claiming that the bear for most Indians dramatically manifests those characteristics distinctive of animal life while simultaneously displaying those capabilities which enabled Indians to conceive of animals as "people," possessing "culture" and even shamanlike powers. It is not surprising, therefore, that rituals involving bears consistently emphasized the interconnectedness of humankind and bearkind. This was a striking feature, for example, of the ancient formal bear ceremony of which we possess the most complete description, the Delaware Bear Sacrifice Ceremony, an annually performed ritual that lasted ten to twelve days.[20]

As Frank Speck reports, the ceremony takes place in a log building known as the "Big House," arranged so that its floor embodies a projection upon earth of the constellation Ursa Major. The center post of the Big House, moreover, is conceived as linking the center of Delaware society on earth to the center of the sky. The core of the ceremony is the selection of twelve men to find the den of a hibernating bear designated by a "blessed" woman who has dreamed of this animal and described to them the location of its den. The men call it out, then drive it to the Big House, where it is killed alongside the center post. The designated chief thereupon formally addresses the bear, saying that he and the Delawares will meet in the sky, admonishing the bear to go there in advance of his killers to inform spirits of the sky that all is right on earth, and that men are being faithful to their obligations to one another and to the deceased. An analogous address begins each subsequent night of the ceremony. The bear is then skinned (beginning with the throat and proceeding to the tail, the reverse of the normal skinning method), and its body provides the meat for a sacrificial feast. The skin is hung on the east side of the center post, replacing the dried skin of the previous year's sacrifice, which has remained tied there until this moment.

On each night of the ceremony the chosen twelve perform a Man's Dance in which each individual sings a song-offering, accompanying himself with a sacred turtle rattle. Other performers include Reciters of Visions, or "Magical Men," who have been blessed by special visionary experiences of which they tell between dances. Doorkeepers, or Sweepers, sweep the dancing track after each round of dancing, and at the coming of dawn they use special brooms, starting from the center post, to sweep out any evil influences through the eastern and western doors of the Big House.

Even so condensed a summary suggests the value of Speck's assessment of the ceremony as constructed around a belief that bears killed by men returned in spirit form to a realm above the earth, whence they descended to be born again during the winter of hibernation. New bears, thanks to the ceremony, would descend into winter dens to appear as cubs in the spring. A visible image of celestial bear life is formed by the four stars making up the rectangle of Ursa Major, also seen as a bear by the Delawares, who regard the three stars we refer to as the handle of the Big Dipper as hunters, the "little star" alongside the second hunter being his dog. Ursa Major in its revolutions around the North Star lies on its back in midwinter, ascends head-up in midspring, is upright in the midnight sky in summer, and descends head-down in autumn, the constellation thus imaging the bear on earth emerging from hibernation in spring and retiring to its den at the end of autumn after a summer of activity.

Of special value to us is the clarity with which this ceremony illustrates the literalness of some Native Americans' most effective ritual symbolism. The post at the center of the Big House that points toward the center of the sky, for example, and the "sweeping out" of evil simultaneously embody and express the interconnectedness of all realms of being, not just the celestial and the earthly but also the realms of practice and mythic imagining. It is this literalness, as anthropologists have noticed with varying degrees of frustration, that tends to be obscured by the very act of ethnographic description. The written report in itself separates ritualized ceremony from its concrete physical manifestation in the total culture practiced by a given people. The efficacy of the symbolism permeating the Bear Sacrifice Ceremony, linking sky and earth, was assured for the Delawares by the presence of a real bear that was physically killed, skinned, and butchered. That terrific literal presence at the center of Delaware society reinforced the tangible power of the words spoken and sung, the dreams recounted, the dances performed. We need to recognize that something of the same "actualness" informs oral tellings of myths to an assembled audience, an actuality that tends unavoidably to be diminished and obscured by their translation into written texts.

The most serious loss in translation is likely to be that of a realized interconnection between what we sharply distinguish as natural and cultural realms. As the Delaware ceremony concretely illustrates, a crucial aspect of that interconnectedness is a process of renewal, which in reported description takes on the false appearance of cyclic reiteration. That ceremony, of course, did repeat the ceremony conducted the previous year; at the same time, however, it *replaced* the previous ceremony, as the new bear skin replaced the old. The renewal of the world is generated by a ritualized reenactment. Yet if we can imaginatively recover the actualities of the ceremonial process, we will recognize that reenactments necessarily will be "inexact." Not only may there be different participants, but there is no way that two bears can be killed and butchered in identical fashion. Such inexactness helps to make the repetition a renewing one. In the ceremony as in myth tellings, variation-within-identity affirms that the world is perpetually renewable as a dynamic organism rather than as a set of mechanically reiterative cycles.[21]

The foregoing suggests that differences between the art of singular literary form and variable mythic forms are rooted not only in the difference between oral and written narrative but also in the different character of ceremonial and rhetorical practices in preliterate and print-oriented societies. Although I sympathize with McClellan's comparison of "The Girl Who Married the Bear" to Greek tragedy, I believe we do more justice to the myth's power by perceiving how different its narrative forms are from what we are habituated to understanding as "tragedy." The ironic denouement of the myth, for example, seems somewhat peculiar from a Western perspective. In the light of the earlier events, what could be stranger than the brothers asking their sister to put on their brother-in-law's skin so they can "play" at hunting with blunt arrows?

I highlight the word "play" because in Tom Peters's Tlingit telling the term seems used to intensify the strangeness (with all its gender implications) to which I have pointed. The word first appears earlier in the story when the bear goes out to meet the brother he knows will kill him. The bear tells his wife:

Be brave,
I will go out
to him.
I will play with your brother.

In the light of this phrasing (including the intriguing admonition to "be brave"), one is almost forced to interpret the later uses of "play" as reinforcing the ironic reversals in the situation which precipitates the final killings, when the brothers plead:

"Mother! please ask
 our sister
 to let us play with her."
 How many times

they must have asked this.
Finally she said to them
"Well, okay, let's go!
Let's go!
Let them play with me."

It would be rash to elaborate an interpretation on counterpoised meanings of a single word, and I am certainly too ignorant of Tlingit to recognize all the implications of the term in these special contexts. But given the vivid psychosocial resonances evoked by the total narrative, it would seem almost perverse to ignore Peters's exploitation of multiple ironic meanings of "play." At the very least, this linguistic detail suggests the teller's self-conscious artistry, possibly even an awareness of his telling as itself a kind of "play." His concentration on psychosocial ambiguities would make it appropriate for him to perceive their relation to the ambiguities of language. The "artistry" of deploying "play" as fatal seems unmistakable in the second use, which so distinctly evokes an intensely gendered situation – the girl is there to be played with – whose horrific reversal recalls through inversion the bear's deliberate self-sacrifice. Peters's telling, in fact, exemplifies almost perfectly Ernst Cassirer's suggestion that "poetry" be defined as language "calling physical reality into itself," an intensifying process that "transforms the world of sense impression . . . into a world of ideas and meanings."[22]

If we knew enough about the language practices of nonliterate peoples, we might with profit apply Cassirer's speculations to the art of mythic storytelling through linguistic analyses. Without that knowledge, we may still follow up suggestive evidence provided by larger forms of mythic discourse. For example, the informant who remarked to McClellan that the girl's transformation into a murderous bear "sounded funny" but was part of the story (a less self-conscious and innovative teller than Peters) reveals the value for Indians of the integrity of mythic narrative, even though this story belongs to no one, is now unconnected with any particular ritual performance, and is enacted in diverse fashions. The illuminating paradox here is that even a teller who feels obliged to recount what he admits puzzles him offers the myth as opening possibilities of interpretation.[23]

Every retelling is also necessarily a reinterpretation. A teller such as Peters may manipulate his material more boldly and subtly and achieve stronger and more precise effects than less capable recitalists, but his practice differs from theirs in degree rather than in kind. This may alert us to the intensity of significance in the seemingly unmetaphoric language of many myths. Were I accused of "reading into" mythic texts significances that are not there, I would argue in reply that Peters's deliberate concentration on the word "play" is supported by his trying for a similar effect at the same point in his narration to McClellan twenty years earlier, when he told the story in English. "I am going to play with my brothers-in-law," he has the bear tell his wife when he goes to his death (26). And the same word recurs when the girl is persuaded to put on the bear skin: "They [the brothers] think they are going to play for fun" (27).

But if I am correct, a more disturbing problem emerges. Despite attention to verbal nuance, Peters's first retelling of the story to the Dauenhauers differed radically from that he had told McClellan. The Tlingit version he told them in 1972 ended with the bear's death and the singing of the two songs about him, leaving out the final episode of the girl killing her brothers. The Dauenhauers were so pleased with Peters's story that they had it printed in booklet form, and the next year read it back to him. He was delighted but then insisted on "completing" the story by telling the final episode, which the Dauenhauers now print as "Part Two," even though in most of the versions we know the last episode is entirely integral – as is implied by Peters's own manipulations of the word "play," as well as his offer to "complete" the story. Yet he was satisfied to tell the myth in truncated form in 1972 – and the Dauenhauers were sufficiently pleased with that version to have it printed.

Nothing could better illustrate that Indian myths are often constituted of distinct narrative units that may be told separately or in differing combinations. This "modular form" of storytelling is another reason to be wary of applying to Indian myths the critical terms applicable to our literature. Narrative modularity complicates, to put it mildly, idealizations of "organic" form. Modularity meets the requirements of different telling situations, however, whether these derive primarily from the psychological interests of the teller or the social milieu in which the enactment occurs.

We need to keep in mind that Indian myths are retellings of stories with which listeners are familiar. A native audience, for example, would certainly have recognized Peters's 1972 telling as "truncated," and might therefore have sought for meaning in such abbreviation. To native listeners Peters offers an "interpretation" of the myth by treating only one part of it as "complete." To my mind, one of his motives for abbreviating it is suggested by his change of having the younger brother kill the sister, although in his earlier telling she was not killed. Throughout both parts of the Tlingit version Peters probes more subtly into differences between bear and human cultures, exploring what the effects would be for a girl to become a bear – a nuanced examination probably assisted by his use of his native language.

He makes an interesting distinction, for example, between the girl recognizing at dawn that the other "people" are bears but seeming to perceive that her husband is a bear only when he wants boughs for bedding. Psychological subtleties of this kind are developed by the disruptions of brief flashbacks and flashforwards complicating the narrative's linear progress – accentuated by judicious insertions of the traditional mythic meta-narrative form "it is said," as well as the provocative question "But then / at what point was it?" Such rhetorical displacements climax at the conclusion of Part One when the girl comes out of the cave, and – instead of hearing her words to her brother about treatment of the bearskin – we hear what the bear *had* told her, primarily his songs that *will be* sung (not just by the girl but all her people) in honor of slain bears. I suggest that Peters, assuming knowledge of the final episode, through temporal distortions focuses his audience's attention on the confusion intrinsic to a crossing of human and animal "cultures." Part Two stresses – far more than his version told to McClellan – the girl's difficulty in becoming reacculturated as a human; in fact, she is never shown becoming fully human again, as she never completely became a bear. In this telling she must be destroyed because her experience is that of a kind of monster, neither entirely human nor entirely bear.[24]

I do not insist on the validity of this interpretation (although at the least it calls attention to Peters' extraordinary rhetorical skill), that it reminds us that audience familiarity with a myth may be taken into account by a skillful teller. We may assume that variations are meaningful, calling for an interpretive, rather than an automatic, passive response. In myth enactments this call to interpret replaces the suspense (what will happen next?) that we expect from stories. Peters, like most Indian myth tellers, downplays suspense by using prefigurations. He passes rather swiftly over the actual killing of the bear, for example, while emphasizing through repetition the forecasts of his death.

Prefiguration effectively concentrates audience attention on the meaning of action as action. For listeners who are from our point of view responding "backwards" (from knowledge of the story's outcome), repetitions are not so much the delays they seem to us as orienting signals toward the significance being developed through variations. Our preference for suspense is symptomatic of our desire to "consume" stories, to discard them as soon as we know their outcomes. For the Indians, reiteration and prefiguration assure the culture-sustaining transmissive vitality of a narrative.

These fundamental characteristics of mythic form are accompanied by another (to us) unfamiliar structuring device, well illustrated by Peters: limitation to no more than two active characters in any given scene.[25] Where there are groups of characters, they tend to be represented as a unit (like a single character) or divided into two (as with the elder brothers and the youngest brother). This feature seems intrinsic to oral storytelling. Listen to yourself the next time you tell someone a story, and you will probably notice that you fall into this pattern of dualistic representation. I suggest that the two-but-not-more technique manifests the dialogic nature of oral storytelling. The teller-audience relation refracts through character presentations, because in neither telling nor what is told is any passivity permitted. As each telling offers a reinterpretation to be responded to interpretively, so every action in the story appears as an interactive encounter equivalent to the "conversational encounter" of addresser-respondent. This rhetorical mode discourages lavish descriptiveness. Anything beyond unelaborated identification of either external sensory phenomena or inner motivation interferes with the encounter-action – which is both the subject of the storytelling and the storytelling itself.

Peters's Tlingit version of "The Girl Who Married the Bear" is exemplary of these traits of myth rhetoric. Aside from literal dialogue, most of the story's actions are "dialogical" – as when the girl rolls the stone first in the bear's food and then between her thighs before throwing it down hill to attract the dog's attention so that he can alert his masters. One may also notice the peculiarity of the bear's admonition, "Be brave," which seems to enunciate ambiguities of the bear-girl relationship. Being puzzled by the statement seems an "appropriate" response, since a major point in Peters's telling is the unresolvable ambiguity of the relation.

The fluidity with which diverse versions of myths proliferate through repeated retellings in a traditional Indian society manifests itself in the rhetorical methods by which a myth manipulates language to "call" natural realities "into itself." Recognition of these mutually sustaining flexibilities reveals how fuzzy is our concept of "versions." When one addresses empirical cases, it is often nearly impossible to decide whether myth B is properly to be called a version of myth A. One reason is that B is likely to appear quite as legitimately a version of myth X. The confusing crisscrossing is exacerbated by the modular structuring of mythic narratives, because that makes it easy, and rewarding, for tellers to rearrange major structural units and slide an episode from myth F into a new telling of myth Q. In such shifting resides much of the "artistic originality" of superior myth tellers, who innovate by restructurings of the familiar. An illustrative instance is described by Robert Bringhurst, who says of a narrative dictated by the Haida teller John Sky (Ksjaii) to John Swanton in 1900:

> To the best of my knowledge, no other version of this story has been recorded in any language or at any time; yet the story does not exist in isolation. Its central characters are known throughout the Northwest Coast; it is part of the large and living body of Haida mythology; and in John Sky's mind it was only a third of an evening's work. Ksjaii liked to tell stories in sets, or suites, the way many solo musicians like to play, and he told this story as the opening movement in a suite of three. The two stories he joined to it are set in Tsimshian country, and both are well-known in Tsimshian versions.[26]

We need to recognize, as too few mythographers have, that oral cultures do not conceive of individual myths as separate and distinct. Any myth telling is understood as enacting a portion of the total mythology. Its individual existence is, as it were, temporary; the telling does not permanently detach what is told from the matrix of the entire mythology, which itself is kept alive (that is, in a state amenable to alteration) by specific tellings of many portions of it.

Every Indian teller may deliberately rearrange what could be termed the genetic code of a mythology. This possibility encourages what I call the exploratory functions of myth telling, the developing of new perspectives and meaning out of entirely traditional materials that continue to be celebrated as traditional. The body of mythology of an oral culture, therefore, is so very shiftingly interconnected that it is never adequately describable by any static, ahistorical system of classification such as Lévi-Strauss has proposed. If we must classify, I prefer Wittgenstein's suggestion about categorizing in terms of "family resemblances." That preference has determined my selection of the other bear myths in this chapter, which I hope may increase appreciation of the skills that go into myth enactments without forcing upon them our preconceptions as to what constitutes aesthetic merit. The Beaver Indian story translated by Robin Ridington under the title "The Girl and Her Younger Brother" displays a family resemblance to "The Girl Who Married the Bear," but to my mind the similarities highlight more impressive distinctions in both plot and style. Through condensation and blunt savagery of presentation the Beaver myth emphasizes the incestual themes subdued in all McClellan's tellings, including Tom Peters's version. The Beaver bear-wife appears as sexually rapacious and inherently violent: she "goes off" with a grizzly rather than being lured away; she bluntly refuses to warn the brothers that the bear is their brother-in-law (which presumably would save his life); then she refuses to come out of the cave until she is allowed to carry her husband's corpse. After gruesomely chewing off the necks of her mother and brothers, she sits with her legs spread suggestively. Such "loose" behavior, however, is symptomatic of self-confident power: this girl is victimized by neither animals nor her supposed social superiors.

But in this Beaver story the girl who marries the bear is dramatically subordinated to a younger sister undergoing her first menstrual seclusion – accompanied, surprisingly, by her younger brother. The purpose of this intimacy is presumably to endow him with hunting power: she is the source of potency. Although the boy does shoot his older sister, it is the younger sister who orders him to do the job and makes the bow and arrows he uses. Against the older sister's more "instinctual" and destructive rather than creative power, the younger sister shapes events by deliberately transforming traditional practices and biological limitations.

It is not possible for us to recreate the responses of Indians familiar with one or more versions of "The Girl Who Married the Bear" who might have attended an enactment of this myth. But I hope that a reader coming to "The Girl and Her Younger Brother" after considering the other will gain through this arbitrary juxtaposition some feeling for how such a relationship might influence responses to a distinct but affiliated narrative. It is conceivable, for example, that "The Girl and Her Younger Brother" would gain affect by echoing the other myth yet "distorting" its focus and tone. With the killing of the older sister, for instance, the remaining siblings are brought back to a primal situation, "the only people alive." This may be thought of as a rhetorical magnification of social circumstances probably not uncommon among small groups of hunting peoples. One can imagine circumstances in which the creation of more people can come about only through incestual relations. Perhaps we are meant to appreciate the impossibility of this story's solution, a woman capable of fertilizing herself. But it seems to me that what the story primarily investigates are relations between biological and cultural potencies. Besides creating offspring by herself, the younger sister bestows on her brother, too feeble to kill animals, "hunting eyes" so that they will have food. Power in this myth is centered in the young woman, not in a "forest animal" (Tom Peters's term of respect for the bear). The brutal sexuality of the older sister (superbly suggested by the dangling paw with swinging claws of her dead husband) is overcome by the younger sister's more elemental female generative power which, by violating "normal" social patterns (men as hunters, incest suppressed), becomes communally productive.

Even these few observations raise the question, what benefit is gained by identifying "The Girl and Her Younger Brother" as a *version* of "The Girl Who Married the Bear?" Do not the indubitable parallels finally accentuate even more meaningful differences? Would it not be as profitable to define the myths contrastively? Leaving aside matters of classification, however, I suggest that taking the two narratives together offers to a modern, nonspecialist reader an experience faintly analogous to that of an Indian hearing a familiar myth reworked for new purposes. Unexpected changes in familiar elements provoke thought about what one has made of earlier tellings and encourage reimagining as a basis for probing different if affiliated psychic and communal problems. As this process of using the familiar to move into new realms advances through subsequent tellings, an enactment may eventually be produced with almost no significant relation to its "original" – a "new" myth.

This is one process that generates myths in oral societies. Failure to recognize it explains some of the inadequacies of categorizations, whether formal or thematic, by Western mythographers. All these classifications fail to consider myth "versions" as forming patterns of *graded* relations. There are various ways in which one narrative establishes itself as a version of another. Affinity in myth telling is intricate, nuanced, and always evolving. These qualities, moreover, contribute to the ongoing cumulative power of an oral society's mythology as a whole. The mythology can be sustaining for a people because in it myths are able to interrelate in a variety of productive ways, each new version a part (but not a fixed part) of a total system refigured by each retelling.

I am, of course, cheating in my illustration by contrasting myths from different tribal peoples. But some drastic device is needed to display for us whose mind-set is print-dominated how continuity and originality of artistry may function in preliterate societies. The vitality of oral mythologies is strengthened (rather than undermined, as our mythographers assume) by variations in the affinity between myth tellings.

Appreciation of the special qualities of particular tellings is enhanced, at any rate, if we focus on how one theme can be developed for quite different purposes – as appears when one places alongside Peters's narrative the Cherokee "Bear Man" myth from far across the continent. In both there is concern for respectful treatment of a hunter's quarry, the magical and telepathic power of bears, and their "civilized" social life. The center of the Cherokee myth, however, is the bear's spontaneous generosity in offering food (ultimately himself), a theme enriched by countercurrents of competition, focused by the bears' vain attempt to use the hunter's bow, and complicated by the feature of the hunter's wife destroying him by bringing him home too soon. The "otherness" of bear nature to human nature here is represented as important because there is no absolutely impassable barrier, only one that ought assiduously to be respected. The final event of the Cherokee myth, therefore, highlights the significance of the very different emphasis on gender in various versions of "The Girl Who Married the Bear," an emphasis carried much further in "The Girl and Her Younger Brother."

The Kiowa "Star Girl" myth (which refers to a game actually played by Kiowa girls, reflecting the practical interest in real bears among many Indian groups)[27] shifts the orientation of "The Girl and Her Younger Brother" toward a mixed-sex sibling group. The Kiowa myth concentrates less on femaleness than on the destruction wrought on a family (and village) by a passion for something beyond the group, suggesting how an "outsider" may liberate destructive passions concealed by apparently harmonious social patterns. Looked at from this perspective, the transformation of the brothers and younger sister into stars is powerfully monitory. The constellation over the tilted, claw-scored rock reminds us of a self-disruption latent within every familial unity constituted (of necessity) from dangerously aggressive personal impulses. Here, in contrast to the Beaver myth, the concentration on family (for most Native American peoples the cornerstone of community) rather than gender helps to account for this younger sister's escaping death not by exertion of direct female power but by going off to a bitch and her pups. The dog family, clearly enough, contrasts with the unsatisfactory human family, thereby extending the mediative hunting role of dogs in "The Girl Who Married the Bear," while tying the "ideal" of family to "natural" familialness.

I hope that even such cursory comments will suggest why we may best recognize intellectual and emotional depths in these myths if we attend more to their individual particularities than to situating them within some sort of invented relational scheme – let alone treating them as all equally illustrative of some factitious universal such as the "savage mind." I admit the difficulties in understanding myths when we approach them as individual imaginings, difficulties that help explain the temptation so many have felt to classify rather than to face up to the uniqueness of each. Yet many of our problems arise from myths' unfamiliar rhetoric, their socially determined forms of affective representation which – because different from those of our literature – we fail to recognize, or misperceive. If we can develop appreciation for alien rhetorical techniques, we may begin to feel the intellectual and emotional profundity of individual mythic stories, however ill informed we are about the cultures that fostered them.

One unfamiliarity appears in the use of proper names, as is illustrated by the ferocious, mass-murdering female in "Grizzly Woman Killed People." In this myth we are presented with a human being who is *named* Grizzly Woman but who does not literally become a bear. The distinction raises some issues that have been insufficiently addressed by mythographers (I comment further on characteristics of Indian naming in the discussion of Trickster myths in chapter 4). Here a principal question concerns the degree to which we should recognize a name as carrying primarily *mythic* connotations, rather than connotations of the natural creature. The research of Melville Jacobs and Dell Hymes suggests that for a Chinook audience the name "Grizzly Woman" would superimpose upon allusive reference to real bears even more powerful affects deriving from a mythic "stereotype" of a murderous, bear-named ogress.

Still, the double referentiality of the name produces formal consequences, as Hymes has demonstrated by his analytic retranslation of Jacobs's original translation.[28] Hymes claims that certain syntactic and lexical patternings in the story prove that a highly repetitive and tightly structured translation more accurately reflects the form of the myth as it would be experienced by a Clackamas teller and auditors. He argues also that changes in the naming of Grizzly Woman (through the use or elision of specific verbal prefixes) further formalizes the ordering of the story and thereby strengthens the power of mythic stereotyping for a Clackamas audience. His proposal that the myth be understood in terms of its deliberately wrought, intensely repetitive construction is persuasive if we think of this formal structuring more in terms of mythic concentration upon action rather than as an analogue to Western metrical orderings. The symmetrical pattern of "Grizzly Woman Killed People" functions to dramatize the complexity animating the deadly conflict between Grizzly Woman and Water Bug, not merely to adhere to a formal pattern of recitation – although if Hymes is correct, conventions of recitation form would serve to make the conflict more vividly meaningful to Clackamas listeners.[29]

Hymes's rigorous formalism splendidly highlights the Grizzly Woman–Water Bug opposition, but his translation is most effective in allowing us to perceive the paradoxical intricacy of the conflict, revealed, for example, when Grizzly Woman accuses Water Bug of lying. Prevarication is plainly one of Grizzly Woman's own characteristics, but *she* is never accused of lying. This odd inversion illuminates the way the story's formal symmetry (emphasized by the many repetitions) refractively intensifies patterns of action. Grizzly Woman, attributing her own fault to Water Bug, surprises us into reconsidering the relation of the two, forcing awareness of parallels between these opponents, such as their power to numb others to sleep. Within the context of the repetitive formalizations that Hymes's translation insists upon, such likeness subtilizes what might otherwise be mere melodramatic contrast of evil villainess to idealized heroine.

Water Bug, the rhetorical form of the myth makes us perceive, can defeat Grizzly Woman because she possesses, and can control, the same powers that distinguish Grizzly Woman – which may explain the odd forcefulness of Grizzly Woman's desperate (because evidentially unfounded) accusation that Water Bug is motivated by a desire to attract men in a narrative that marginalizes male influence. The myth's "thematic form" leads us toward thinking of the "monstrousness" of murderous Grizzly Woman as a distortion (too complete realization?) of impulses and capacities that are "normal" and that perhaps distinguish even a "good" female like Water Bug. Awareness of this affinity between opponents permits one to carry farther Hymes's argument that linguistic signals, such as presence or absence of a specific prefix, reinforce the complex social implications of a character like Grizzly Woman. Contrastive affinities articulated by rhetorical form make it possible to perceive Grizzly Woman also as a kind of victim, however fearful an aggressor. To put the matter in the opposite way, the myth's structure enables us to perceive young Water Bug's success as dependent upon qualities that could develop her into a Grizzly Woman. This thematic inverting, I suggest, supports and extends the relevance of the distinctions detected by Hymes between naming a character and referring to that character by a pronoun. Indeed, some such complexity of naming and reference seems almost necessary, if what makes Grizzly Woman finally most fearful is identifiable with what enables "good" Water Bug to defeat her.

The point illustrated here cannot receive too much emphasis. We ought to examine American Indian myths in and for themselves as carefully wrought artifacts; the artistry of their making, however, depends on aims and techniques we are likely to overlook or misunderstand because of their unfamiliarity. Until we have undertaken such examinations, *any* system of myth classification we employ will diminish our appreciation of individual myths, thereby obscuring their deepest cultural significance – as well as depriving us of the chance to learn from authentically alien modes of discourse.

NOTES

1. The Tlingits were a populous and powerful nation of the Northwest, occupying the southeastern Alaska coastline, living in cedar plank houses with elaborately carved center posts and gabled roofs. A carved post in front of the house might have a lower figure with an open mouth that served as a doorway. The carvings represented the lineage of the family, and sometimes the ashes of deceased members were kept in the pole. In the back of the house there was often a wooden screen decorated with totemic crests. Lineage involved inherited privileges – including exclusive rights to particular songs, dances, and ceremonies as well as territorial possessions and fishing and sealing grounds – which were the basis of Tlingit social prestige, along with ownership of slaves. Potlatches (see note 5 on the Chinook group, below) were means of asserting prestige. Other ceremonies often included dances performed by elaborately costumed and masked dancers. There was an abundant food supply in the territory – above all, fish, which the Tlingits caught from red cedar dugouts. They were also active traders, particularly with tribes from inland. Beginning in the mid-eighteenth century, Europeans trading with the Tlingits introduced epidemic diseases. The Tlingits strenuously resisted Western encroachments on their traditional commercial rights, early in the nineteenth century destroying a Russian base at Sitka, and fifty years later a Hudson's Bay Company post in the Yukon Valley.

Frederica de Laguna's monograph *Under Mount St. Elias*, Smithsonian Contributions to Anthropology 7 (Washington DC, 1972), is invaluable; see also her contribution to vol. 6 *The Handbook of North American Indians*, ed. William Sturdevant (Washington DC: Smithsonian Institution. Dan Kaiper and Nan Kaiper, *Tlingit: Their Art, Culture, and Legends* (Seattle: Hancock House, 1978), includes information on ceremonialism and potlatch, as does Aurel Krause – reporting on fieldwork from the 1880s – in *The Tlingit Indians*, trans. Erna Gunther, Monographs of the American Ethnological Society 26 (Washington DC, 1956);

John R. Swanton, *Tlingit Myths and Texts*, Bureau of American Ethnology Bulletin 39 (Washington DC, 1909).

2. The not very numerous Beaver (Dunne-Za) Indians roamed the vast Peace River area of Alberta and British Columbia, living in tipis made from the skin of moose or caribou, animals they killed with bows and arrows, sometimes after attracting them with birchbark trumpets. Buffalo they hunted communally. Fish were caught in the summer with nets, in the winter by hook-and-line through the ice. Snowshoes and toboggans were used for winter travel, canoes in the summer. Loosely organized into small hunting bands based on kinship, the Beavers expected newly married couples to live with the wife's family, but the children were regarded as belonging to the man's family. Dreaming was always an important aspect of Dunne-Za practical life. Hunters could be successful only if they first dreamed of their animal quarry. The vision quest for a guardian spirit was fundamental to Beaver religious belief. Shamans who acquired their power from especially strong guardian spirits cured the sick and supervised ceremonies.

See Earle Pliny Goddard, "The Beaver Indians," *Anthropological Papers of the American Museum of Natural History* 10 (1917): 201–93; Robin Ridington, *Little Bit Know Something* (Iowa City: University of Iowa Press, 1990), and *Swan People: A Study of the Dunne-Za Prophet Dance*, National Museum of Man, Mercury Series, Canadian Ethnology Service Paper 38 (Ottawa, 1978).

3. The Cherokees were the most powerful southeastern Indian tribe when De Soto's exploring party encountered them in 1540. Through more than sixty towns they controlled a vast area including good portions of the Carolinas, Virginia, Tennessee, Georgia, and Alabama. Many Cherokee towns, whose dwellings (including a large council house) were of pole framework covered with woven mats plastered over with clay, were fortified with palisades. These towns were largely independent, ruled by a chief, a council, and a war chief. The Cherokees divided themselves into seven matrilineally defined clans, forbidding marriage within the clan. They hunted with blowguns as well as bows and arrows; they were also skillful farmers, originally growing corn, squash, and sweet potatoes. Shamans played an important part in Cherokee life, undergoing long training in the use of medicinal plants, learning sacred formulas both for curing and inflicting injuries, and officiating at religious festivals. The most important of these was the Green Corn Dance at the time of the ripening of corn each year.

The Cherokees learned rapidly from the Europeans, and by the end of the eighteenth century, despite serious population losses due to smallpox epidemics, had become successful farmers, had developed plantations, and, following the European model, had become slaveholders. Recognizing the importance to Europeans of writing, the Cherokee Sequoyah in the early 1820s devised a syllabary for his native language which was quickly adopted and adapted for printing, including the publication of a successful tribal newspaper. In 1827 the Cherokees established themselves as a republic, printing in their own language a constitution modeled on the United States Constitution. Discovery of gold on Cherokee lands in Georgia served as an excuse for whites supported by President Andrew Jackson to dispossess these people who seemed so threateningly effective at adopting and adapting to white ways, even though the Supreme Court declared the dispossession illegal. Forced to migrate on foot to Arkansas and Missouri and finally Indian Territory (now Oklahoma) – the "trail of tears" on which hundreds of their people died – most of the Cherokees relocated in less fertile land. Though factionally divided, they nevertheless gradually reestablished themselves and are again today one of the most populous Indian tribes, some living in the North Carolina mountains where their ancestors hid out to avoid migrating west.

James Mooney, in *Myths of the Cherokees*, from which "Bear Man" is taken, includes a sketch of early Cherokee history and 126 myths with copious notes. Mooney's earlier work "The Sacred Formulas of the Cherokees," *Annual Report of the Bureau of Ethnology* 7 (1885–86): 301–97, contains valuable material on incantations and healing practices. On later Cherokee history, especially the displacement, there are many books, among them Thurman Wilkins, *Cherokee Tragedy*, 2d ed. (Norman: University of Oklahoma Press, 1986); and John Ehle, *Trail of Tears: Rise and Fall of the Cherokee Nation* (New York: Doubleday, 1988).

4. The Kiowas, migrating from western Montana at the end of the eighteenth century, in the early nineteenth century reached the Arkansas and Red Rivers. Although never very numerous, they were divided into seven bands, each with its own peace and war chiefs, which lived separately during the winter months. High status was attained by the possession of wealth or religious power or special achievements in warfare – above all, "counting coup": touching but not killing an enemy in battle. Kiowa social life was shaped by a variety of special societies – associations for women, warriors, dancers, and even young boys – some of which had special responsibilities for healing and prophecy. Religion, focused by the annual summer Sun Dance, integrated personal vision quests with ceremonies connected with the "Ten Grandmothers." These were ancient bundles sanctified by their linkage to a cluster of myths about culture heroes called the Half Boys. Those charged with the responsibility of caring for

a bundle were not allowed to examine its secret contents, each bundle being opened once a year by a specially trained priest.

Like many Plains tribes, the Kiowas depended primarily on the buffalo, not only for food but also for clothing, tipi coverings, and the like. Like the Sioux, they painted pictographic calendric records on buffalo skins. Intertribal warfare, principally against the Osage, Cheyenne, and Arapaho tribes, had been ended by peace treaties by 1840. Thereafter the Kiowas proved their reputation as fierce and relentless warriors by their effective resistance (despite their small numbers) to white encroachments into their territory until after the Civil War.

See Alice Marriot, *The Ten Grandmothers: Epic of the Kiowas* (Norman: University of Oklahoma Press, 1945), and *Saynday's People: The Kiowa Indians and the Stories They Told* (Lincoln: University of Nebraska Press, 1963). N. Scott Momaday – a Kiowa whose novel *House Made of Dawn* (1968) heralded the beginning of the "Native American Renaissance" in fiction and poetry – in *The Way to Rainy Mountain* (Albuquerque: University of New Mexico Press, 1969) beautifully intertwines the retelling of Kiowa myths with the story of his own pilgrimage to his birthplace.

5. The Clackamas, Kathlamet, Clatsop, and Wishram peoples are all considered part of the Chinook group, the principal traders among the Indians living along the Columbia River and the nearby coastal area. "Chinook jargon" became the main language of trade among a large body of northwestern Indians, and when white traders appeared, English and French words were added to this lingua franca spoken from California to Alaska. Some of the Chinooks constructed fine boats, usually made of a single cedar or fir log, as much as fifty feet long and carrying thirty people, with carved wooden figures at stem and stern. Slaves (seized in raids) were among the items of Chinook trade. There were more than thirty substantial Chinook towns, composed of cedar plank houses. The main source of food was fish, supplemented by the camas roots, berries, and grapes gathered by the women. Guardian spirit quests were a major feature of religious practice. Although probably the most important public ceremony was the First Salmon Rites, the Chinook like many other northwestern Indians practiced the potlatch, in which valuables are given away – not merely as a competitive display of wealth, and hence of prestige, but also as a form of recompense to those from whom the donor had previously received benefits, economic or otherwise. The lavish ceremoniousness of the potlatch has made it a matter of public record. It may also be seen as a kind of investment of wealth, since in future years recipients were expected themselves to offer a "reciprocal" potlatch of superior size.

The Wishrams, who occupied the north bank of the Columbia River five miles upstream and downstream at The Dalles, were primarily fishermen, whose defined fishing stations were owned and inherited by families. Fish dried, smoked, and then pulverized would keep for several years and, so processed, was used as reserve food supply and for trade. Occupying perhaps the most important trading point on the Northwest Coast, the Wishrams were vigorous middlemen, buying and reselling blankets, robes, horses, slaves, canoes, skins, and furs.

One may consult Robert H. Ruby and John H. Brown, *The Chinook Indians: Traders of the Lower Columbia River* (Norman: University of Oklahoma Press, 1976); and Melville Jacobs, *The People Are Coming: Analyses of Clackamas Chinook Myths and Tales* (Seattle: University of Washington Press, 1960). Hymes, *In Vain I Tried to Tell You*, from which "Grizzly Woman" is reprinted, contains analyses of other texts. Verne F. Ray, "Lower Chinook Ethnographic Notes," *University of Washington Publications in Anthropology* 7, no.2 (1938): 29–165, includes extensive reports on ceremonial practices.

6. Karl Kroeber, "Scarface vs. Scar-face: The Problem of Versions," *Journal of the Folklore Institute* 18, nos.2–3 (May–December, 1981): 99–156.

7. Catherine McClellan, *The Girl Who Married the Bear*, Publications in Ethnology 2 (Ottawa: National Museums of Canada, 1970); page numbers are cited in the text. Because of the fame of this collection and its centrality to my discussion, and to avoid unnecessary confusion, I refer to all versions – including Tom Peters's later telling of the myth to the Dauenhauers, which they published as "The *Woman* Who Married the Bear" – by the title McClellan used, which has become the accepted referential title for ethnologists discussing these stories.

For ethnographic background, see McClellan's *My Old People Say: An Ethnographic Survey of the Southern Yukon Territory*, 2 vols., Publications in Ethnology 6 (Ottawa: National Museums of Canada, 1975).

8. For the "aiming" of tellings, see the classic study by Keith H. Basso, "Stalking with Stories," in his *Western Apache Language and Culture* (Tucson: University of Arizona Press, 1990), 99–135. David Rockwell, *Giving Voice to the Bear* (Niwot CO: Roberts Rinehart, 1991), presents an impressive compendium of information on Native American myths about bears and descriptions of ritual practices concerning them. Clara Ehrlich, "Tribal Culture in Crow Mythology," *Journal of American Folklore* 50 (1937): 307–408, although following the lead of Boas in his analyses of Tsimshian and Kwakiutl mythology, recounts some of the difficulties in ascertaining actual practices from oral tellings. American anthropologists, because of the diversity of North American cultures, have been

particularly conscious of the dangers in generalizing about the relation of mythology to practice. Ruth Benedict, for example, in "The Concept of the Guardian Spirit in North America," *American Anthropological Association Memoirs* 29 (1933): 1–85, makes the point regarding the killing of a guardian spirit animal that two antithetical attitudes were irregularly distributed among Native American peoples: one that the tutelary animal must not be killed, the other that it should be the primary prey.

Within the enormous (and fascinating) literature on hunting, I suggest as particularly valuable Robert A. Brightman, *Grateful Prey: Rock Cree Human-Animal Relationships* (Berkeley: University of California Press, 1993); Adrian Tanner, *Bringing Home Animals* (New York: St. Martins, 1979); and the collection *Man the Hunter*, ed. Richard B. Lee and Irwin DeVoe (Chicago: Aldine, 1968).

9. Pierre Bourdieu, *The Logic of Practice: Outline of a Theory of Practice*, trans. Richard Nice (Cambridge: Cambridge University Press, 1972), 89.

10. Ralph Maud, discussing different reactions in *The Porcupine Hunter* (Vancouver: Talonbooks, 1993), 40, cites a telling recorded by Frederica de Laguna in which the girl expresses with vivid naturalism her anger when she slips on the bear turd: "Big flappy foot, always pooping in a place where you can step on it."

11. Rockwell (*Giving Voice to the Bear*) has collected a considerable body of data on these matters, and the observations of de Laguna (*Under Mount St. Elias*) on Tlingit attitudes toward diverse animals are especially valuable.

12. This is one reason I dislike the abstract and implicit universalism of "other" and "otherness" that has become current intellectual jargon and too often is employed by metaethnographers and discourse critics to obscure the kind of specific difference I am here sketching.

13. "Magic" is the point at which the Judeo-Christian tradition of separating supernatural from natural collides in bafflement with the Native American identification of natural with supernatural. An enormous body of Indian "magic" we can today understand as activating in a concentrated manner what we term "ecological forces." Having come to recognize the value of many of their herbal remedies, we may be prepared to perceive that Indians were not misguided in respecting the potency of less specific interplayings of ecological balances and imbalances – suggested by their tendency to term magic "medicine" or "power." A valuable analysis of shamanism as a dramatically focused form of environmentalism is provided by David Abram, himself trained as a magician in our sense, in *The Spell of the Sensuous* (New York: Random House, 1994).

14. Terence Turner's commentary in "History, Myth, and Social Conscious-

ness among the Kayapó of Central Africa," in *Rethinking History and Myth*, ed. Jonathan D. Hill (Urbana: University of Illinois Press, 1988), 196–97, describes this concentration upon events in myth as constituting "the forms of appearance through which cultural actors define the subjective meanings of the collective structures and situational patterns that provide the general framework and orientation of their acts." Myths are often best understood as "programs for the orientation of action . . . and as keys for the interpretation of interaction within that context. . . . the structure of the [social] situation becomes the schema through which interanimation of individual act and traditional form is realized." Myths concentrate on action as action because, in contrast to our "aesthetic" discourse, they embody actual processes of communal living. Focus purely on events facilitates myth's superimpositions of diverse but simultaneously operative relationships, both social and natural.

15. The development of the dog motif in the Kiowa myth is obviously germane. McClellan discusses the role of dogs in *The Girl Who Married the Bear*, 9, and offers a more general commentary in *My Old People Say*. I am not aware of any broad study of Indian dogs (at what point, for example, were they first given names?) or of their interesting roles in mythology.

16. Still the best discussion of this psychological intricacy (too little examined by recent reader-response theorists) is Simon O. Lesser, *Fiction and the Unconscious* (Chicago: University of Chicago Press, 1957).

17. See Richard Dauenhauer, "The Narrative Frame: Style and Personality in Tlingit Prose Narrative," *Folklore Forum: Bibliographic and Special Series* 9 (1976): 65–81.

18. Irving Hallowell, "Bear Ceremonialism," *American Anthropologist*, n.s. 28 (1926): 1–175. Hallowell's scope is circumpolar, not merely New World.

19. De Laguna, *Under Mount St. Elias*, 826.

20. The fundamental description appears in *The Celestial Bear Comes Down to Earth*, by Frank G. Speck in collaboration with Jesse Moses (Reading PA: Reading Public Museum and Art Gallery, 1945). The most thorough analysis is Jay Miller, "A Structuralist Analysis of the Delaware Big House Rite," *University of Washington Papers in Anthropology* 21, no.2 (1980): 107–33. Miller's study is the basis for the account given by Rockwell, *Giving Voice to the Bear*, 164–74. Rockwell draws attention also to the Winnebago Bear Dance, the Zuni Winter Solstice Ceremony, and Huron healing rituals involving bear rites. Claude E. Schaeffer, *Bear Ceremonialism of the Kutenai Indians*, Studies in Plains Anthropology, Museum of the Plains Indians (Browning MT, 1966), compares Kutenai practices, especially the Grizzly Bear Ceremonial, with those of the Assiniboins,

Blackfeet, and Utes. Martha Beckwith includes a valuable story of a bear ceremony in her *Mandan and Hidatsa Myths*, Memoirs of the American Folklore Society 32 (Philadelphia, 1937), 255–63.

21. An excellent study of Plains Indians' world-renewing ceremonies and the psychology that animates them is to be found in Howard L. Harrod, *Renewing The World: Plains Indian Religion and Morality* (Tucson: University of Arizona Press, 1987). He too insists that Native American oral traditions were "a system of dynamic meaning structures which exhibit considerable pluralism" and that "these traditions did not take the form of a normative account, one which was controlled by a professional elite. . . . these were sacred stories, to be sure, but there was no one official version" (47).

22. Ernst Cassirer, *The Philosophy of Symbolic Form*, trans. Ralph Mannheim (New York: Dover, 1953), 1:189.

23. Several of Dennis Tedlock's most valuable contributions to our understanding of mythic tellings as inescapably reinterpretive acts appear in *The Spoken Word and the Work of Interpretation* (Philadelphia: University of Pennsylvania Press, 1983).

24. I gather from both her notes and the text that Peters's audience at this time was Nora Dauenhauer alone; so personal a telling may have led him to be ruminative and self-reflective. In any event, we ought to remember that a storytelling occasion provides a teller the opportunity to reflect on the story through the enactment.

25. To the best of my knowledge, Axel Olrick was the first to describe this two-but-no-more characteristic of oral storytelling in his "Epic Laws of Folk Narrative," now most conveniently available in *The Study of Folklore*, ed. Alan Dundes (Englewood Cliffs NJ: Prentice-Hall, 1965), 129–41. It is odd that over the years folklorists have done little to develop Olrick's important insight.

26. Robert Bringhurst, "John Sky's 'One They Gave Away,'" in *Coming to Light*, ed. Brian Swann (New York: Random House, 1994), 227.

27. A considerable number of Native American tales describe children playing at being bears: for example, an Apache story, "The Girl Who Turned to Bear," in the collection made by Morris Opler, *Myths and Legends of the Jicarilla Apache Indians* (1938, Lincoln: University of Nebraska Press, 1994), 113–16.

28. A full discussion of Melville Jacobs's original translation and comments appears in Dell Hymes's essay containing the translation used in this collection, part of his very important volume *In Vain I Tried to Tell You*, 342–81. A psychoanalytic reading of the role of Grizzly Bear Woman in the mythology of the nearby Nez Percés is presented in Dell Skeels, "Grizzly-Bear Woman in Nez Percé Indian Mythology," *Northwest Folklore* 3, no.2 (1969): 1–9.

29. In effect, Hymes presents an appealing argument that the characters' names are not so much distinguishing signifiers as functions of the action. Part of the argument's appeal is that this enactment does not supply any "external" or "objective" logic for Grizzly Woman's repeated actions – whose increasing complexities of deception suggest that dramatizing the nature of deception is one of the myth's functions.

4
Trickster-Transformer's Orality

Winnebago[1]

Trickster Tales

SAM BLOWSNAKE

As he went wandering around aimlessly he suddenly heard someone speaking. He listened very carefully and it seemed to say, "He who chews me will defecate; he will defecate!" That was what it was saying. "Well, why is this person talking in this manner?" said Trickster. So he walked in the direction from which he had heard the speaking and again he heard, quite near him, someone saying: "He who chews me, he will defecate; he will defecate!" This is what was said. "Well, why does this person talk in such fashion?" said Trickster. Then he walked to the other side. So he continued walking along. Then right at his very side, a voice seemed to say, "He who chews me, he will defecate; he will defecate!" "Well, I wonder who it is who is speaking. I know very well that if I chew it, I will not defecate." But he kept looking around for the speaker and finally discovered, much to his astonishment, that it was a bulb on a bush. The bulb it was that was speaking. So he seized it, put it in his mouth, chewed it, and then swallowed it. He did just this and then went on.

"Well, where is the bulb gone that talked so much? Why, indeed, should I defecate? When I feel like defecating, then I shall defecate, no sooner. How could such an object make me defecate!" Thus spoke Trickster. Even as he spoke, however, he began to break wind. "Well this, I suppose, is what it meant. Yet the bulb said I would defecate, and I am merely expelling gas. In any case I am a great man even if I do expel a little gas!" Thus he spoke. As he was talking he again broke wind. This time it was really quite strong. "Well, what a foolish one I am. This is why I am called Foolish One, Trickster." Now he began to break wind again and again. "So this is why the bulb spoke as it did, I suppose." Once more he broke wind. This time it was very loud and his rectum

Paul Radin, *The Trickster: A Study in American Indicn Mythology* (New York: Philosophical Library, 1956), 25–27.

began to smart. "Well, it surely is a great thing!" Then he broke wind again, this time with so much force that he was propelled forward. "Well, well, it may even make me give another push, but it won't make me defecate," so he exclaimed defiantly. The next time he broke wind, the hind part of his body was raised up by the force of the explosion and he landed on his knees and hands. "Well, go ahead and do it again! Go ahead and do it again!" Then, again, he broke wind. This time the force of the expulsion sent him far up in the air and he landed on the ground, on his stomach. The next time he broke wind, he had to hang on to a log, so high was he thrown. However, he raised himself up and, after a while, landed on the ground, the log on top of him. He was almost killed by the fall. The next time he broke wind, he had to hold on to a tree that stood near by. It was a poplar and he held on with all his might yet, nevertheless, even then, his feet flopped up in the air. Again, and for the second time, he held on to it when he broke wind and yet he pulled the tree up by the roots. To protect himself, the next time, he went on until he came to a large tree, a large oak tree. Around this he put both his arms. Yet, when he broke wind, he was swung up and his toes struck against the tree. However, he held on.

After that he ran to a place where people were living. When he got there, he shouted, "Say, hurry up and take your lodge down, for a big warparty is upon you and you will surely be killed! Come let us get away!" He scared them all so much that they quickly took down their lodge, piled it on Trickster, and then got on him themselves. They likewise placed all the little dogs they had on top of Trickster. Just then he began to break wind again and the force of the expulsion scattered the things on top of him in all directions. They fell far apart from one another. Separated, the people were standing about and shouting to one another; and the dogs, scattered here and there, howled at one another. There stood Trickster laughing at them till he ached.

Now he proceeded onward. He seemed to have gotten over his troubles. "Well, this bulb did a lot of talking," he said to himself, "yet it could not make me defecate." But even as he spoke he began to have the desire to defecate, just a very little. "Well, I suppose this is what it meant. It certainly bragged a good deal, however." As he spoke he defecated again. "Well, what a braggart it was! I suppose this is why it said this." As he spoke these last words, he began to defecate a good deal. After a while, as he was sitting down, his body would touch the excrement. Thereupon he got on top of a log and sat down there but, even then, he touched the excrement. Finally, he climbed up a log that was leaning against a tree. However, his body still touched the excrement, so he went up higher. Even then, however, he touched it so he climbed still higher up. Higher and higher he had to go. Nor was he able to stop defecating. Now he was on top of the tree. It was small and quite uncomfortable. Moreover, the excrement began to come up to him.

Even on the limb on which he was sitting he began to defecate. So he tried a different position. Since the limb, however, was very slippery he fell right down into the excrement. Down he fell, down into the dung. In fact he disappeared in it, and it was only with very great difficulty that he was able to get out of it. His raccoon-skin blanket was covered with filth, and he came out dragging it after him. The pack he was carrying on his back was covered with dung, as was also the box containing his penis. The box he emptied and then placed it on his back again.

Navajo[2]

Coyote and Prairie Dogs

YELLOWMAN

A (1) Ma'i was trotting along [having always done so]. [*slowly*]

-4-

(2) At a place I'm not familiar with called "Where the Wood Floats Out" he was walking along, it is said.

-4-

B (3) Then, also in an open area, it is said [!!!], he was walking along in the midst of many prairie dogs [!!!].

-1-

(4) [!!!] The prairie dogs were cursing him, it is said [!!!], all crowded together, yelling.

-1-

(5) He went along further into their midst.

-1-

(6) Then he walked further.

Trans. Barre Toelken (with help from Tacheeni Scott), in *Traditional Literatures of the American Indian: Texts and Interpretations*, 2d ed., comp. and ed. Karl Kroeber (Lincoln: University of Nebraska Press, 1997), 116–22. Main units of meaning are indicated as "scenes" by capital letters. Within scenes, each line represents completion of a thought or phrase as indicated by narrator's pacing; utterances too long for one line of print are carried over indented. Longer pauses are given in seconds between "verses," which are identified by number. On the right margin are descriptions of narrator style (in italics and brackets) and audience response (in italics only). Parentheses in the text represent the narrator's formulaic variation in volume and pitch as he gives an explanation; brackets in the text are the editors' explanations of untranslatable implications. The marker [!!!] represents a long Navajo word that signals intensification, urgency, importance in the phrase preceding or following. Ma'i is Coyote; Golizhi is Skunk; *shiłna'ash* means "one who walks with me," implying trust and interdependence but made ironic when used by selfish Ma'i.

-3-

(7) [!!!] He got angry and soon began to feel hostile.

-2-

(8) After a while it was noon.

-1-

(9) He wanted [implied: looking upward] a cloud [*slower, nasal*]
to appear
(His reason was that he started hating the prairie dogs),
so he asked for rain.

-2-

smiles, quiet laughter

(10) Then a cloud appeared, it said.
"If it would only rain on me," he said. *smiles, heavy breathing*
And that's what happened, it is said.

-2-

(11) "If only there could be rain in my footprints."
And that's what happened, it is said.
"If only water would ooze up between my toes
as I walk along," he said.

-3- *open amusement*

(12) Then everything happened as he said, it is said.

-4- [*clears throat*]

(13) "If only the water would come up to my knees," he said.
And that's what happened.

-2-

(14) "If only the water would be up to my back
so that only my ears would be out of the water." [*nasal*]

-13- *heavy breathing; baby cries*

(15) "If I could only float," he said. [*nasal*]
Then, starting to float,
"Where the prairie dogs are,
if I could only land there," he said.

-3- *quiet laughter*

(16) He came to rest in the midst of the prairie dog town, it is said.

-3-

(17) Someplace in the *diz* – *smiles, quiet laughter*
(*diz* is the name of a plant that grows in clumps) –
he landed [implied: along with other debris] hung up
in the clump, it is said.

-4- *quiet laughter*

C (18) And there he was lying after the rain.
And then Golizhi was running by to fetch water. [*slower*]
(Ma'i was pretending to be dead) *smiles exchanged*
Then he [Golizhi] was running. *glances*
He [Ma'i] called out to him, it is said.
"Come here," he said, and Golizhi came to him, [*very nasal*]
it is said.

-6- *suppressed giggling*

(19) "Shiłna'ash," he said [very seriously]. [*nasal*]

-2- *quiet laughter, expelling air*

(20) "'The hated one has died, and has washed up
where the prairie dogs are,' tell them that shiłna'ash."

-3-

(21) "'He's already got maggots,' you tell them" he said. [*nasal*]

-2-

(22) "Slendergrass, it is called – shake that Slendergrass
so the seeds fall off.
In my crotch, in my nose, in the back part of my mouth,
scatter some around, then put some inside my ears,"
he said.
"'He's got maggots,' you tell them. *quiet laughter*
'The hated one has been washed out.'"

-3- *quiet laughter*

(23) "Make four clubs and put them under me.

-3-

(24) 'We'll dance over him.
We're all going to meet over there,'
you tell them," he said.

-1-

(25) "This is how," he said.
. . . . [wording indistinct] . . . .
. . . . "dancing around" . . . .
[implied: Golizhi is to join in these actions]
. . . "'Hit Ma'i in the ribs'" . . . . *breathing*

-1-

(26) "Be careful not to hit me too hard!
'Slowly, gently, like this,'
you tell them," he said.

-5- [*clears throat*]

D (27) This happened. [*normal tone*]
He ran home, and gave out the word to the prairie dogs, it is said.
"The hated one is washed out [!!!].

-2-

(28) There were rabbits and other animals [there], and even groundsquirrels.
(Those animals which are food for him were gathered [!!!].)
[!!!] Now the people were dancing, it is said, at the meeting.

-3-

(29) First, he [Golizhi] said, "It's true! It's true! [*tones exaggerated*]
Let's have one of you who runs fast run over there to find out."

-1-

(30) Then Jackrabbit ran and, "It's true!" said, running back, it is said. *quiet giggling*

-1-

(31) Then Cottontail ran and, "It's true!" said, running back, it is said.

-1-

(32) Then Prairie dog ran and, they say, "It's true!" said, running back, it is said.

-1-

E (33) At that time there was a big gathering [!!!].
They were dancing [implied: couples periodically stepping into circle], it is said.
Whatever they were singing, I don't know.

-2-

(34) "The hated one is dead," they were saying [!!!];
the club is beside him; they were hitting
him in the ribs, it is said. [*delivered in one long breath*]

-REST- *expelling of air*

– [*narrator rests for about five minutes, drinks coffee*] –

(35) Then they continued with what they were doing, and more and more people came.
Then Golizhi-ye-ne said (remembering Ma'i's plan)
"You are all dancing;
While you are looking up, while you are saying,

you say 'Dance in that manner,' you tell them [!!!]
'while you're in charge there, shiłna'ash,' he said."

-2-

(36) Then they were dancing.
Then, "Waay, waay up there at *t'aadziłgai* is running through the air," he said,
Golizhi said. *one girl: hn!*

-1-

(37) Then, when they were all looking up,
he urinated upward
so that it fell in their eyes, the urine.

-3- *open laughter*

(38) His urine the animals were rubbing from their eyes [!!!].
"'The one who is hated is dead?'" he [Ma'i] said, jumping up [!!!].

-1- *laughter, giggling*

(39) He grabbed the clubs from under him [!!!].

-3- *laughter, giggling*

(40) He used the clubs on them [all in a row, in one circular swing].
They were all clubbed to death. [*laughter*]

-8- *laughter*

F (41) Then
"Let us cook by burying, shiłna'ash," he said.
"Dig right here," he said [!!!].
And he dug a trench, Golizhi did.

-2-

(42) After he dug a ditch, he built a fire.
He put the food into the pit.
Then he [Ma'i] thought of something new.

-1-

(43) "Let's have a foot race, shiłna'ash.
Whoever comes back first,
this will be his," he said *light laughter*
"No," he [Golizhi] said, but he [Ma'i] won the argument.
"I can't run fast," he [Golizhi] said.
"While I stay here, you start loping," he [Ma'i] said.

-1-

(44) . . . [indistinct] . . . while Ma'i pretended to do something to his ankles, he [Golizhi] started to run,

then, over the hill he ran,
    and ran into an abandoned hole.

-2-

(45) In a little while, he [Ma'i] suddenly spurted away.

-3-

(46) A torch he tied to his tail
and the smoke was pouring out behind him
    as he ran. [*laughter*]

-17- *laughter*

G (47) While he was running over there;
Golizhi ran back, it is said,
    there where he had buried the food [!!!].
He dug them up and took them up into the rocks,
    it is said. *amusement*
Four little prairie dogs he reburied,
then he was sitting back up there, it is said.
[!!!] Ma'i ran back, it is said, *light laughter*
    back to the place where the prairie dogs were buried.
He leaped over it.

-4- *increased laughter*

(48) "Hwah!" he said. [*laughter*]

-8-

(49) "Shiłna'ash – I wonder how far back he's plodding,
    Mr. His-Urine," he said.

-6-

(59) [!!!] Sighing, he lay down,
    pretended to lie down, in the shade.
He jumped up and leaped over to the pit. [*laughter*]

-1- *laughter*

(51) He thrust a pointed object into the ground
    and grabbed the tail of the prairie dog first, it is said.
Only the tail came loose. [*chuckle*]

-1- *light laughter*

(52) "Oh no! the fire has gotten to the tail," he said.

-2- *loud laughter*

(53) So he grabbed the stick and thrust it into the ground again;
    a little prairie dog he dug up, it is said.
    "I'm not going to eat this [meat]," he said,
    and he flung it away toward the east.

-2- *light laughter*

(54) He thrust it into the ground again; [*slower*]
a little prairie dog he dug up.
"I'm not going to eat this," he said,
and he flung it away toward the south.

-2- *light laughter*

(55) He thrust it into the ground again; [*slower*]
a little prairie dog he dug up.
"I'm not going to eat this," he said,
and he flung it away toward the west.

-2- *breathing*

(56) He thrust it into the ground again; [*sleepily*]
a little prairie dog he dug up.
"I'm not going to eat this," he said,
and he flung it away toward the north.

-1- *breathing*

(57) He thrust repeatedly in many places, it is said,
and couldn't find any.
Nothing, it is said.
There weren't any, it is said.

-2- *expelling breath*

(58) He couldn't, he walked [frustrated] around in circles.
He went around and he picked up those little prairie dogs he had thrown away.
Then he picked up every little bit
and ate it all.

-2- *quiet laughter*

H (59) Then he started to follow [Golizhi's] tracks, *amusement*
it is said, but he couldn't pick up the trail.
He kept following the tracks, back and forth,
to where the rock meets the sand. *boy: hn!*
(He didn't bother to look up.)

-2-

(60) He [Golizhi] dropped a bone and he [Ma'i] looked up, it is said.
It dropped at his feet.

-1- *quiet laughter*

(61) "Shiłna'ash, share with me again
[implied: what I shared with you previously]." [*brief laughter*]

-5- *brief laughter*

(62) "Certainly not," he said to him, it is said. [*slowly, seriously*]
He was begging, to no avail, it is said.
Golizhi kept dropping bones down to him.
He chewed the bones, it is said.

-4- *small burst of quiet laughter*

I (63) That's how it happened, it is said.

Nez Percé[3]

Coyote and Bull

WAYILATPU

Coyote was going along upstream hungry, as usual. He came upon a big, fat buffalo bull. Coyote said to him, "Friend, I am hungry. Is it so impossible that you change me into a bull just like you, so that I, too, could become fat and sleek?" Bull heeded him not the least. He only wandered away grazing and not a word would he reply to Coyote. Coyote was insistent. He said again and again, "I wish that I, too, were a bull so that I could get fat." Finally Bull got tired of hearing this and said to him, "Coyote! You are inveterately foolhardy in the things you do; you could never do what I might ask of you. You are becoming a great bother." Coyote replied, "No, friend, I will do exactly what you tell me to do. Here I see you fat and sleek. Here is much grass and you live well, while, you see, I am painfully hungry. I will do just anything you tell me." Bull then said to him, "Then go over there and lie down." Coyote accordingly went and lay down. "Absolutely do not flee; do not move when I dash at you. You must, absolutely, remain still and I will heave you upward with my horns." – "Yes, friend, why should I flee?" replied Coyote as he lay down. Bull went off to the side and there he incited himself to terrific anger. He tore up the turf; he threw dirt upward; he bellowed and breathed clouds of vapor from his nostrils. He became terribly angry and then he dashed upon Coyote. But Coyote had been glancing at Bull and had seen him become so terrible. He saw Bull come at him and he jumped quickly aside. "Now that is what I spoke of – that you would run away," Bull said to him. "Let me try again, just once more," Coyote said. "I will not move next time." But Bull went away even though Coyote beseeched him weepingly. Coyote followed,

Trans. Archie Phinney, *Nez Percé Texts*, Columbia University Contributions to Anthropology 25 (New York: Columbia University Press, 1934), 9–10.

tearfully entreating him, "Once more, just once more; I will not run away again." Bull said to him at last, "You are most bothersome to me. Now I will try you once more and if you move do not beg me anymore, for I will heed you never again. We are trying for the last time." Coyote placed himself on the designated spot again and Bull went aside, as before, to become terribly angry. Now he dashed at Coyote. This time Coyote steeled himself and Bull threw him high into the air with his horns. Coyote fell and suddenly became a buffalo bull. He walked away and went along grazing. He would see all kinds of things and eat them. Then finally he parted with the other bull which now wandered off somewhere feeding. Here now another coyote met him and recognized him as erst Coyote. "Oh, friend, how is it, friend, that you have become like that? I am terribly hungry; I wish that you would make me like that, too." Coyote-Bull only looked at him sullenly, and walked away to feed, unmindful of what the other said. The coyote insisted, "Friend, make a bull of me, too. I fare piteously and you are very fat." Coyote-Bull then spoke to him. "You are very bothersome. You would never do those things which I would ask." "Yes, friend, I will follow out absolutely every word you say. Try me." – "You have been a nuisance to me," Coyote-Bull said to him. "But place yourself there and I will dash upon you angrily and toss you into the air with my horns. You absolutely are not to move. If you run away do not tearfully entreat me for another chance." The coyote now placed himself there while Bull made himself angry. He bellowed and pawed the ground. He imitated in every way those things that he had seen the other bull do. Now Bull dashed upon him, and oh! he picked him up and hurled him upward with his horns. Now coyote fell – *thud*! To the ground he fell still a coyote. At the very same moment Bull, too, changed back into a coyote. Here they were suddenly standing there, both coyotes. They stormed and they scolded each other. "You! You have caused me to change back into a coyote. There I was a bull living happily and you caused me to change back into a coyote." "Ha, you imitator! You thought you could make me into a bull too, as the other one did to you." Now one chased the other up the valley. The coyotes chased each other. There one lost interest and forgot that. "Thus I was acting silly – had become a bull." He went along up the valley from there unmindful of all that had happened.

Lipan Apache[4]

Wasps Catch Coyote's Head in an Old Horse Skull

ANTONIO APACHE

Coyote started out again. As he was going along the road he came to a big dance that was being held in the skull of an old dead horse. In the skull were some wasps and they were making a big noise and dancing.

Coyote put in his finger. He made his finger dance through the hole at the back of the skull by moving it in time to the singing. They were having a good time in there. They invited him to come in.

"It seems too small," he said.

But still they invited him in. They stretched it so he could put his head in. They made it just large enough for that and then let him get his head stuck in there. They all ran out through the eye sockets. Coyote was caught. He had to wear that old skull and look through the eye sockets to see. He couldn't get his head out. He walked around like that.

He came to a camp. He said to the people there, "I am holy; I have supernatural power. You must give me something."

They lined up and marked him with pollen as he was sitting under a tree. All the people of the camp did that, even the children.

He just wanted one of them to take the skull off for him, but none of them thought of it. The line had almost passed when one of the last ones came forward. He was a crazy boy. He had a stick hidden under his arm. He put the pollen on, then, instead of going on, he lifted the stick and hit the skull. It split open and fell off.

"Oh, that is what you should have done long ago!" said Coyote. "But instead you all wanted too much supernatural power."

Coyote was somewhat ashamed because all those people had marked him with pollen. He went on and came to a group of men playing hoop and pole. He didn't do anything there. He continued on his way without doing anything more.

Trans. Morris Opler, *Myths and Legends of the Lipan Apache Indians*, Memoirs of the American Folklore Society 36 (Philadelphia, 1940), 169–70.

Sioux (Dakota)[5]

Blood-Clot Boy

ANONYMOUS

A rabbit lived happily until a bear and his young came and took possession of his home, driving him out. So he was obliged to dwell in a makeshift hut near by. And each morning the bear stood outside his door and said, "You Rabbit with the ragged muzzle, come out. Your buffalo-surround is full." Then Rabbit came out with his magic arrow and, with one shot, sent it piercing through each buffalo in turn till all were killed. Then the bear would rush up with his young, and take all the meat home. They never gave the rabbit any meat, and the result was that he was now very thin. Once again they were cutting up the meat; so he came and stood to one side, but before he even asked for a piece, they ordered him off, so he turned to leave. Somewhat removed from the scene was a blood clot on the ground. So, as he went over it, he pretended to stumble, and picked it up, thrusting it under his belt. And the bear called out, "Hey, there, you worthless wretch, you aren't taking anything, are you?" So the rabbit answered, "No, I only stagger because I am weak from hunger." Then he came home. Immediately he made a sweat-bath over the blood clot. He was busy pouring water over the hot stones when someone within heaved a deep sigh, and then said, "Whoever you are who are thus kind, open the door for me." So he opened the door, and a young man, red (from the heat), stepped outside. Rabbit was very happy. "Oh would that my grandson had such and such things," he would say, and instantly they would appear, so that all in the same day, he had everything desirable. Everything he wished for him was his. But Rabbit couldn't offer him food, for he had none. Then Blood-Clot Boy said, "Grandfather, how is it that you starve while a rich man lives near by?" So Rabbit related everything to him. "Alas, grand-

Ella Deloria, *Dakota Texts*, Publications of the American Ethnological Society 14 (Washington DC, 1932), 113–20. Reprinted with permission of the American Ethnological Society.

son, what do you mean? Why, the fact is that it is I who shoot all the game, and then when I am through, the bear comes with his young and they take the meat all away. They always call me by saying, 'Say you Rabbit with the ragged muzzle, come out; your surround is full.' So I come out, and do the shooting for them." On hearing this, Blood-Clot Boy was very angry. He took a piece of ash and burned it here and there, and made a club, and sat ready with it. As usual, the bear stood outside very early in the morning and, "Hey, you Rabbit with the ragged muzzle, come on out; your surround is full," he said, so he answered as his grandson had taught him. "*Hoh!* Get out, what are you talking about? I suppose you'll be claiming all the meat again!" And he didn't come out. The angry bear came in, thinking to force him out, but Blood-Clot Boy was ready for him, and killed him with one blow of his club. Then he sent his grandfather to the bear's wife, telling him what to say. He said, "Bear sends for extra help." And the wife called out, "Is that so? How many is he carrying?" – "He is carrying two buffalos." – "That's funny. I never knew him to carry so few!" So the rabbit tried again. "He is carrying three buffaloes," he said. "How funny. He used to carry more than that," she said. So Rabbit said, "He is carrying four buffaloes." And this time the wife said, "Is that so? Well, wait, then." And she started to come out of the tipi but Blood-Clot Boy was ready for her and the moment her head appeared, he struck her with a resounding blow and killed her. Then he entered the bear's home, and found all the bear children sitting in a circle, eating their meal. So he said to them, "Now, if anyone here has been kind to my grandfather, let him say, I," and they all yelled, "I." And then one said, "Do they think that, simply by saying the word 'I,' they will be spared? He who was kind to your grandfather sits over here!" he said. And in the corner they saw him sitting, the very youngest little bear wearing his very brown coat. The rabbit spoke up, "Grandson, he speaks true. Ever so often, he dragged a piece of meat over to me, and pushed it with his snout into my hut." So Blood-Clot Boy said, "In that case, step outside; you shall live." After he had gone out, the boy killed all the other cubs. The rabbit now moved into his old home and as he still had his magic arrow, he provided meat in abundance so that the three, including the little bear, lived without want. And then one day Blood-Clot Boy declared his plans. "Grandfather, in what direction do the people live?" he asked; so he told him they lived in the west. Then he said he planned to go there on a visit. The rabbit advised against it vigorously. "No, grandson, I dread it for you. Something very deceptive lives on the way." But that made him all the more eager to be off, and he started. He hadn't gone far before he saw a man shooting at something. "Ah! This must be what grandfather warned me of as not to be trusted," he thought, and tried to go around him, but he called, "My younger brother, come over here and shoot this for me before you go." – "Impossible! I am on a rush trip, I haven't time to loiter and shoot your game for you!" he said. But he begged so earnestly that he persuaded the boy to turn and come back to him. The boy sent an arrow which pierced the bird; and then he started to go on. But he called again, "That's a fine arrow, younger brother; who would discard it this way?" He shouted back, "Well then, take it and own it," and would go on, but, "My younger brother, please climb the tree and get if for me," he pleaded; so, as the best way to get rid of him, the boy came and prepared to climb the tree. But the man said again, "My younger brother, you better take off your clothes. They are very beautiful; it would be a pity to tear them on the branches." With that he persuaded the boy further, until he removed all his clothes and started to climb the tree in his naked state. He got the arrow and was coming down when he heard the one below saying something under his breath. "Are you saying something?" he called out. "I just said, Hurry down, brother!" he answered. So, "Oh, all right!" he called and continued down. Then, just as he was about to step to the ground, the man called in a great voice, "Stick to the tree!" And at once Blood-Clot Boy became glued to the tree. It was Ikto who had thus deceived him, and now he hurriedly dressed himself in the boy's finery and flung his old garments at him saying, "There, Blood-Clot Boy, put those on!" Then he went towards the village. In that village was a young woman, the eldest child of her parents, and greatly loved by them. "She-dwells-within-the-Circle" was what her name meant. He was going to her. As soon as he entered the tribal camp, the cry went up, "Blood-Clot Boy comes on a journey, and *C'oka'pT'i'wį̹* is the one he comes for!" The parents immediately gave their daughter to him and placed their tipi within the circle. So Ikto, all in a day, settled into the rôle of the son-in-law. The next morning he proceeded to demonstrate his supernatural powers. "Let all the young men remove the hair from a buffalo-hide and scatter it about in the bend of the river, beyond the hill." It was done accordingly. Next day he told them to send scouts to see the result. They went; but came back to report that nothing had happened. Now, *C'oka'pT'i'wį̹* had a young sister who stayed around her tipi. She didn't like her around, and ordered her off each time, saying, "Go on away! I don't want her to even look upon my husband!" Finally the girl went crying into the woods and gathered firewood. There she came upon a youth, very handsome, stuck fast to a tree. He said to her, "Young girl, if you have pity, free me from this tree. Ikto has dealt thus badly with me and gone into camp leaving me to my fate." So the girl took her ax and peeled the man off from the tree; and then, sharing her blanket with him, she took him home. And then he said, "Now go to the one who is living inside the circle and bring my clothes to me; Ikto has worn them long enough." So the girl stood at the door of her sister's tipi and said, "Ikto, you have worn certain clothes long enough; I have come after them for their owner." But her sister said, "Go away. I don't want you to look upon my husband!" But all the while Ikto repeated without a pause, "Hand them out, hand them out." At last then, the young woman realized that Ikto himself had duped her; so she began to cry. Now Blood-Clot Boy put on his own clothes and sat looking very handsome, and said, "Let all the young men remove the hair from a buffalo-hide and scatter it about in the bend of the river beyond the hill." They did so; and the next morning when they went to see, the bend was packed with buffalo, so the people had a real killing, for this young man had true supernatural power. That evening everyone took part of his killing to the council tent where men sat about and feasted and talked; and they say all Ikto took was a shoulder-piece; it was all he managed to secure (from some hunter). Soon after, Blood-Clot Boy announced that he was going home, taking with him the girl who saved him. So they made preparations. And the once-proud elder sister who had been so mean to her younger sister, now rejected Ikto and went following the girl and her young husband. They in turn ordered her back, but she did not have any ears. And so they came on until they neared Blood-Clot Boy's home. The little bear who was sitting on a hilltop saw them. He had been sitting there alone, viewing the country round about. He started up, evidently having seen them, and disappeared downhill in the other direction. Breathlessly he arrived home and said, "Grandson is now returning; but he brings a woman home." Immediately the rabbit, very happy, ran hopping out to meet them; and taking his grandson on his back he carried him the remainder of the way. The little bear also came to meet them, and he took the daughter-in-law on his back; but she was so heavy (for him) that he could not lift her entirely off the ground; so her feet dragged behind. As for the proud elder sister, nobody took any notice of her, so she came along behind them, and lived with them there. They kept her to take out the ashes for them. . . . That is all.

Chinook-Wishram

What Coyote Did in This Land

LOUIS SIMPSON

THE ORIGIN OF FISH IN THE COLUMBIA

Coyote heard about two women who had fish preserved in a pond. Then he went to them as they were collecting driftwood from the river. He turned himself into a piece of wood trying (to get them to pick him up). He drifted along. But then they did not get hold of him. He went ashore, ran off to way yonder up river, and transformed himself into a boy. He put himself into a cradle, threw himself into the river, and again drifted along. The two women caught sight of him wailing. They thought: "Some people have capsized, and this child is drifting towards us." The younger one thought: "Let us get hold of it." But the older woman did not want to have the child. Now it was drifting along. The older one thought: "That is Coyote." Nevertheless the younger woman took the child and put it in a canoe.

The two women started home towards their house. The child was wailing, and they arrived home with it. They took off the cradle from it and looked closely at it. As it turned out, the child was a boy. The younger one said: "A boy is better than driftwood." And then she went and cut an eel and put its tail in his mouth. Then straightway he sucked at it and ate it all up. She gave him another eel, and again he sucked at it, (eating up) only half. Then he fell asleep, and half the eel was lying in his mouth. The two women said: "He is asleep; now let us go for some more wood."

And then they went far away. He arose and saw them going far off. Then he made himself loose and seized their food. He roasted the fish on a spit; they were done and he ate. He caught sight of the fish, which were their food, in a lake. Then he examined (the lake) carefully, and discovered a spot where it would be easy (to make an outlet from it to the river). "Here I shall make the fish break out (from the lake), and

Trans. Edward Sapir, *Wishram Texts*, Publications of the American Ethnological Society 2 (Leiden: Brill, 1909), 1–47. Footnotes are those of Sapir.

then they will go to the Great River."[†] He made five digging-sticks, made them out of young oak. And then he put them down in that place. He started back home towards their house. Again, just as before, he put himself into the cradle. Again there (in his mouth) lay the eel's tail. Again he fell asleep.

Now the two women arrived. "The boy is sleeping," they said; "very good is the boy, being a great sleeper." And then they retired for the night. Daylight came, the boy was sleeping. Again they went for wood. Again he saw them going far away. Then he got up and took their food. He roasted it on a spit and ate it all up. Then straightway he went to where his digging-sticks were. He took hold of one of his digging-sticks. Then he stuck his digger into the ground; he pulled it out, and the earth was all loosened up; his digging-stick broke. He took hold of another one and again stuck it into the ground. Then he loosened up the earth, and his digger was all broken to pieces. He took hold of another one of his digging-sticks. Again he stuck it into the ground; he loosened the earth all up, and his third digger was all broken to pieces. He took hold of the fourth one; again his digger broke. Now at last he took hold of the fifth and stuck it into the ground; he loosened the earth all up. And then the fish slid over into the Great River.

Now then the older woman bethought herself. She said to her companion: "You said, 'The child is good'; I myself thought, 'That is Coyote.' Now this day Coyote has treated us two badly. I told you, 'Let us not take the child, that is Coyote.' Now we have become poor, Coyote has made us so." Then they went to their house, and he too went to them to their house.

He said to them: "Now by what right, perchance, would you two keep the fish to yourselves? You two are birds, and I shall tell you something. Soon now people will come into this land. Listen!" And the people could be heard "du'lululu" (like thunder rumbling afar). "Now they will come into this land; those fish will be the people's food. Whenever a fish will be caught, you two will come. Your name has become Swallows. Now this day I have done with you; thus I shall call you, 'Swallows.' When the people will come, they will catch fish; and then you two will come, and it will be said of you, 'The swallows have come; Coyote called them so.' Thus will the people say: 'From these two did Coyote take

[†]That is, Columbia River. The word wi'mał of the text is never used to refer to any other river. All other streams are denoted by wi'qxał.

away their fish preserved in a pond; now they have come.'" Thus did Coyote call those two.

COYOTE AND THE MISCHIEVOUS WOMEN

Then Coyote travelled up the river. He went and went and arrived at a certain land. He caught sight of two women across the river. And then each shouted out to him from across the river: "How fond I am of you!" Thus the women spoke to Coyote. Then he thought: "Well, now I should like to have the women." He threw himself into the river and dived under. He came to land where he had seen the two of them. He looked about; there was nothing to be seen. He turned about to where he had thrown himself into the river. There they are still. Again he threw himself into the river and dived under the water. He thought: "Truly, they like me; but I for my part have left behind a fish-line." He put his head above water; there was nothing to be seen.

Across yonder were the two women where he had first caught sight of them. He thought: "Truly, they make me crazy." Now he feels cold. He thought: "How now! they are really two birds, but they make me crazy." He thought: "Never mind, now!" and called out to them: "Now you two there have for all time become birds in the water. People will say, 'These two have made Coyote crazy, so he called them birds.' For all time you two shall be birds in the lake."

COYOTE AS MEDICINE-MAN

A certain old man was sitting in the trail with his penis wrapped about him just like a rope. And then Coyote passed by him and went on a little beyond. He saw some women jumping up and down in the water. And then he thought: "I shall borrow from the old man his penis." He went over to him and said to him: "Friend, would you not lend me your penis?" And then (the man) said to him: "All right, I shall lend it to you." So then (Coyote) took it and carried it along with him. Then he put it on to his own penis.

Then he shoved it under water right where the women were jumping up and down. One of the women jumped up, the penis got between her legs, and it remained stuck a little ways. And then she became ill.

Then the (other) women took hold of her and brought her yonder to shore. They saw that something was sticking to her, but they could do nothing with her; they could not cut it out of her with anything. And then they took hold of her and carried her a little farther away from the water. Coyote was far off across the river, and they dragged him into the water. Coyote shouted: "Split a stone (as knife); with it you will cut it off." They said: "What did some person tell us? He said, 'Cut it off with a stone knife.'" And then they looked for it and found a stone. They split it, and with the same they cut off the (penis) from her. It had run up right into her. That Coyote over yonder cut it all off. Then he turned his penis all back (to himself).

Immediately Coyote went on again; he arrived somewhere, and laid himself down there. Now this woman is sick; they took her with them and straightway carried her (home). They looked for a medicine-man and found the Raven. They said to him: "Now you will treat (her)"; then he assented. He went to treat her; he had consented to do so. And then he doctored and doctored (until) he said: "There is nothing in her body, there is no sickness in her body." Thus did speak the Raven.

And then the people said: "Yonder is a certain Coyote, who is a medicine-man." Then they went and said to him: "What do you think, will you treat her? We have come for you." And then he said: "Well, I could not go so far on foot; there must be five women without husbands. No! five women will have to come for me; they will just carry me on their backs." And then they went and said to five women who had no husbands: "Now you will go and bring the old medicine-man." Coyote yonder split some alder-bark and chewed at it. Then the women came to meet him, and he said to them: "I am sick in my breast." Then he spat; he showed them that what he had spit out was red and pretended that it was blood.

"You will just carry me on your backs so that my head is downward, in order that the blood may slowly go down to the ground. If my head is turned upwards, my mouth will perhaps become filled with blood, (so that) I shall die. It is good that my head be down; (so) I shall not die." One of the women straightway took him on her back; the youngest one carried him first; she carried him with his head turned down. She went along with him. And then straightway he put his hands between her legs. Immediately he stuck his hands into her private parts and fingered them. She thought: "Oh! the old man is bad; the old man did not do good to me." So then she threw him down on the ground. Then he spat blood when she had thrown him down. One of the older sisters spoke, and said to her: "It is not good that you have hurt the old man."

And then one of the women again took him on her back. She went along with him. Straightway again, as before, he treated her; again he put his hands into her private parts. She did not carry him long; she also threw him down. Again one (of the sisters) said to her: "It is not good that you have thrown him down; you have hurt the old man. Look at him; again blood is flowing out of his mouth, he is coughing." And then she also put him on her back; now she was the third to carry him. To her also he did as before; he fingered her private parts. She did not carry him long, but threw him down also. And then again one of the women said to them: "Oh! you have not treated the old man well. Now he is continually spitting out much blood, the blood is flowing out of his mouth; you have hurt him badly."

And then the fourth woman took him on her back. That woman also went along with him. He treated her also as before, fingering her private parts. She also threw him down. Behold, now they were approaching to where the girl was lying sick in the house. Now another one of the women, the oldest of all, – she was their oldest sister, – said to them: "How you have treated the old medicine-man! Look, blood is flowing out of his mouth; now he is close to dying. Why have you done thus to the old man?" The four women said among themselves: "Thus has the old man done to me myself." One again said in like manner: "He fingered my private parts." They said to one another: "Now she too will find out; she will think that the old man is bad, after all."

Now also the other one, the fifth, took him on her back and went along with him. Her also he treated as before. Now the house was near by, and there she threw him down. And then people were gotten where the woman lay sick who should sing for him, while he was to treat (her); they obtained animals of such kind from the land, large deer who could make much noise; they were to sing out loud.

Coyote, the medicine-man, said: "Now lay her down carefully." And then they laid her down; the people who were to sing for him seated themselves. The medicine-man said: "I alone would treat her. Put something around her here to hide her from view, so that I may treat her well." And then they took rushes and put them over her to hide her from view. Now there he sat by her, and said to them: "If I turn my hand up, then you shall sing."

Then he took up the song, and they started in singing. And then he treated (her); he spread apart her legs. He stuck his penis into her and copulated with her. She called out: "The old one is copulating with me." He put up his hand and said to them: "Now go ahead, sing hard." And then hard they sang and sang. The two (parts of the) penis stuck together. Truly, that was the same penis which they had cut off with the stone knife; that (Coyote) penetrated her halfways, thus he copulated with her. The two (parts of the) penis recognized each other, they stuck together.

And then he pulled it out of her. Straightway she became well. Her mother asked her: "How are you feeling now? Have you now become well?" – "Now I have become well, but the old one has copulated with me." – "Well, never mind, just keep quiet; now the old one has done well to you." And then the old man was told: "Now she has become your wife." He said: "I do not want a woman. I am walking about without particular purpose; I desire no woman." Then he went out of the house; he left them.

COYOTE AND THE MOUTHLESS MAN

Again Coyote travelled up the river. In the water he saw the canoe of a certain person, as it turned out, a man. He saw how (the man) dived into the water. He came up out of the water, his hands holding one sturgeon on that side and one sturgeon on this; he put the sturgeons down in the canoe. Then (Coyote) looked on and saw him count them with his finger, pointing about in the canoe. He thought: "When he dives, I shall take hold of and steal from him one of his sturgeons; let us see what he'll do."

The person dived under water. And then (Coyote) swam towards his canoe. He seized one of his sturgeons. He went and took the person's sturgeon with him, and hid it in the bushes. And then that (Coyote) seated himself there and hid. Then the person came up out of the water into his canoe; he put his sturgeons down in the canoe, again one and one. And then he counted them; again he counted them. Quite silently he counted them; there was (only) one sturgeon in his canoe.

And then he pointed his finger out, first up high, (then) a little lower, again a little lower still, finally a little lower still on the ground. There he pointed, where (Coyote) was sitting. Quite silently (he held) his finger there. (Coyote) tried (to move) to one side, there again was he finger. No matter which way (he moved), there was his finger (pointing) at him, Coyote. Where his finger was (pointed to), there he went straight up to him. Straightway he went to meet him; straightway he came quite close to him.

He kept pointing at him; (Coyote) kept dodging from side to side; the person kept him well in eye. And he also looked at the person; the person was strange in appearance. As it turned out, he had no mouth; he had only a nose and eyes and ears. He spoke to (Coyote) with his nose, but he did not hear him; just deep down in his nose (could be heard): "DEN dEN dEN dEN." In fact he was scolding that (Coyote) in this way. Thus he said to him with his nose: "You are not good." Thus the person kept telling him; his heart was dark within him. "But perhaps now this man desires the sturgeon; perhaps he is going to kill me." Thus thought Coyote.

And then the person went back to his canoe. (Coyote) made a fire when he had gone. He gathered some stones and heated them in the fire. And then they all became heated up. He cut the sturgeon in two, cut it all up, and carefully made ready the stones. He laid the sturgeon out on the stones and steamed it; it was entirely done. And then he removed it and laid it down. Then that same man who had no mouth went back to him; he met Coyote as he was eating.

And then he took hold of that good well-done sturgeon. Then thought Coyote: "Wonder what he'll do with it!" He looked at him; he took the good (sturgeon). He just sniffed at the sturgeon, then threw it away. And then Coyote thought: "It is not well." He went and brought the sturgeon back and brushed it clean. Now Coyote is thinking: "What is he going to do with it?" Once again he took hold of it and did with it again as before.

He went up to him and looked at him closely. And then he thought: "I don't know what I shall do to make him a mouth." Secretly he took a flint and chipped it on one side; it became just like a sharp knife. And then he went up to him with the flint secretly in hand and looked at him closely. In vain the man tried to dodge from side to side. Now he put the flint down over his mouth. He sliced it open, and his blood flowed out. He breathed: "Haaaa." He said to him: "Go to the river and wash yourself." When he had come up out of the water, he stopped and spoke to Coyote.

Coyote was spoken to (thus): "You do not seem to have steamed a large sturgeon." And then Coyote said: "Well, you would have killed me; you wanted the sturgeon for yourself. You got after me for the sturgeon." Now the people told one another: "There is a man whose mouth has been made for him." In truth, all the people of that same one village were without mouths. And then they betook themselves to him. He made mouths for all the people of that same one village. He called that same land Nimîcxa'ya. They said to him: "We will give you a woman." He said: "No! I should not care for a woman; I'll not take one."

COYOTE AND THE PREGNANT WOMAN

Coyote again went on and travelled up the river. He met a man whose feet were tied together, and whose legs were full of pieces of wood. He was turning somersaults and standing on his head, and he kept crying: "Alas!" (Coyote) met this same man (and said): "What are you doing?" – "Not of my own accord am I doing thus. My wife is soon to beget a child; therefore have I thus come for wood."

(Coyote) took hold of him and disentangled him. He put the pieces of wood in order, and tied them together with a hazel-bush rope. And then he asked him: "Where do you live?" – "Yonder I dwell," said the man. "Let us go," said Coyote; "go first while I carry these pieces of wood on my shoulders." And then he said to him: "Thus you should handle it – look at me – whenever you go for wood."

And then he packed it on his head; Coyote put it around on himself. Then they two went towards the man's house, and arrived at the house. He had packed the wood good and strong. "Moving along in this way, man, should you handle the wood. You should pack it good and strong, moving along thus." They entered the house. He saw the woman; her body was sound, only she had one of her hands covered up.

He examined her hand carefully; it turned out that a small thorn was sticking in her little finger, and that it had white pus in it. He turned it over and made (the swelling) burst, and pulled the thorn out from it. "No!" he said to him, "not in this way is she to become pregnant; this which has been sticking in her is what people call a thorn. Thus should you treat her from now on, and you will cause her to be pregnant. See me copulate with her!" And then she became pregnant with a child in her womb. Then she gave birth to it. "In this way should you deal with a woman. Now this infant has become your own child. Thus should you people do in this one village."

COYOTE MAKES A FISH-TRAP

Then Coyote went on; straight on he went. He saw white salmon in the water. Then he thought: "How shall I catch them?" And then he thought: "I shall make a fish-trap." He saw the white salmon jumping along, and made a fish-trap. And then he tied the fish-trap, tied it on to the string. He jumped straightway right into the fish-trap.

And then Coyote said to the fish-trap: "If, fish-trap, you become filled, if your mouth becomes filled with white salmon, then you shall cry out, 'Uuuu, I am full'; you shall cry out, 'Now the fish-trap is quite full of white salmon.'" And then it cried out: "Uuu, I, the fish-trap, am full"; Coyote shouted: "Uuuu." And then Coyote went and saw that it was full now. Then he unloosened the fish-trap. Then Coyote said: "For all time shall you people catch them thus; thus did Coyote do." (The name of this land is "Eating Place" or "Water-Keeps-Tearing-Out.")

COYOTE SPEARS FISH

And then again he went on. He went and went (until) he arrived (at a certain place). And then he said: "Now I am extremely thirsty for water." They said to him: "There is no water." Then he saw the river, and said: "I desire some of the water." And then a woman went for the water. She dipped down the bucket and lost hold of it. Coyote saw that she was crying. And then Coyote went and got hold of the bucket; he went to the water and dipped it down. And then he took some water along with him to the house. Then it was drunk without knowledge of the (other) people.

He saw white salmon with their mouths agape. And then Coyote made a salmon-spear. He said to an old woman: "Give me a string; I am going to prepare a salmon-spear." And then she gave him some large beads. He did not want them. So then he went and cut up some wild-cherry bark in thin strips; he wound it around on the salmon-spear.

And then he speared a white salmon. Then he brought it to the house and steamed it. Then it was done, and they ate a side of split fish; they ate it without knowledge of the (other) people. And then Coyote said: "Thus shall you people get white salmon in this land." – "Now you shall get a woman." Coyote said: "I do not want any woman. Never mind! I'll not take her."

COYOTE EATS DRIED SALMON

And then he went on. Over there he saw in the trail some dried salmon. And then he ate it. Then he fell asleep and died. The salmon went out through him at his nostrils, at his mouth, and at his ears. In truth, it was a flea which Coyote had swallowed. It had killed him, (so that) he fell asleep. And then he named the land. He said: "Now the name of this land shall be Dried Salmon. Now forever shall you people call its name Dried Salmon." Thus is its name: Lmuyaqsoqu.

THE STORY CONCERNING COYOTE

And then he went on. He went and went (until) he seated himself. And then Coyote looked all around. Then Coyote sucked himself. Thus he did: he turned up his penis, and bent down his head (so that) he stooped down. Coyote said: "You have not done me good." And then Coyote locked up the story (of his obscene act); he did not wish that people should find out about it. So he headed the story off. But then the story loosened itself; they† caused it to break out (from its prison).

And then everybody found out what Coyote had done to himself. Now Coyote became hungry. Then he thought: "Now I shall eat." And then he went among the people. But they said: "Coyote has acted badly; he has sucked his own penis." And then Coyote went on again. He thought: "Yonder I am not known; truly now they shall not find out about me."

He went on (until he came) to another house. But again the people were laughing among themselves; "Now Coyote has sucked his own penis," again the people were saying to one another. And then he thought: "Truly now I am found out." So then he went on. Then again he entered a house (where) an old person was dwelling. He went in to this one and saw that the person had sores all over.

And then he said: "I am hungry." Then the person said to him: "I have no food. I have this flesh of mine which you see, my ugly flesh." And then she gave him to eat of this flesh of hers, she gave it to him in a plate. She said to him: "I have no food. This bad flesh of mine I shall give you to eat." So then she gave him it to eat. Then he ate, (but) did not eat in real truth; he did not swallow it. He let it fall down (until) there was a little left of it. And then he put it into his quiver and tied and took it with him. He took a little of the (sores) with him. He went out of the house and went on.

He went and went (until) he came to (some people). He got scent of something to eat. And then he said: "You are eating alone, but you will save a little for me also; I too will swallow and eat some." And then he

†The text is obscure. It is said that Coyote requested all things present not to carry off the "story," but forgot about the clouds (itka′), just then sailing above the spot. Not bound by a promise, they tore out the "story" from its fastness and conveyed it to the people. Thus was explained how all had heard of Coyote's obscenity, though no one had witnessed it, and though he himself did not tell any one of it. North of the Columbia and opposite Mosier may still be seen a long, high mountain called Idwô′tca or "Story," in which Coyote attempted to lock up the "story." Its clefts are due to the sudden force with which the "story" broke out.

went for some stones; Coyote bored them through with holes. He said: "You are eating alone."

And then he sat down, he was tired out. Then he turned and got hold of his quiver. He untied it and pulled out (what was inside). Behold, there in his quiver was one entire salmon. He put it down; he had taken out an entire salmon. There was another entire salmon inside, and he put that down. He started in eating, and ate it all. He ate up his whole quiver, ate his bow.

And then he sat down; he had eaten them all up, (including) his quiver. Then he thought: "I shall go back; truly it was a salmon which she had given me to eat." So then he went. Straightway he arrived there. And then he entered where she had given him to eat; there he went again. But she said to him: "I shall give you no food whatever. Just now Coyote has been here. I gave him to eat, (but) he threw away all my flesh. He did not like it, (so) he threw away all my flesh. Now I shall give you nothing to eat." And then Coyote scolded the old woman because she did not give him anything to eat. Then Coyote became angry. And then Coyote went on again. He arrived (at another place).

COYOTE AND ATATÁLIA

And then Coyote heard that Atatália and Owl were stealing people. So then Coyote went; Coyote cut up some rushes. And then he dried them; he tied the rushes on all over himself: on his head and on his hands – on every possible part. And then Coyote went along. Atatália was coming. And then Coyote caught sight of Atatália. He tried to turn aside, but without success; now Atatália headed him off.

And then Coyote stood still; Coyote's body was rattling in all its parts. Then Atatália said to him: "What did you do to yourself?" Then he said to her: "I would not tell you. I would first have to do that same thing to you yourself before I should tell you." And then she said to him: "What did you do to yourself to make your body rattle?" Then he told her: "I put pitch all over my body, then burnt myself in the fire." Atatália said: "It is good that you do that same thing to me, you shall put pitch on my body." Coyote said to her: "Well, I'll put it on you."

And then both of them went on. Very soon both Coyote and Atatália arrived at the furnace.† Coyote saw many people mourning; there in

†Or "Barbecuing Place," reckoned as the extreme eastern point on the river of the Wishram (hence also Chinookan) country.

the furnace their children were sitting two by two. And then Coyote said to the people: "Do you all stand up." And then the people stood up. Then he said to them: "Do you all get some pitch." The people went, and then they got some pitch. And then they came bringing pitch. Then Coyote said: "Do you rub it on over her body." He rubbed it over the eyes of Atatália.

And then he said to her: "If I shall do thus to you also, O Atatália, (if I) shall put the pitch over you, you will burn all over your body. And then you will become strong, and the people will all be afraid of you." And then Atatália said: "Now it is well that you put the pitch on my body also."

And then they two went to the furnace, and he put the pitch on her. He said to her: "I, Coyote, must let you know just when you, Atatália will be burnt (sufficiently)." And then he pushed her in, and she burned. Then said Coyote: "Do you (people) cut four pieces of wood so that they be forked." And then they fastened the pieces of wood on to her – to the front part of her neck and to both her arms and to her legs. Then they turned her over, and Atatália burned.

And then Atatália said: "Now I am burning." Then said Coyote to her: "I, Coyote, must (tell you when you're done), not you." He turned her over and said: "I must tell you." And then said Atatália: "I am burrrning!" Coyote said to her: "Soon I shall let you know." She burned all up; Atatália died. And then Coyote said to the people: "Now do you all go home!"

Now he caught sight also of Owl, of whom, in truth, Atatália was the wife. And he also, Owl, was bringing along some more people. And then Coyote took hold of some ashes. Then Coyote said to him: "By what right, perchance, would you, Owl, do thus to people? No! This day your name has become Owl." And then he threw the ashes at him; Owl became all ashy gray.

And then Coyote said: "Very soon will come here the Indian people. Whenever an owl (is heard), the people shall say, 'Now an owl is hooting; now surely some person will die.'" And then said Coyote: "Now do you people go home; I have now killed Atatália. And then Coyote said: "No longer would you, Atatália, do thus to the people. Now I am Coyote, you have this day died, Atatália." Thus he did at Wishram.

COYOTE IN *SKIN*†

And then Coyote went on; he travelled up the river. Straightway he ar-

†*Skin* was the country immediately north of the Columbia and east of the Falls or "Tumwater," inhabited by Sahaptian tribes.

rived at *Skin*, in *Skin* he urinated on the people.† Coyote went across to the Falls; he went thither by means of a round-pointed canoe. He shouted. And then he said: "Mind, now, that you always do thus; you shall shout; whenever you cross over, then you shall shout. You are the Iłka'imamt; thus I have named you."

COYOTE AND ITCÉXYAN††

And then Coyote went on again. Straightway he arrived (at another place). Coyote heard that the Merman was always swallowing people. Wheresoever a canoe went, straightway the Merman seized it; every one he swallowed. "Now let him swallow me also," thought Coyote. And then Coyote went and got a big tree. Then he came into view. The Merman caught hold of him, and he was swallowed down.

Straightway Coyote fell down under the water (apparently) to the bottom. And then he saw many people; many canoes were piled together there under the water. Then Coyote caught sight of the Merman's heart hanging. And then Coyote was told: "That is the Merman's heart." Then he cut it off; the Merman's heart was çut off.††† And then everything floated up to the surface – all the canoes and the people and Coyote.

And then Coyote said: "By what right, perchance, would you alone, Merman, do thus to the people? This day you will have had enough of doing thus to the people. I, Coyote, have told you. Soon the people will come into this land, and then they shall say, 'Thus did Coyote transform the Merman.' And then you, the Merman, will do no harm."

COYOTE AT LAPWAI, IDAHO

Now Coyote goes toward the uplands, and he approaches truly a bad place, the land of the mountain monster. Anything with wings would try to fly overhead, but still he would swallow it without difficulty; should it try to go by underneath, he would swallow it likewise. Then

†Coyote is supposed by the Wishram to have urinated on their Sahaptian neighbors to show their inferiority to themselves. This inferiority consists, among other things, in the use by the Sahaptians of a smaller and more rudely constructed canoe as contrasted with the long, elaborately built iknî'm of the Chinookan tribes.

††This word is used only in reference to the swallowing of anything by an Itcéxyan [a monster being, such as the Merman – KK].

†††Coyote used the tree to climb up to the heart, which was dangling high up out of reach.

(Coyote) thought: "What shall I do?" He saw a hill and thought: "I shall make a hazel-bush rope."

Then he made it and tied it on to the (hill); then he tied it about himself also. Now he saw the (monster) lying down, lying with face and belly down. He tied some hazel-bush ropes all together and made a long rope. Then he went up to him; his rope ran out, falling somewhat short. Again he made another rope; again he went up to him and came a little nearer, yet fell short. Again he made a rope; again he went up to him and fell short. Thus he kept doing, and at the fifth time reached close enough, about five steps off.

Then Coyote said: "O mountain monster! I am challenging you that we two swallow each other." The mountain monster lies silent. He did not say anything at all. Again (Coyote) spoke to him; it was the fifth time before he looked up at him. He said "Yes" to him, although (Coyote) was tied on to the hill by means of his rope.

Now the mountain monster drew in his breath, – fūu[†] – the (rope) was stretched out somewhat forcibly. In a little while he let it come to rest. Then Coyote also drew in his breath – fūu; the mountain monster became somewhat shaky. Again he also tried to draw him to himself – fūu. The fifth time the two did thus. The mountain monster went at it with great force. Oh, dear! Coyote became uneasy. Somehow he kept rising straightway; he kept getting higher and higher, and his rope almost snapped. Now the hill is worn far in at that part in which it had (the rope) tied to it. Long he tried to draw him to himself – "fūu," and so on for quite some time before he let him come to rest.

Now Coyote, in his turn, drew in his breath, – fūuuu, also for quite some time. Then the (mountain monster) was heard groaning; "Āaaaa, Bu'x̣u," he was heard; his belly burst, and his guts went out of him. It is for this reason that he was always lying down, – lying down on his belly. If he were to be turned over, his belly would straightway burst. And that Coyote tried to draw him to himself, – fūu; straightway he turned over. And that (monter's) guts were spilt out. Thus was his character.

And then he skinned him. Then he made people out of that same (monster's) flesh. (He) cut off a little, threw (it) away, one village (came into being). In this way he made people. Then he discovered that he had no more flesh, (yet) he had not yet made the Wishram people. There was only the tongue lying down. "Well, then I shall make the

[†]The monster had been wont to devour all beings that passed by by drawing them to himself with his breath. Fūu represents the sound made by sucking in air.

Wishram people out of it." And indeed (he made) the flat-headed Wishram people out of the tongue. Therefore the people dwelling farther up say that the Wishrams' heads are like a tongue, flat.

Again he looked around. Behold! As yet he had not made any people belonging to that place, to Lapwai; but there was nothing left at all. And then he felt sorry. There was only blood on his hands. Then he plucked some grass, wiped his hands with it, and threw it away. He said: "Out of that you have become the Nez Percés people." Thus do men say: "Nez Percés are brave warriors, a people made out of blood. They are a dangerous people of warriors."

COYOTE AND THE SUN

Now Coyote is going towards the sun. Then he arrived (there). "Well," he said to the Sun, "it is good that I shall be your slave and that I shall follow you about. I shall work for nothing, you are chieftainess." So she said "Yes" to him. Early next morning the Sun arose. (Wherever) she went, there he also, Coyote, followed her. Oh, dear! he looked on and saw everything.

Early next morning they two went again. Again, as before, he saw various things, – in what various ways people were acting, how women were eloped with, or what was stolen, what bad things (were done), who was killed, – everything Coyote saw. At last he became uneasy. Then he cried out: "I see what you people are doing."

Again he saw them. As before, he cried out again: "I see you." Then she did not want him. She said to him: "Now I shall have taken you with me long enough. You are too mean. It would not be good that you should always tell on people. There would soon be trouble." It is because of this that we do not find everything out. But if Coyote had become (the sun), everybody would to-day be betrayed in his secrets. In this way did Coyote in vain try to become (the sun). And then he gave it up. There he stopped; he had arrived at the end.

Chemehuevi[6]

How Wolf and Coyote Went Away

GEORGE LAIRD

Wolf and his younger brother, Coyote, were living together in a cave on Nɨvagantɨ. Having Snow.

Wolf always spoke in a chant. In this way he said to Coyote, "Cɨn-awávipɨɨtsí, Respécted Óld Coyó-oté, go get some grass seed from our aunt."

"Haiky*a*, haiky*a*, I did not know we had an aunt-aiky*a*!" Coyote said. "But I'll go anyway-aiky*a*, I'll do as you say-aiky*a*!"[†]

Coyote went down the slopes of the mountain almost into the valley. There he found a little brush house. No one seemed to be at home. Coyote thought it would be well to build a fire, and he did so. Then he picked up one of a number of little poker sticks that were lying in a row and poked the fire with it.

"Arɨrɨrɨh, that burns!" the little stick cried.

Coyote dropped that stick in a hurry and poked the fire with another, and it also said, "Arɨrɨrɨh!"

He dropped that one and tried the next, and it also cried out in pain.

While Coyote was going down the line, poking the fire with one little poker stick after another, his aunt came home. She was Papaw*a*, Bear, and she had been out seed-gathering. She saw in one glance what the visitor was doing, made a lunge at him, caught him with her powerful claws, and stripped the flesh from his loin.

Coyote went home.

Wolf was out hunting. By this great power he was aware of everything that went on. When he perceived what Coyote had done and

Trans. Carobeth Laird, *The Chemehuevis* (Banning CA: Malki Museum Press, 1970), 192–207. © 1970 Malki Museum, Inc.

[†]"Haiky*a*" and "aiky*a*" are intranslatable identifiers of Coyote's peculiar mode of speech – KK.

what had befallen him, he killed a mountain sheep, cut off the loin, and brought it, together with the blood, home with him.

He found Coyote lying by the fire, trying to conceal his hurt.

"Respécted Óld Coyó-oté," Wolf chanted, "do not lie there on your back; take this flesh and make yourself a loin. . . . Respécted Óld Coyó-oté, I did not tell you to make a fire at our aunt's house, I did not tell you to poke it with those little poker sticks. They are our aunt's children. Becuase she lives all alone, the Fire Poker is her only husband. Those poker sticks are our little cousins."

Coyote took the piece of meat. "Yes-aiky*a*, yes-aiky*a*, I'll make myself a loin-aiky*a*!" he said. "I don't know how you see everything-aiky*a*! I don't know how you know so much-aiky*a*!"

Coyote made himself a loin out of the loin of the mountain sheep. (And that is the reason that even to this day the loin of a coyote tastes like the loin of a mountain sheep – or at least, so it is said.)

Then Wolf said: "Respécted Óld Coyó-oté, tomorrow you must go down towards the valley again. You must take this blood with you and these flint-chippings. When you have come to our aunt's house, you will make a fire and put this blood into a pot and cook it, stirring in the flint-chippings. Then you will feed some to the little poker sticks, and they will all die. Presently our aunt will come home, and you will offer her some. She will eat it, because all the Bear People are very fond of blood pudding. As she eats, you must watch her carefully. When her eyes begin to change, be ready to dodge! She will try to leap upon you and kill you. Then she will die.

"When she is dead, you must pack up her body and all her possessions and bring them back with you. Bring everything. Oh Respécted Óld Coyó-oté! Bring everything! Do not leave one little thing behind you, Respécted Óld Coyó-oté!"

"All right-aiky*a*! I'll do as you say-aiky*a*!" Coyote promised. "I'll bring everything back with me-aiky*a*!"

The following day he went down to his aunt's house, taking with him the blood and the flint-chippings. He was careful to do everything just as Wolf had directed. He prepared the blood pudding poisoned with flint-chippings and fed it to the little poker sticks. When they were dead he laid them out neatly all in a row on top of a rock.

Then Bear came home.

"Haiky*a*, haiky*a*, haiky*a*! My aunt-aiky*a*," Coyote exclaimed very quickly, before she had time to attack him. "Look at the nice blood pudding-aiky*a* I have cooked for you-aiky*a*! Your children-aiky*a* have already had theirs-aiky*a*, and now they are asleep-aiky*a*!"

The sight of her favorite food made Bear's mouth water. She sat down and began to eat. She ate and ate, while Coyote watched her closely, especially her eyes. By and by they began to roll wildly and to glow with a red and angry light. Coyote rose up on tiptoe.

Bear lunged at him ferociously.

Coyote dodged. "Haiky-aiky-aiky*a*!" he screamed. "you can't catch me-aiky*a*!"

Bear came after him. Coyote kept out of her way, screaming and yelping with excitement. She pursued him in great awkward lunges, growling terribly, her eyes rolling wilder and wilder. She was already in her death struggle.

Suddenly she tumbled over dead.

Coyote skinned her, cut up her body, and put it in his carrying net. He set fire to her little brush house. He packed up all her baskets and cooking pots, and all the rest of her belongings, together with the little dead poker sticks. Then he started home.

When he had gone about halfway, he had a sudden thought, "I wonder if I got all those little poker sticks?" He went back to check. There on the rock was one little poker stick that he had forgotten.

Coyote put out his hand to pick it up. The little poker stick slipped off the rock. He tried again to grasp it, and it eluded him. He ran after it, and away it went, tumbling end over end, bouncing and skipping down the valley like a feather in the wind. As it went, it called out in its tiny little voice, "I am going to tell-sikwikwikwi!" I am going to tell-sikwikwikwi!"

Coyote gave up. "All right-aiky*a*!" he called after the little poker stick, "go on and tell-sikwikwikwiaiky*a*! Tell everything-aiky*a*!"

Coyote took up his pack and went home.

Wolf already knew what had happened. He rebuked Coyote, telling him how grieved and disappointed he was. Wolf had put up with Coyote's carelessness and disobedience ever since the earth was made, and now he was getting very weary of the way things were going.

Coyote hung his head in shame. He tried to excuse himself by telling how it had all come about. "The little poker stick went off down the valley-aiky*a*," he said, "it went away saying 'I am going to tell everything-sikwikwikwiaiky*a*!'"

"Respécted Óld Coyó-oté," Wolf sang. "Straighten arrows! Straighten arrows!"

Now the word that Wolf used for "straighten" was one which would more usually be taken to mean "rub." Coyote knew perfectly well what his brother meant. Nonetheless he pretended to misunderstand and went about rubbing the reeds which were to be made into arrow shafts against various objects in the cave.

"I did not mean for you to do that," Wolf chanted, "I meant for you to straighten your arrows."

Coyote pretended great surprise. "Haiky*a*, haiky*a*! Is that-aiky*a* what you meant-aiky*a*? Why didn't you say so in the first place-aiky*a*?"

Coyote then built a fire and threw his arrow-straightening stone into it. When the stone was hot, he took it out, sat down by the fire, and began to rub the reeds one at a time back and forth in the little groove, straightening each separate reed very carefully.

Wolf looked on for a long time in silence. Then he said, "That is not the way, Respécted Óld Coyó-oté! That is too slow. This is the way you should do." He grasped a bunch of reeds and pulled them through his closed fist, straightening them perfectly all at once.

"No-aiky*a*, no-aiky*a*!" Coyote protested. "This way is better-aiky*a*! Your way is unnatural-aiky*a*, magical-aiky*a*! It is more seemly and proper that Man-aiky*a* shall sit by his fire-aiky*a* straightening arrows as I am doing now-aiky*a*!"

When the shafts were all straightened, the brothers began to feather them. Wolf merely touched the feathers to the arrow, and they were instantly and perfectly affixed to it. But Coyote wrapped each one with sinew, taking infinite pains, holding up the arrow and squinting along it to see that every feather was on straight. "It is more natural-aiky*a* that Man-aiky*a* should feather his arrows thus-aiky*a*!" he said. And it was the same with attaching the flints: what Wolf did without effort, Coyote did with much labor so that he might set a proper pattern for Man.

After all the arrows were finished, Wolf chanted, "Respécted Óld Coyó-oté, go dig in the mountain."

"All right-aiky*a*, all right-aiky*a*, I'll go dig-aiky*a*," Coyote said.

He went higher up on the slope of the mountain and began to dig vigorously with his paw-like hands, but he did not accomplish anything. After he had been digging for a long time, he could still be seen on top of the ground. He was just raising a dust.

Wolf came to him and said, "Respécted Óld Coyó-oté, this is the way to do." He thrust his *poro* into the earth, gave it a single twist, and immediately a tunnel opened, slanting upwards through the mountain to the other side. (And if we had followed Wolf, we too could dig without effort; but we followed Coyote.)

Wolf then said, "Respécted Óld Coyó-oté, pack up our belongings and carry them into the tunnel."

"All right-aiky*a*! I'll do as you say-aiky*a*!" For once Coyote did exactly as he had been told.

Wolf's next command was, "Respécted Óld Coyó-oté, stand out in the sun! Stand out in the sun!"

"All right-aiky*a*! I'll stand in the sun-aiky*a*! It's very hot in the sun-aiky*a*! I don't know why I should stand out here-aiky*a*!" Coyote kept up a noisy protest, pretending he did not know that Wolf meant for him to stand guard at the mouth of the tunnel.

"All right-aiky*a*, all right-aiky*a*! Whatever shall I be watching for-aiky*a* out here in the sun-aiky*a*? I don't know why you want me to stand in the sun-aiky*a*! I think you want to cook me-aiky*a*! Whatever should I be watching for-aiky*a* out where it is so hot-aiky*a*. . . .

"Haiky*a*, haiky*a*, haiky*a*!" he cried suddenly, "It is dark to the southwest-aiky*a*! There something lies like a rainstorm-aiky*a*! Like dark fog-aiky*a*!"

"That is what I want you to watch," Wolf chanted. "Watch well, Respécted Óld Coyó-oté! Watch well what becomes of it."

"It is coming toward us-aiky*a*! It is getting nearer-aiky*a*!"

"Watch carefully, Respécted Óld Coyó-oté."

"Haiky*a*, haiky*a*! Under the dark cloud-aiky*a* things are moving-aiky*a*! They are people-aiky*a*! I can see sparks flashing-aiky*a* like lightning from their arrowheads-aiky*a*! Haiky-aiky-aiky*a*! They are our aunts-aiky*a*!"

Coyote had recognized the Bear People. They were approaching like rain under a dark storm cloud, and the sparks that glinted from their flint arrowheads were the lightning.

"Watch them closely, Respécted Óld Coyó-oté! Do not abandon your post."

But as the approaching army became more clearly visible, Coyote was overcome by fear. "Haiky*a*, haiky*a*, haiky*a*!" he yelped, turning tail and running back into the tunnel.

"Respécted Óld Coyó-oté," Wolf commanded, "put on these clothes and go out to fight!"

With that he gave Coyote a suit of beautiful pink armor. Coyote put it on, and at once he felt big and brave. He took a bow and four arrows and showed himself at the mouth of the tunnel.

The Bear warriors were massed below him on the mountain side.

"There is Wolf!" some of them shouted.

"No," cried others, "it is not Wolf! Do you not see his squinting, slanted eyes? It is that Coyote!"

Coyote shot three times and missed. With his fourth arrow he wounded one of the Bears. Then he broke his bow, dropped it, and ducked back into the tunnel.

Now Wolf gave him a red suit of war clothes, and Coyote felt grander than ever. Again he went out, armed with a bow and four arrows.

"Ah, that one is Wolf!" some of the enemy exclaimed. Coyote heard them. He was grinning all over his face because he was being taken for his brother.

But others were looking more closely. "Don't you see his pointed nose?" they asked. "It is that same Coyote!"

Coyote missed three times, wounded one warrior with his last arrow, broke his bow, and ran back into the tunnel.

Wolf gave him yellow armor, and he wore it very proudly as he went out with still another bow and four arrows.

Again he fooled some of the Bears. "Surely that is Wolf!" they cried. Coyote smiled as he fought, hearing what they said.

"But no," others said, "don't you see his stubby, dog-like paws? He has no proper hands. It is just that Coyote again!"

Coyote wounded one Bear with his last arrow, broke his bow, and dodged back into the tunnel.

He brother gave him green war clothes. He showed himself again and heard voices calling, "There! At last Wolf has come out!"

But others answered in disgust, "Just look at his bushy tail! It is that same miserable Coyote!"

As before, Coyote used up his arrows and retreated.

Then Wolf chanted: "Respécted Óld Coyó-oté, make a bundle of all my belongings, and pack it on your back. Go through the tunnel. When you come out, keep on going straight north. Under no circumstances must you look back."

"All right-aiky*a*! I'll pack everything-aiky*a*!"

Wolf waited till Coyote was well on his way. Then he took his own armor from the place where he had hidden it, put it on, and went out to do battle. His fighting clothes were of all colors at once, every color of the primary rainbow, including, but far outshining, all the colors that Coyote had worn – which is why, to this day, we call the primary rainbow "Wolf's war clothes" and the secondary rainbow "Coyote's war clothes."

The brilliance of this armor of light dazzled the eyes of the Bear warriors. They gasped in amazement. A great sigh went up from all of them, and they cried out with one voice, "Ah, that is Wolf! See how glorious he is to look upon! How unmistakable! How different from that Coyote!"

Wolf strung the whole length of his bow with arrows and, discharging them all at once towards the right flank of the enemy, he mowed them down. Again releasing innumerable arrows at one time, he mowed down the entire left flank. And shooting thus the third time, he destroyed half of those who were left standing in the center. Had he ever discharged his fourth volley, the battle would have been over.

But while Wolf was winning gloriously, Coyote was toiling through the tunnel. He came out onto a high ridge beyond it and wondered to himself, "Why did my brother tell me not to look back?" Then he turned around and looked. He saw Wolf in his dazzling rainbow armor mowing down whole masses of the Bear People.

Coyote's heart was filled with bitterness and envy. "Oh, why did he withhold that suit from me?" he thought. "If he had given it to me, I too could have dazzled the enemy, I too could have wiped them out with many arrows discharged at once. I cannot endure to watch him." Then Coyote thought, "Mangasuyaganu (would that that one) might get shot in the calf of his leg!"

Coyote intended only to humble his brother and tarnish his splendid image, but no sooner had he made his wish than an arrow pierced Wolf's heart. Immediately the Bears fell upon him and butchered him.

Coyote squatted down and howled: "Kayuyayuyayuuwaiky*a*! Kayuyayuyayuuwaiky*a*! Oh, what made me think that? Oh, why did I make that wish? Kayuyayuyayuuwaiky*a*!"

After he had kept this up for a while, his curiosity began to get the better of his grief. "Well-aiky*a*, my brother is dead-aiky*a*," he said. "I might as well go through his things-aiky*a* before I burn them-aiky*a*! I might as well see what he had-aiky*a*! He would never let me-aiky*a* do this while he was alive-aiky*a*!"

Talking to himself, Coyote began to rummage among Wolf's belongings. Soon he found a bundle well wrapped and securely tied. This seemed like something worth looking into. He untied the string and removed the buckskin wrapping, only to find an inner wrapping just as well secured as the outer one. He untied that and found another; and another, and another, and another. He got tired of untying knots and used his knife to cut the string. Still there were more wrappings to remove, and more, and more, till only a tiny little bundle was left. Coyote cut the last string, spread out the last little scrap of buckskin – and immediately it was dark, completely, impenetrably dark! It was the Night itself that Wolf had kept in that bundle.

This time Coyote's mourning was long and sincere, because he was crying for himself. "Kayuyayuyayuuwaiky*a*! Kayuyayuyayuuwaiky*a*! Whatever made me-aiky*a* go through my brother's things-aiky*a*? Now how shall I live-aiky*a*? How shall I see to get my food-aiky*a*? Now I must surely die-aiky*a*? Kayuyayuyayuuwaiky*a*!"

Coyote howled a long time. But he could not keep this up forever. Finally he felt around, found some pieces of wood and made a little fire. Then he squatted down beside it and began to make arrows. He had hope, because he knew that among his brother's possessions was a bag containing the feathers of every sort of bird that flies upon the earth. Coyote thought to himself that he would use them all if necessary.

Coyote finished an arrow, feathered it with crow feathers, and shot it up into the sky.

"Haiky*a*! It just got darker-aiky*a*," he said, "that won't do-aiky*a*!"

On the next arrow he put buzzard feathers. He shot it up and immediately exclaimed, "Haiky*a*! I believe it has become still darker-aiky*a*!"

Coyote kept on trying arrows feathered with the feathers from a very great number of different kinds of birds, and the darkness lifted not at all. Then he used feathers from the red-tailed hawk, and there came a faint light!

"Haiky*a*! Haiky*a*! Cɨnaarɨsɨant-aiky*a*! Coyote-dawn-aiky*a*!" Coyote was wild with delight because the false dawn had come – and that is why to this day coyotes howl early in the morning.

The darkness thickened again. Undismayed, Coyote made another arrow, feathered it with seagull feathers, and shot it into the sky. The light came back.

"Haiky*a*! Haɨtɨtasɨant-aiky*a*! True dawn-aiky*a*!" Coyote cried.

Then the sun came up.

Coyote carried all his belongings and all his brother's belongings back to the cave and hung them up in their accustomed places. Then he went down to the battlefield to see if he could find any pieces of his brother's body. He found one small sliver of bone, one little hair, one speck of dried blood, and one flake of flesh. These he gathered up carefully and put under a large basket.

Then he went back into the cave and once more sat himself down to make arrows. He made an enormous stack of them. Then he began to make bows, one bow for every four arrows. When he had all the bows and arrows that he could possibly carry, he started out on the enemies' trail.

After travelling a long, long way it seemed to him that he had come to the proper place to leave a cache. He hid a bow and four arrows in such a way that they were well concealed but accessible in a hurry. Then he ran as fast and as far as he possibly could, and when his breath completely gave out so that he could not take another step, he again hid a bow and four arrows. Again he ran as hard and as far as he could, and left another bow with four arrows, and so he continued till he had only one bow an four arrows left. By that time he was getting well into enemy country.

"Haiky*a*, my penis-aiky*a*! Oh, my penis-aiky*a*! What shall I do-aiky*a*? Coyote asked. "How shall I manage this business-aiky*a*?"

Coyote's penis advised him how to proceed.

As he came near to the camp of the Bear People he saw two old women coming out to gather wood. He sat down and hastily painted himself so that he would not be recognized, and he also disguised his manner of speaking.

Then he approached the old women. "How are you-siviyaukwi*i*?" he asked politely. "Are you well-siviyaukwi*i*? I am a traveller-siviyaukwi*i*," he explained, "and have not seen anyone for a long time-siviyaukwi*i*, and I do not know what is going on in the world-siviyaukwi*i*."

"Ye-es," the old women answered slowly and with relish, "what shall we tell you? Well, there is nothing to tell except that they have been to kill our nephew Wolf –"

"Ye-es-siviyaukwi*i*?"

"– and now they are having the Scalp Dance, and we are gathering wood for their fire."

"Yes-siviyaukwi*i*. And how do you two do after you gather the wood-siviyaukwi*i*?"

"We go grunting under our loads, unh, unh, unh. And when we are come near to the dancing place we sing:

yawaiya' yawaiyawai ha
yawaiya' yawaiyawai
tuwamɨ'

tuwamɨ'
yawaiya' yawaiyawai ha
yawaiya' yawaiyawai

Then people say, 'Our mothers are acting like Coyote – Coyote has got into our mothers!" And we answer. 'How could he? He is all alone now, he has no one to come with him.' Then after this kind of talking and joking, we put our wood down and go to our house to lie down. Then our granddaughters go to the dance. Towards morning they come home, and we get up and go to the dancing place again. As we draw near, we sing. Then we get inside the circle of dancers and dance and sing. The scalp is passed from person to person till at last it comes to us, and we have it on our heads for a while. Then we stoop lower as we dance and sing louder and act more fiercely. And people say, 'Now surely Coyote has got into our mothers! Just see how they are acting!' And again we answer, 'No, how could he do so? He is all alone!'"

"Yes-aiky*a*!" shouted Coyote in his own voice, as he fell upon the women and killed them.

He skinned the old Bear women and put himself into one skin and his penis into the other; then having become two, he picked up the loads of wood and went along grunting towards the dance circle. And as he approached that place, Coyote and his penis sang the women's song just as they were accustomed to sing it. The people made sport, saying, "Look! It seems that Coyote has got into our mothers! Perhaps he has killed them and has put himself into their skins!" Whereupon Coyote and his penis replied in the voices of the old women, "How could he do so when he is all alone and has no one to come with him?"

Coyote and his double put down their loads and went into the old women's brush house. It was already sundown. The granddaughters came in, and all ate supper together, and the young women noticed nothing peculiar about their grandmothers. Then the false grandmothers lay down to rest, and the girls went to the dance. Towards morning they returned. Coyote and his penis sprang on them and killed them.

Still in the form of two old women, Coyote went to the dance ring. Oh, now he was singing with all his might!

"Just look at our mothers!" the people said. "They were never so fierce before – surely Coyote has got into them!"

"Oh, no," two cracked old voices answered, "he couldn't do that, he has no one to help him."

Coyote and his penis entered the circle and began to dance vigorously. Slowly the scalp progressed toward them. It was put first upon the head of Coyote's penis, which then stooped lower and danced harder and sang louder. Meanwhile Coyote, apparently absorbed in the frenzy of the dance, was selecting a good place to break out of the circle. He timed himself so that Wolf's scalp would come to him just as he danced by the Badger People, who were much shorter than their allies, the Bears. When he felt it on his head, he got a firm grip on it, cried "Haiky*a*" loudly, took a tremendous flying leap over the heads of the Badgers, and made off at a dead run. In that instant the second "grandmother" vanished, and his penis was joined to him in its proper form.

Now Coyote was running for his life with his enemies close on his heels. He finally made it to his last cache of a bow and four arrows, tied the long hair of the scalp around his waist, snatched up his weapons, and stood off the Bears while he caught his breath. He only wounded one of them with his last arrow. Then he ran again, as hard as he could.

It was a long, long run to the next weapon cache. Coyote barely made it. He used his arrows as slowly as possible, to give himself time to breathe. When he had wounded one warrior with his last arrow, he broke his bow and began to run again.

In this way Coyote travelled till he had used up all the bows and arrows that he had hidden. Then there was nothing left for him to do but to run and run and keep on running. He became so tired that he could hardly put one foot before the other. Wondering what in the world he could do to save himself, he darted down into a dry wash where the bank concealed him momentarily from the Bears, who were now gaining on him rapidly. His eye lit on an old coyote track, and he turned himself into it.

His enemies rushed into the wash. "Which way did Coyote go?" they asked. "He can't have got very far!"

They scattered to search for him, but there was no sign. At last someone noticed the track and exclaimed, "Look! There is an old coyote track."

"That must be Coyote himself!" another surmised. "Get a rock and smash him quickly!"

"Haiky*a*! How do you see me when I have made myself vanish-aiky*a*?" Coyote leaped up and went away from that place. He had had a good rest, and for a while he left all his pursuers far behind.

At last he began to lose his breath again, and little by little they gained on him. This time they were sure they had him. But down in a hollow he spied an old coyote rolling-place and turned himself into it.

The Bears swarmed all over looking for him. "Where did he go? He can't have got far because he was pretty nearly done for." After a time someone exclaimed, "Look here! Here is an old coyote rolling-place – get a rock, it may be he himself!"

"Haiky*a*! It is I-aiky*a*! It is I-aiky*a*!" yelped Coyote, starting off on another long run.

And so he travelled, running all out, running till he could run no more, then using his power as an imitator to gain himself a little breathing space. All the time he was getting more and more tired. There came a time when he could barely stagger along, but he could see no shape to assume, no way to disguise himself.

He rounded the point of a little hill and was hidden for a moment. "Haiky*a*, my penis-aiky*a*," Coyote begged, "what shall I do-aiky*a*?" His penis advised him.

Quick as thought he collapsed into a heap and became invisible, projecting his semblance to run far off on the slope of a distant mountain.

The Bear People came rushing around the point. "Where can that Coyote have got to? Not far surely, because he was just barely creeping along." They looked in every direction and finally caught sight of what seemed to be Coyote running like the wind, far, far ahead of them.

"Look how he has out-distanced us!" they said in disgust. "He must just have been pretending to be tired. We'll never catch him now."

"Oh, well," some of them suggested, "let us call up a snowstorm and freeze him to death."

"Yes, that is what we shall do," they all agreed.

The Bears turned around and started home. Of course all the time the real Coyote had lain there right under their feet, listening to every word.

"Haiky*a*! My penis-aiky*a*, what shall I do-aiky*a*?" he said. "It would be better for me to hunt myself a cave-aiky*a*! It would be better to gather up a quantity of wood-aiky*a*! They say it is going to turn cold-aiky*a*!"

Coyote ran all around till he found a nice, dry cave. Then he gathered a great pile of wood. By this time it was late afternoon. Soon cold, gray clouds spread all over the sky. It began to rain, and then the rain turned to snow. The night was dark, snowy, and bitterly cold. But there lay Coyote, snug and warm in his cave, waking up from time to time just long enough to put another piece of wood on the fire.

When he opened his eyes in the morning the storm was over. The sun shone brightly on a cold, white world. As far as he could see in every direction, the earth was covered with snow. "If I try to travel through that snow-aiky*a* I'll freeze to death-aiky*a*!" Coyote said. He went back and lay down by the fire to try to figure out a way to get home. Looking up at the roof of the cave, he saw where a very small spider had spun a very small web. In it was caught a tiny puff-ball, such as one sometimes sees blowing along for miles over the desert.

"Haiky*a*! That looks like it might be useful-aiky*a*!" Coyote said.

He took down the puff-ball, weighed it in his hand, and felt how light it was. Then he took his awl and punched a little hole in it and looked in. Yes, just as he had thought, it was hollow! He placed the puff-ball near the opening of the cave, where the wind could catch it and swirl it away. Next he turned himself into a tiny little creature, no large than the smallest ant, and crawled inside the puff-ball through the hole that he had made. When he was all curled up securely, he began to call the North Wind:

Kwiyamayamayuuyuuwaiky
kwiyamayamayuuyuuwaiky!

Coyote kept this up for a long, long time. At last he could hear the wind, but he could not feel it. He called harder than ever and heard it roaring above him, but still he could not feel even a tremor in the little puff-ball. Then Coyote crawled out of his place and made himself as tall as the sky, and with his *poro* he hooked the wind down so that it raced along just above the ground. (Before this time all winds had stayed high up in the sky; it was Coyote who brought them down to sweep the earth.)

Quickly Coyote made himself small again and crept back inside the puff-ball. Soon it began to bounce and quiver. Then the wind picked it up and swept it away, and it floated light as a feather over mountains and valleys and across deep canyons. "Haiky*a*, haiky*a*," Coyote said, "this is a fine way to travel-aiky*a*!"

But then the movement stopped. Coyote was puzzled. "Haiky*a*, what can be the matter with this thing-aiky*a*?" he said. "I wonder if it can be caught in a crevice-aiky*a*?"

He took his awl, punched a small hole, and peered outside. "Haiky*a*! That looks like my bundle hanging on the wall of the cave-aiky*a*! That other one looks like my brother's bundle-aiky*a*!" Coyote got himself out in a hurry. The puff-ball had come to rest back in his home cave on

Nɨvagantɨ. "Haiky*a*! What a good way to travel-aiky*a*! And quick too – I didn't even get tired-aiky*a*!"

Coyote went back to his normal size. He lay down and rested for a while, then he got himself some food. After that he went outside the cave and placed Wolf's scalp beside the other fragments of his body, and replaced the large basket on top of the remains. Then he returned to the cave, lay down, and slept.

At midnight he awoke and lay listening. There was silence till the time when the morning star emerges. Then he heard a faint call: "Huuuu!"

"Haiky*a*! That is my brother-aiky*a*!"

Coyote listened intently. He was happy, because this time he had done everything exactly right. Now that his brother had come back to life, they would go on living together in the cave, and everything would be as it had always been.

The sound came again: "Huuuu!"

"Haiky*a*! That is from the wrong direction-aiky*a*!" Coyote cried. "It sounds as if he was going north-aiky*a*! Why doesn't he come to the cave-aiky*a*?"

And then a third time the call sounded, very faint and far: "Huuuu!"

"Haiky*a*! He's going away-aiky*a*! I am going to follow him-aiky*a*! Coyote started running in the dark, guided only by those distant, mournful wolf howls.

The two brothers ran on and on and on, always towards the North, the Storied Land where the Ancient Telling starts and ends. Coyote ran far behind. We are not told if he ever caught up with Wolf or ever saw his brother's face again. But even after he could no longer hear the guiding voice, Coyote knew he was on his brother's trail because he came upon a rock beside a spring which retained the clear imprint of Wolf's hand. Perhaps Wolf stopped to drink and rested his palm upon the rock; or perhaps he left the sign to guide his errant brother. However that may be, there was the print of the well-formed hand Coyote knew so well. Always the imitator, he put his own doggy paw-mark on the rock beside it (where those handmarks may be seen to this day) and ran on, even though ever so far behind.

That is all. That is the end of the tale and of the ancient telling.

COMMENTARY

No character in Native American myths has provoked more confused ethnological comment than Trickster-Transformer, whose most popular guise is that of Coyote. Nothing more upsets conventional Western logicians than this buffoonish embodiment of self-destructive greed – who simultaneously is the creator of culture.[7] There has arisen around this contradictory figure a heap of commentary that threatens to overwhelm him as he is overwhelmed by his own feces in the stories from the Winnebago Trickster Cycle collected by Paul Radin.[8] Rather than attempting a measured survey of such a malodorous mass, I bring forward evidence that the Trickster-Transformer uniquely reveals essential qualities of mythic imagining in preliterate societies.

One of the most important of these qualities has been beautifully defined by Barre Toelken in a thirty-year-long study of a single Navajo Coyote tale: the compatibility of profound cultural significance with humorous enactments. Toelken, so far as I know, is alone in having fully explored this productive combination in all its detailed specifics. After publishing in the early 1970s a translation and analysis of a telling of "Coyote and the Prairie Dogs" which he had recorded in 1966, Toelken returned to his tape ten years later with the collaboration of a native Navajo to revise and reassess his presentation – and then to report with rare scholarly honesty that there were mistakes and omissions in his original transcription. If so patient and conscientious a scholar as Toelken finds "mishearings" in a much-studied tape recording, consider the possibilities for differences in both telling and hearing between two different enactments of the same story! Oral myth's vitality arises from the diversity of "uncertainties" created by retellings and rehearings.

Because Toelken also carefully reported all aspects of the audience's response to the telling he recorded, his text illuminates how critical is the immediate presence of specific listeners in reenactments of oral myths. He shows it to be this interparticipation of teller and audience that allows fundamental principles of Navajo culture to be sustained through communal enjoyment of an amusing Trickster story. He asked the teller:

Why, then, if Coyote is such an important mythic character (whose name must not even be mentioned in the summer months), does Yellowman tell such funny stories about him? Yellowman's answer: "They are not funny stories." Why does everyone laugh, then? "They are laughing at the way Ma'i does things, and at the way the story is told. Many things about the story are funny, but the story is not funny." Why tell the stories? "If my children hear the stories, they will grow up to be good people; if they don't hear them, they will turn out to be bad." Why tell them to adults? "Through the stories everything is made possible."[9]

Toelken's judgment that Coyote stories bring to realization a Navajo's deepest sense of the order of all things was confirmed a few years after he had published his revised translation of "Coyote and the Prairie Dogs." He was invited to discuss his work with a group of Navajo medicine men. They taught him that he had profoundly underestimated the religiosity of the story. Toelken learned finally that "stories about Coyote are themselves considered so powerful, their recitation in winter deeply connected to the normal powers of natural cycles, their episodes so reminiscent of central myths . . . that elliptical reference to them in a ritual can . . . summon forth the power of the entire tale and apply it to the healing process . . . to reestablish reality and order.[10]

Emphasized by the Navajo explanation of the potency of Trickster stories is their multiple intersecting allusions to natural, physical systems and to mythic, cultural systems. Only when we have confronted the extraordinary density of such interanimating references (equally applicable to individual and community life, that equivalency undergirding Navajo healing practices) will we perceive the schematism of conventional explanations of how oral myths function. "Intertextuality" is a dismally inadequate term – but our print-dominated world offers none better – for the confluence of traditional imaginings with new actualities, both social and environmental, which determine the dynamic form of any given myth enactment.

By unwavering focus on one telling, Toelken offers us access to an understanding of how that confluence functions. The character of such an enactment is determined by its audience's active participation, obviously signaled by laughter but more subtly registered in the continuity of amused attentiveness. From a sense of this participativeness arises Gerald Vizenor's insistence that Trickster exists *only* as an utterance of communal discourse. The Trickster, Vizenor asserts, is "a sign in a language game" that is purely oral, a game vital to the continuity of tribal communality. "The trickster is real in those who imagine the narrative. . . . the trickster is imagination." Trickster "is 'within language' and not a neutral instrument that reveals codes and structural harmonies in tribal cultures." Rather, the "trickster narrative situates the participant audience . . . in agonistic imagination: there, in comic discourse, the trickster is being, nothingness and liberation, a loose seam in consciousness; that wild space over and between sounds, words, sentences, and narratives."[11]

A simple but entertaining and elegantly constructed illustration of Vizenor's description is the Nez Percé story "Coyote and Bull." In several ways it epitomizes Trickster narrative, displaying its protagonist as the antithesis of a scapegoat. Trickster undergoes a sequence of boundary crossings and identity changes culminating in no synthesis but a dissolving impasse, unforgettably confirmed for the audience by dropping so swiftly out of the protagonist's memory. The essentially self-reflexive quality that Vizenor concentrates upon is also here charmingly dramatized in the disastrous meeting of Coyote with coyote. But the story may most significantly illustrate how aural imagining is fundamental to Tricksterism. If one thinks of the tale transposed into an animated cartoon, its essentially oral character stands out in bold contrast. We are amused by the behavior of the irritated bull and of the nervous Coyote, for example, less by visualizing the two figures in conflict then by imagining the physical opposition as culminations of the characters' psychological processes. This imagining sustains our acceptance of a recognizably impossible transformation – destroyed in any visual form, which by its very mode of representation would eliminate the impossibility.

The principle that seems to underlie the difference between visual and aural imagining is suggested by the accompanying illustration. This is the famous "duck-rabbit" from the nineteenth-century Viennese comic paper *Die Fliegenden Blätter*, which E. H. Gombrich made famous in his discussion of the nature of visual illusion. His point is that we can see the drawing as either a duck or a rabbit, but we cannot *see* both at the same time.[12] Aurally, however, we can and do imagine Trickster – Coyote – simultaneously as human and as animal. Aural perception, significantly, has received none of the attention lavished on visual perception in recent years, and how we imagine aurally remains virtually unexplored territory.

Vizenor's definition of Trickster as a trope, specifically a "comic holotrope," of oral narrative usefully shifts the ground of traditional analyses. In essence, he describes Trickster as sound, which exists as it

Rabbit or duck? (From Joseph Jastrow, *Fact and Fable in Psychology* [1901; Freeport NY: Books for Libraries Press, 1971], 295.)

vanishes, and as the sound of language, which to be meaningful requires not mere physical perception but also a socially trained imagination. Trickster as linguistic sound operates comically by engaging teller and audience in absurd realities of chance and contingency and improbability in our physical experience. In no way does this engagement diminish the "seriousness" or "importance" of the Trickster story, as Toelken has been so careful to demonstrate. Vizenor, analogously, claims that the final "significance" of the Trickster tale derives from its liberating and healing qualities. These are dependent on the narrative's embodiment of an agonistic reality shared by narrator and audience outside the orderliness that is the basis of Western constructions of reality. This orderliness, or logic, gives Western culture its bias toward tragic modes. Vizenor (188) aptly cites Paul Watzlawick's observation that our accepted construction of reality "rests on the supposition that the world cannot be chaotic – not because we have any proof for this view, but because chaos would simply be intolerable."[13] The possibilities opened up by Trickster are liberative and healing qualities because they derive from acceptance of the possibility that reality may be chaotic. "Chaotic" here means not incoherent but so complexly interdependent as to be irreducible to simple, unchanging principles of cause and effect. Chaotic reality, then, is not merely a mess; rather, it is constituted of diverse systems of coherence whose irregularities of interaction exceed the organizing capabilities of Western logic.

To come to terms with that view, we should begin by recognizing how cramping are traditional Western analyses of the fluid fecundity of Trickster narratives – even those by commentators who describe their "antistructural" character. Tricksters do not inhabit merely "the tolerated margin of mess,"[14] but enable us to imagine "mess" – everything from psychic confusion to feces – as a primary condition of being, depicting how new vitalities emerge out of unmappable interpenetratings of contingent interfaces.

Vizenor rightly says that Trickster is only imaginable; he exists in, and only in, oral narrative forms. Since narrative is a social transaction, Trickster comes into being only through processes of people imagining together – which one may fairly call, with Vizenor, "comic," as opposed to tragedy's monologic, isolative mode. An implication of the gregarious festivity that is Trickster-Transformer's mode is that only aural imagining permits the meaningfulness of chance which is the peculiar achievement of his stories. Evidence for this point appears in the enfeeblement of Trickster when he is translated even into written language. As I have suggested in relation to "Coyote and Bull," there can be no genuine visual Tricksters – despite some current commodified, Disneyesque pseudoversions.

Oral verbalizations are obviously "incomplete," dependent upon implications beyond what is actually said. Oral discourse makes unmistakably apparent (not least because its addressivity is shaped by expectations of response) how human thinking always involves interplay of unconscious as well as conscious processes and thereby makes apparent the impossibility of total cognitive explicitness. This paradoxical (from a logician's perspective) feature of human speech situations makes knowing how to speak appropriately more important than speaking "competently" (as Bourdieu has tirelessly insisted) – and it is out of this rift of indeterminacy that Trickster emerges.

When we perceive Trickster as a process of aural imagining, his illogicality begins to make sense. Sound, because so different from that which is visible or tactile, best represents a world characterized in Walter J. Ong's words by "dynamism, action, being-in-time," because it exists only while going out of existence (exactly as Trickster does to permit his unfailing reappearances). Human understanding "involves process" (above all, the process by which conscious and unconscious psychic components interact), and "sound is the process sense par excellence." The evanescent sound of spoken words, for example, enables the listening audience to escape imprisonment in the spectator's role forced upon it by visual representations, including print. These, as Ong says, drive the reader "outside the action" that is the "agonistic framework of real life, of decision and action" – into engagement with which an audience of listeners (interacting with the speaker) is inevitably attracted.[15]

Father Ong's observations derive not only from his analyses of processes of orality in culture but also from his perception of the unconscious bias of Western civilization toward conceiving of thinking in predominantly visual terms. That bias, strengthened in recent years by deconstruction's theatricalized privileging of "writing" over "speech," may be the most important unexamined presupposition orienting contemporary literary criticism. Ong points out: "Structuralism has said little about differences between oral and written discourse and has seldom adverted to the fact that texts must be recycled back through sound to have meaning. What is needed is a knowledge of the phenomenology of orality, including an understanding of oral noetics" (309–10). The significance of this observation (especially the insight that only by being literally or imaginatively "recycled back through sound" can a written text mean anything) is negatively attested to by the minimal treatment of Trickster myths as such in Lévi-Strauss's voluminous work. This slighting is impressive because Trickster tales, besides constituting the largest single body of New World myths, are also by far the most widely distributed; they would seem *the* primary body of data for a project purporting to explain so comprehensively "the savage mind." But for all our recent theorizing about discourse, we still have not admitted the depth of the Western unconscious commitment to representing cognitive processes in imagistic and spatial terms. Structuralist and even poststructuralist methods have been popular because most of our "explanatory" terms derive from words with visual rather than audial roots.[16]

Deconstruction, ironically, through its concentration on the primacy of text conceived as graphic object, has exacerbated our criticism's concern with closure. Issues of closure arising from concentration on language in printed forms, Ong points out, are ultimately death-oriented, whereas "spoken utterance comes only from the living." Working from the Bourdieuian understanding that the logic of practice is not the logician's logic, he dramatizes the contrast of the oral to the written to assure that we remember the productive and sustaining qualities of open or "unstable" social organizations. To poststructuralist demonstrations that if all implications of a text are examined, it will be found to be inconsistent with itself, Ong asks why "should all the implications suggested by language be consistent? What leads one to believe that language can be so structured as to be perfectly consistent with itself, so as to be a closed system? There are no closed systems and never have been. The illusion that logic is a closed system has been encouraged by writing and even more by print. Oral cultures hardly had this illusion, though they had others."[17] For us, it may be specialists such as Kurt Gödel who have exploded the delusion of closed-system thinking, but for Indians, Tricksters did the job. Trickster embodies those processes that make all systems – including language systems and Trickster-created social systems – ultimately self-inconsistent, but do so in a fashion that can be culturally renewing and healing rather than nihilistic. Cultural healing becomes possible, for example, when the way is opened to increasing dynamic interplay between social and natural communities.[18]

Trickster, however, can so operate as productive destabilizer only in oral discourse. Even the best Trickster stories are distorted when written down. How the loss occurs appears in the weakening of Tricksters used (as many have quite effectively been used) as retaliatory weapons by oppressed peoples against their oppressors. Valuable as such stories are, something of the true Trickster energy is lost by the mere fact of constraint within an oppositional mode. Orality, we should realize, creates what many now think of as "deconstructive" conditions, so it is unfortunate that proponents of "deconstruction" refuse to consider the noetic functions of oral discourse. Written language vainly struggles against the self-refiguring, productively catachretic tendencies intrinsic to spoken discourse. Trickster stories draw their power from their overt exploitation of spoken language's self-dismantling and hence ever self-reconstructive potencies – most obvious in puns and other forms of wordplay. The peculiar appropriateness of deconstructive aspects of spoken language in Trickster narratives appears when we are reminded that marginality (which defines Trickster's situation) is necessary to any ordered system.[19] Vizenor's observation that Trickster *is* verbalized imagining begins to seem obvious when one considers, for example, the wordplay that creates the shiftiness between human and animal forms of a figure such as Coyote. Coyote can be entirely human or entirely animal, or change shapes within a single phrase, without disturbing (indeed, even enhancing) the functioning of our imaginative understanding, because he embodies intangibly (!) the infinite flexibility of a participatively engaged aural imagining.

The communal, participative, comic quality of Trickster as aural trope helps to explain why he is diminished when used purely as a counterideological or countercultural weapon. Loss of essential Tricksterism appears, for example, in Louis Aripa's attractive "Coyote and the White Man." Aripa is a gifted teller, and his performance as reported by Rodney Frey is hilarious and brilliantly pointed.[20] Yet it lacks the wild openness, the liberative quality that distinguishes apparently more trivial and less carefully wrought Trickster tales. Speaking in English, Aripa talks *at* his primary audience, whereas Yellowman talks *with* his Navajo audience. By speaking English, Aripa surrenders the essential communality of his and his Indian fellows' native language, which is their Trickster's habitat – what Bourdieu would call the Indians' "habitus." "Coyote and the White Man" is a fine story, but it cannot possess the deeper paradoxes of structure and allusiveness that make "Coyote and the Prairie Dogs" so profoundly resonant for the Navajo.

Oral cultures depend heavily on narrative discourse to sustain themselves, and narrative transactions have a marked tendency to emphasize social, rather than purely private, psychology. Narrative is the discourse of encounter, and it foregrounds psychological truths emerging from social interfaces. This is one reason Vizenor turns for contemporary theoretical support to Mikhail Bakhtin, who relies on a psychological approach radically distinct from the self-analytic, monologic, privatized bias of the modern Western Freudian tradition. It's less Bakhtin's too simply celebrated emphasis on "carnivalizing" that makes his thinking helpful in understanding Trickersterism than his explanation of processes of verbal generation. He shows how new ideas and expressions emerge out of "unoriginal" language within determinative nonverbal contexts. He demonstrates that every utterance's unique intonation is created out of language constituted by *other* speakers' usages, verbal and social habits, intonations, and purposes. His observations can be applied to the use of myth within societies whose highly traditional character is nourished by purely oral discourse. Emphasizing as he does the "dialogic," moreover, Bakhtin frequently develops his ideas through descriptions of speech situations, as when he illustrates the determinative nature of the nonverbal circumstances of any speech, however brief.

Two people are sitting in a room. They are both silent. Then one of them says "Well!" [*Tak!*] The other does not respond. For us outsiders this entire "conversation" is utterly incomprehensible. Whatever pains we take with the purely verbal part of the utterance, however subtly we define the phonetic, morphological, and semantic factors of the word "well," we still shall not come a step closer to an understanding of the colloquy.

Let us suppose that the intonation with which this word is pronounced is known to us: indignation and reproach moderated by a certain amount of humor. The intonation fills in the semantic void of the adverb "well," but still does not reveal the meaning of the whole.

We lack the "extraverbal context" that made the word "well" a meaningful locution to the listener.

At the time the colloquy took place, both interlocutors *looked up* at the window and *saw* that it had begun to snow; both knew that it was already May, . . . *both* were *sick and tired* of the protracted winter. . . . On this "jointly seen," . . . "jointly known," . . . "unanimously evaluated" [information], . . . on all this the utterance *directly* depends . . . [for] its very sustenance. And yet all this remains without *verbal* specification or articulation. . . . nevertheless all this is assumed in the word *well*.[21]

This description applies almost perfectly to the retelling of myths, especially to their allusive components. For example, the congruence of Bakhtin's analysis to Toelken's recording of Yellowman's telling of "Coyote and the Prairie Dogs" is remarkable. Analyzing an utterance larger than *Tak*, Toelken makes more explicit how the shaping "extraverbal context" is reciprocally animated by the verbal regeneration of the myth in an enactment. Yellowman's explanation of the potency of the myth and why he tells it as he does, moreover, emphasizes the "addressivity" intrinsic to the telling situation.

This leads us into another paradox: Trickster's enabling, generative powers often seem in odd ways marginalized, not fully participative within the wholeness he creates. For example, Trickster (so far as I can determine) is virtually always male. His gendering may represent cultural "generation" as metaphoric rather than naturalistic, although probably more important is the fact that to create something is inescapably to become separated from what one has created. This is why even unambiguous culture heroes are so often portrayed as becoming in one way or another excluded from the very culture they establish, as Aeneas at the end of the *Aeneid* disappears from his creation, which will become the realm of Rome.[22] American Indian Coyote tales always represent the Trickster-Transformer moving away from what he has created, whether a mess or a new way of life. Coyote is always on the move, unable to remain with what he has generated; or, more extremely, he dies or is put to death, only to return to life totally freed of any memory of or obligation to his previous productions. He is, like spoken words, pure presentness. Trickster in fact embodies the paradox of tradition in oral societies, where the past exists only through novel retellings of it as present experience.

Because the Trickster story is oral, it exists solely in terms of its affects on a participating audience. The transience of Trickster's irresponsibility (however great his gifts to the people who delight in stories about him) permits an audience to enjoy his discomfiture and disapprove of his bad behavior without having to assume the rigidities of self-righteous moralism. Greed, selfishness, lack of respect for others, lust (indeed, every sin) in Trickster stories is condemned amusingly rather than with prim piousness. Trickster's generative marginality permits the teller to articulate not merely praise or condemnation of specific behavior but also awareness of how difficult, yet therefore how important, it is to live up to such values. This paradox explains why Trickster is so commonly both human and animal yet never in the Western sense "divine" – never an object of worship, however awesome his performances. He embodies the openness that exists at the heart of the Indian refusal to distinguish, as the Western Judeo-Christian tradition so insistently does, between natural and supernatural. (One form of the distinction, of course, results in the denial that there can *be* anything supernatural, the unexamined presupposition of virtually every contemporary literary critic.) The Indian is free to perceive every creature as existing in a condition of wonderful ambiguity, contributing to a wondrous, everlastingly ongoing vitality in its most "natural" – hence sometimes scandalous – behavior. Trickster, therefore, enables us to recognize the absurdity, the dangerousness, even the vileness of natural behavior without sacrificing any appreciation for the goodness of natural life.

I suspect that the Western habit of discriminating decisively between natural and supernatural reinforces our tendency to insist that "reality" and "imagination" are opposites. That idea poses a major difficulty for Western commentators on Trickstersim, as appears even in the important essay "A Tolerated Margin of Mess" by Barbara Babcock-Abrahams, which is especially useful in its descriptions of trickster's marginality and ambiguousness. Picking up Mary Douglas's observation that where there is "dirt," there is a system defining what is "dirty," Babcock-Abrahams describes Trickster as the disorder that is the defining condition of order, offering the "threat and possibility of chaos." The positive "possibility" in such a threat is that chaos not only is the matrix of forms but after their establishment also remains as the potential for their dissolution, the potential for change that constitutes vitality. This is an important dimension of Trickster's ambiguousness, which as Babcock-Abrahams observes is a cultural condition: animals don't dwell consciously in such ambiguity; culture can create beyond what already exists naturally primarily by nurturing conditions of intense contradiction and ambivalence.[23]

Another dimension of Trickster ambiguity lies in his peculiar appearance as an intruder into the very culture for which he may be responsible. Babcock-Abrahams shrewdly analyzes this function in terms of Trickster's socially counteractive potency – especially vivid where he negates cultural negations, taboos. Placing the "marginal" at the center of social reality allows for a simultaneous identification and disidentification by auditors, who laugh at imaginary realizations of their desires which at the same time validate the empirical reality of those desires – a validation requiring that they be faced.

Such considerations should lead to a recognition of how Indian conceptions of individuality differ from our own, and how the discourse of myth mediates the relation – in Emile Durkheim's formulation – of "social authority and individual consciousness" in ways different from those characteristic of our print-dominated, highly rationalized culture. But at this point Babcock-Abrahams retreats into the reductive universalizing that enfeebles so much modern criticism. For her, there is no essential difference between the Trickster in Paul Radin's Winnebago Cycle and the protagonist of Renaissance picaresque novels. Doubtless there is a relationship of some kind, but the differences and their causes need to be recognized if we are not to misunderstand, even distort, the forms of discourse of the less familiar cultures.

Such distortion appears in Babcock-Abrahams's insistence in going beyond even Radin in imposing upon the Winnebago Cycle a thoroughly Western conception of logical form. Radin believed that the forty-nine tales told by his informant constituted a developmental (almost a *bildungsroman*) sequence in which the Trickster figure emerges from unconsciousness and arrives finally at a deep sense of social responsibility. He admitted, however, that the final episodes might have been tacked on as a deliberate effort to satisfy his Westernized expectations. Babcock-Abrahams dismisses this idea in laying out a rigorous unity for the entire series. Her critical insistence is striking, because so much in her essay displays awareness of the "formless form" of Trickster narratives: for example, their effacing of ordinary temporal and spatial boundaries, signaled by the elision of any overt relation between episodes.

"Formless form" *within* a story is illustrated by the splendid Lipan Apache tale of Coyote and the wasps. Most Western tellers would happily conclude with Coyote's stunning condemnation of the people's desire for too much supernatural power. But the "point" of all Indian Trickster stories is their ongoingness. The anticlimactic final paragraph restores the episode to the continuity of life, especially Coyote's: he condemns yet he is ashamed, but neither attitude is definitive; he wanders on as pointlessly (making good points) as when he encountered the wasps.

Babcock-Abrahams's blindness to the value of such formlessness displays the unwillingness of contemporary critics to recognize fundamental distinctions between discourse structures and discourse functions in literate and oral societies. Some sense of the importance of such differences may be gained by considering the Wishram "cycle" of Coyote stories collected – and arranged – by Edward Sapir. Unlike Radin and Babcock-Abrahams, Sapir does not claim to be reproducing any "deep-structured," Indian-originated pattern. He suggests that the linear sequence of various episodes created by Coyote's progress up the Columbia River provides a convenient linkage between otherwise unconnected episodes. My guess is that Sapir was drawn to this arrangement by the wonderful little story "Coyote and the Sun," which he says forms an appropriate conclusion for the series, even though he admits it was not among the episodes of "What Coyote Did in that Land" told him as a unit by Louis Simpson.

From a Western point of view, Sapir is dead right: "Coyote and the Sun" offers perfect closure to Coyote's progress. The trouble is that from an Indian point of view, such a perfect conclusion is antithetical to what Coyote does and what he means. We may begin with a very simple point: whereas the clarity of progressive sequence seems to us meaningful and satisfying, a distinct beginning logically leading to specific subsequent results, these Wishram stories deliberately blur and confute such clarity. In the narratives of the mouthless man and of the Merman, for instance, the people who *will* be coming appear already to be present. Here, as in so many Indian myths, the idea of a single beginning is superseded by a more complicated, relativistic vision. As a transgressor of boundaries, Trickster-Transformer of necessity appears "episodically." He downgrades the importance of all linear sequence (including that of cause-effect and science's "arrow of time") because he violates all categories of time and space as well as of social distinction. In the normal oral telling situation, which is largely a matter of retellings, some "confusion" of temporal order – of where any beginning is to be located – is quite appropriate, for the audience already knows simultaneously both the beginning and what happened "afterward." This asequentiality (from our perspective) is closely linked to the narrative form in which Coyote flourishes, since the Trickster exists *only* in stories, and stories in oral cultures (as I earlier observed) are constituted of modular units: episodes that can be told as separate stories in themselves but can also be combined and recombined in diverse ways.

A clear instance appears in the Sioux story "Blood-Clot Boy," in which the second half, which centers on the adventure with Ikto, a Trickster, has no necessarily "logical" relation to the first part, the hero's rescue of the oppressed rabbit. Either part could be (and surely sometimes was) told separately. But when joined, each episode takes on a special coloring from its "arbitrary" juxtaposition with the other. The nature of the boy's heroism with Rabbit is intriguingly qualified when we see him fooled by the Trickster and dependent on the assistance of an outcast girl. The function here of the Trickster story is repeated again and again in different tribal groups: Trickster serves as a complex measure or definer of "model" figures.[24]

Mythic form as well as content is the bearer of meaning, but (as Trickster stories bafflingly display) mythic form to us is likely to appear as formlessness. I am not asserting that there is *no* connection between episodes in, say, a series of Trickster stories such as Sapir's Wishram collection. I am saying that it is usually wrong to identify that connection with the linear logicality that Western narrative and scientific thinking encourage *us* to search for and specially to value. The principle of "modular" structuring of Indian oral stories, because it is created by shifting positionings of integral narrative units, suggests that meaningful linkage between episodes may often be more complex than is revealed by the unidimensional interpretations of Radin, Babcock-Abrahams, and Sapir. Were this not the case, in fact, the profound meaningfulness of the Coyote story that Toelken has analyzed could not exist for the Navajo.[25]

Given the variety of intersecting themes and paralleled motifs in the Wishram Coyote series, any adequate analysis of it would be quite lengthy. But we must be wary about imposing systems of significance contrary to Wishram perspectives, about which we in fact know very little. This is why study of the *forms* of the Wishrams' storytelling may be as helpful for understanding their culture as study of their culture is helpful for understanding their myths. The "progress" in the series, for instance, from Coyote as animalistic sexual adventurer to a "noble" exterminator of monsters for the benefit of people, is at the least disordered, for we see Coyote teaching copulation only after he has been involved in a situation where it, and its consequences, are quite well understood. Or what is one to make of the "Dried Salmon" episode? If we restrain our preference for logical sequence and consistent development, in fact, the interplay of several motifs appears more interesting. Very intriguing, for example, are the interlaced motifs of speaking and of giving names, because these representations of verbalizing build up an illuminating commentary on storytelling – myth telling – itself.

The myth Sapir puts first is particularly challenging in this regard, since it begins "Coyote heard . . ." – from whom? This problem of origins at the beginning of the "first" story is not solved by the account of how fish originated in the Columbia, because the story is also about swallows as the *sign* of the annual return of salmon. It seems possible to say that the naming of swallows gives a cultural meaning to a natural recurrent simultaneity (annual return of swallows and salmon) basic to the continuous self-renewal of Wishram society. That draws attention to how significant are names and naming throughout this series, starting with the older woman's thought in the opening tale about the false baby: "That is Coyote," who becomes the prime "namer." Interestingly self-reflexive is the belated naming of the Wishram as "flat-headed" because made from the tongue, which organ of course makes possible the naming and story making that the series keeps returning to, and which is perhaps anticipated by Coyote as infant with the eel projecting out of his mouth.

The most provocative articulation of these motifs appears in "The Story Concerning Coyote," where he is "found out" because he fails to "head off" the story of his obscene act or keep it imprisoned. As often in Trickster myths, humorous vulgarity here gives form to very complicated social issues. To oversimplify grossly, this episode deals with the fact that we *are* very much what is known *about* us. What we are named and the stories told of us effectively define us for society, yet that definition necessarily contains inadequacies, because no single linguistic representation of us can do justice to our contradictoriness and capability to change – qualities epitomized in the Trickster. To find out the worst about Coyote is not to know everything about him. In a Christian community that point might be made in a pious story. For the Wishrams, who do not conceive of another world distinct from the material natural world, ribaldry is an effective way of enabling us to think about these intricacies of human existence. It would be pleasant if our metaphysicians learned from them.

"The Story Concerning Coyote" permits us to understand "Coyote and the Sun" less as conclusive than as a different way of developing the self-reflexivity of this series to elucidate the meaning of Tricksterism. This "final" story, which might easily be adapted as an "introduction," deepens the problem central to "The Story Concerning Coyote" by considering why some things should not be told. If, for example, one thinks of the group's being strengthened by the escape of the story of Coyote's obscenity so that everyone knows what he is capable of, one should remember that the daughter with whom Coyote secretly copulates is advised by her mother not to tell of her experience. Social well-being may be sustained by not telling. The complexity of that truth is given bite by the irony of having it dramatized by uncomprehending Coyote.

This twist allows the "final" episode to define Coyote's unfinalizing functions. As the sun's slave (a reversal of most gender relations in the series) Coyote undermines his role as Trickster-Transformer by moving out of the realm of potentiality – he "stops" at the sun because it is outside the earthly world of chance and contingency. The sun sees everything. Coyote on earth sees specifics: where mouths should be, where to fish, the alterations required by particular desires – in short, concrete possibilities within limitations. The sun is a place of abstractions; in this episode particularities of place and specificities of name disappear. As the sun, ironically, Coyote could not have kept moving.

This account of the unacceptability of Coyote's "naming" unacceptable human behavior perhaps justifies a general observation about names in American Indian societies. In every one of these with which I am acquainted, names are condensed stories. What an individual is publicly called invariably refers to, if it does not summarize, some event associated with that person: it may represent a complete and even complex narrative, or the name may simply commemorate an observation or idea about the person by the one who bestows the name, either formally or as a nickname. For the Indians, therefore, every name has what may be called a narrative significance; its "story" helps bind the society together by being common property while serving as a convenient nexus for linking the diverse narratives of society's members, a linking that creates the vital unity of the community. In short, a name does not for the Indians, as for us, separate the individual by distinguishing him or her from everyone else; instead, it literally socializes distinctive individuality. One of the most interesting features of this use of names as narratives is that names are often changed as the "story" of an individual's life unfolds. Such occurrences indicate the dynamism of Indian narrative-names: they reflect the constant shifting of individual-social relationships of societies whose stability depends on being flexible, capable of constant self-transformations – of accommodating tricksters.

The deep potencies of Coyote tales, described by Toelken and implied in the Wishram Coyote series, are revealed in a different fashion by the beautiful Chemehuevi "How Wolf and Coyote Went Away," which seems self-consciously to dramatize the bafflingness of Coyote's ambiguities as the source of his endless fascination. On the central mountain of the Chemehuevi world, the opening exchange between mythological Wolf (always in this story the perfect man) and Coyote immerses us at once in the slippery reciprocities that enable the storyteller to represent what Tedlock has called the "betweenness" of complex relationships as seen by Indian observers. Coyote addresses Wolf, appropriately, as "Elder Brother." But Wolf addresses his brother as "Respected Old Coyote," which in fact implies that Coyote is the elder. This is not merely Wolf's impeccable politeness, evidenced by his always speaking in a chant, but a way of complicating the priorities of "brotherhood." Wolf is the superior: "I don't know how you see everything-aiky*a*! I don't know how you know so much-aiky*a*," whines Coyote. Yet may it not be that the stupid, physical, bumbling Coyote *is* in one sense the "elder," like the chaos out of which divinity shaped creation? It is a problem that recurs in a different form with the arrow making, for example, because one function of this Coyote story is to raise the question of postmythological people's relation to their mythological forebears.

That relation is more lightheartedly illustrated by the conclusion of the first episode, when omniscient Wolf supplies Coyote with a new loin, and we are told that this is why even today coyote loin tastes like mountain sheep loin – or (a very important qualifier) "at least so it is said." The teller, moreover, respects the understanding of his audience, perhaps paying them the compliment of their being Wolf-like, by skipping explanations of motive, exactly as Wolf does with Coyote. One deduces that Coyote's killing of the poker-stick children of the Bear will produce grave consequences, which Wolf tries to preclude by sending Coyote back to wipe out the bears. When Coyote fails, thanks to the merry little poker stick that evades his grasp (as perverse small objects still love to do), Wolf foresees, without explicitly announcing, the bear invasion and orders preparation for defense: "Straighten arrows." He assumes that Coyote will be bright enough to make the connection.

Wolf is justified in becoming weary of Coyote's slowness to comprehend, his carelessness and disobedience, but it is difficult for us not to sympathize with Coyote when he deliberately misunderstands his morally ever righteous, know-it-all brother, who seldom explains and never condescends to speak colloquially. Nor is that sympathy misplaced, for we do not possess the powers that allow Wolf to straighten arrows and feather them perfectly without effort. Such powers are not "seemly" or "natural" for human beings, who make straight, well-feathered arrows only by the conscientious labor of craftsmanship. Those who have worked with their hands will not deny that it is Coyote who has "set a proper pattern for Man."

Yet one can't help wishing for supernatural gifts, perhaps especially when digging in rocky ground, and that Coyote's bitterness and his envy of his spectacular brother are all too comprehensible is superbly dramatized by primary and secondary rainbow clothing. Who would not be jealous of the splendor that draws gasps of admiration even from Wolf's enemies, as well as his headline-making archery? Who, having been ordered to do all the dirty work such as carrying the hero's baggage, would not be envious? Alas, jealousy is not rationable; it is always deadly.

Coyote is truly sorry he has "accidentally" killed his brother, but he does have the chance now to examine all his brother's wonderful secrets. So he struggles through that marvelous, diminishing bundle, only to plunge the world into darkness as he releases night. At this lowest point of his career Coyote begins to display his virtues. After howling for a long time, he sensibly starts a fire. He straightens arrows (his way) and determines to make use of the other contents of Wolf's luggage to repair the damage he has done. Which, after some mistakes and a near miss, he succeeds in doing – with the brilliance of a desert sunrise.

In fact, with Wolf gone, Coyote becomes organized and effective, in part because he consults his penis; there are times, especially when supernatural support has vanished, when one does best to trust one's instincts. Coyote's escape from the Bear People has something of the quality of a chase sequence in a comic western movie (his arrows may be straight, but his shooting isn't), yet he and his penis display stamina and ingenuity. His last trip, however – in the puff-ball, after he awakens surrounded by a world of snow – seems to be Coyote without even penis help, and his harnessing of the wind for earth purposes is entirely his own work (and a fascinating inversion of the ordinary use of the *poro*, a crooked stick, to pull animals out of holes in the ground).

After the wild chase scenes and the puff-ball trip, the quietness of Coyote's waking at midnight, the tense waiting, and finally, just as the morning star rises, the first sound of his revived brother's voice grip our imagination as strongly as his. One shares Coyote's happiness: at last he has done everything exactly right, and "everything would be as it had always been." Then the sound comes from the wrong direction: his brother is going north, and Coyote runs out after "those distant, mournful wolf howls," running "on and on and on, always toward the North . . . where the Ancient Telling starts and ends."

This conclusion haunts the imagination as profoundly as that of any story I know. Yet it seems to me in Vizenor's sense comic rather than tragic in that there is no closure, no finality; its pathos is of continuing aspiration, as Coyote runs on and on, "even though ever so far behind." The conclusion also reveals – precisely because Coyote here as elsewhere in Indian storytelling is a creature of oral imagination – how unique visual details may acquire stunning emotional impact through verbal realization. The perfect handprint in the rock alongside the "doggy paw-mark" truly "may be seen to this day" – if not in Nevada, in the memory of anyone who has heard this tale.

NOTES

1. When first encountered by the French in 1634, the Winnebago people occupied the south shore of Green Bay, Wisconsin, down to Lake Winnebago, hunting, fishing, practicing some agriculture, and harvesting wild rice from birchbark canoes. Their principal ceremonies were a Winter Feast, a Spring Buffalo Dance, and a Summer Medicine Dance. The Winnebagos in the seventeenth century were one of the tribes severely pressed by peoples from the East, such as the Illinois, themselves under attack from the powerful Iroquois Confederacy, and by the middle of the nineteenth century most had been forced to relocate west of the Mississippi. Miners searching for the rich lead deposits in northwestern Illinois and southern Wisconsin in the 1820s stimulated the Winnebagos to dig and sell lead – so profitably that whites were determined to force them off their land. This provoked the Winnebago Uprising of 1827, which was suppressed by federal troops and territorial militia. Although Chief Red Bird prevented bloodshed by voluntarily surrendering himself for his people, continued white encroachments and land seizures provoked the Winnebagos under the leadership of the prophet White Cloud to join clandestinely with the Sauks in the subsequent Black Hawk War against the whites.

See Paul Radin, *The Winnebago Tribe* (Lincoln: University of Nebraska Press, 1990), and *Crashing Thunder: The Autobiography of an American Indian* (New York: Appleton, 1926), the second version of Sam Blowsnake's life history by Radin. Nancy Lurie Oestrich, ed., *Mountain Wolf Woman* (Ann Arbor: University of Michigan Press, 1961), presents the life history of Crashing Thunder's sister.

2. The Navajo tribe is today the most populous tribe in the United States, occupying the general area of Arizona and New Mexico that it inhabited in the late seventeenth century after having migrated from northwestern Canada, possibly sometime after 1200 A.D. There are over sixty Navajo clans, with marriage forbidden to a person of either one's mother's or father's clan. Although the Navajos came into the Southwest as a hunting people, they learned agricul-

ture from the Pueblo people and later took up sheep herding. Skillful potters and basketmakers, Navajo women also learned weaving from the Pueblos and the Mexicans and soon began producing their famous blankets and rugs. Navajo men learned silversmithing from the Mexicans and became expert makers of silver and turquoise jewelry. The characteristic Navajo dwelling was a hogan, which developed into a square framework of poles, with walls built up to taper toward the center, forming a dome-shaped roof with a smoke hole.

Borrowing some religious practices from the Pueblos, the Navajos developed their own complex polytheistic religion, which includes a vast number of deities; it is centrally focused on healing ceremonies performed for individuals physically or psychically ill. Some of these elaborate curing ceremonies, conducted by specially trained singer-doctors, occupy nine days and nights; they involve hundreds of special songs, and rituals of purification and exorcism – including the creation of "sand" paintings, which the patient literally enters. On the final night there is communal singing and dancing, with some of the performers costumed as deities, because healing the individual is perceived as inseparable from sustaining the harmony of the community with the natural universe.

In the wake of the Mexican War the United States government determined to locate all southwestern Indians on reservations. When in 1863 the Navajos refused to move, U.S. troops destroyed their orchards, herds, crops, and homes. Some eight thousand starving Navajos were forced on a march of 350 miles from Fort Defiance, to Fort Sumner, where they were interned for four years and nearly a quarter of the number died. The Navajo reservation was established in 1868, and the Navajos returned to their land, but in the 1880s much of the best grazing land was taken from them for railroad rights-of-way. Despite these events, the Navajos (like many other Indians) volunteered for military service in the First World War (in which they were used to send radio messages, their native language providing a code), and in the twentieth century have steadily increased their population and begun to reestablish a viable economic tribal base.

Useful information will be found in Clyde Kluckhohn and Dorothea Leighton, *The Navaho* (1946), rev. ed. (New York: Doubleday, 1962); Washington Matthews, *Navaho Legends*, Memoirs of the American Folklore Society 5 (Philadelphia, 1897), which introduces the cultural background of the creation myth; Aileen O'Bryan, *The Diné: Origin Myths of the Navaho Indians* Bureau of American Ethnology Bulletin 163 (Washington DC, 1956); Gladys Reichard, *Navaho Religion: A Study of Symbolism*, 2 vols. (New York: Pantheon, 1950); Walter Dyk, *Son of Old Man Hat: A Navaho Autobiography* (New York: Harcourt Brace, 1938), a life history of Left Handed, born in 1868.

3. Among the Nez Percés, the most numerous and powerful Sahaptian tribe located along the lower Snake River and its tributaries in Idaho, southeastern Oregon, and Washington, religious leaders were shamans who cured the ill, controlled the weather, exorcised ghosts, and presided at funerals. Fish was the staple food, though women gathered berries and bulbs, and men hunted game, sometimes using bows made of mountain sheep horn. The Nez Percés constructed regular dwellings of pole frames with mat coverings, and villages usually contained a communal longhouse. Earth-covered sweat lodges and dance houses were also common. The Nez Percés bred with care the horses they acquired early in the eighteenth century and developed excellent breeds, including the famous Appaloosa. These herds became objects of raids by Plains Indians, and the Nez Percés were continually involved in intertribal warfare, yet from their first acquaintance with whites in the Lewis and Clark expedition they maintained friendly relations with these invaders. When gold was discovered in the 1860s on lands ceded to them by treaty in 1855 and 75 percent of it was seized, however, the Nez Percés forcefully resisted white violations of their legal landholdings. After six months of fighting in 1877 Chief Joseph's band of about 450, including the elderly and young children, eluded the pursuit of thousands of soldiers for several weeks in making a twelve-hundred-mile retreat toward Canada but were finally seized near the border.

See Herbert J. Spinden, *The Nez Percé Indians*, *Memoirs of the American Anthropological Association* 2 (1907): 165–274 (rpt. Lincoln: University of Nebraska Press, 1974); Haruo Aoki, *Nez Percé Texts*, University of California Publications in Linguistics 90 (Berkeley, 1979); Alvin M. Josephy, *The Nez Percé Indians and the Opening of the Northwest* (New Haven: Yale University Press, 1965).

4. The two main cultural divisions of the Athapaskan-speaking Apache tribe – which from around 1200 A.D. ranged from eastern Arizona into Texas and from northern Mexico into Colorado and Kansas – are now classified as Western and Eastern, the latter including the Lipan Apache who were concentrated in Texas until being driven out in the 1840s. All the Apaches were feared and respected as dangerous raiders and fierce warriors. Unlike the Navajos, other Athapaskans who moved into the southwestern area at about the same time, the Lipan Apaches never took up a pastoral life-style, remaining largely nomadic. They originally lived in wikiups or skin tipis when hunting buffalo, and were chiefly hunters and gatherers.

The Lipan Apaches practiced polygamy, which usually involved a man marrying sisters or his brother's widow. Although loosely organized socially, forming into two bands for buffalo hunting but normally functioning through several groups constructed around extended families, the Lipan like other Apaches possessed a richly complex religious mythology. Numerous deities, including the Mountain Spirits, were impersonated by masked dancers in some ceremonies. Shamans played an important role in this matrilocal society, officiating, for example, at puberty rites, in rainmaking rituals, and in curing the ill and injured. Two of the most famous Apaches, of course, were Cochise and Geronimo, who were Chiracahua Apache. Geronimo and a tiny band of followers eluded capture by as many as five thousand expensively equipped United States troops for several years – illustrating how skillfully the Apaches had adapted themselves to their latest homeland.

Keith H. Basso, *Western Apache Language and Culture* (Tucson: University of Arizona Press, 1990), provides splendid essays on language and culture. See also Grenville Goodwin, *Myths and Tales of the White Mountain Apache*, Memoirs of the American Folklore Society 33 (Philadelphia, 1939). Morris E. Opler has published extensively on research among most of the Apache groups; one may note his *Apache Odyssey: A Journey between Two Worlds* (New York: Holt, Rinehart & Winston, 1969), a life history of an Apache named Chris. Angie Debo, *Geronimo* (Norman: University of Oklahoma Press, 1976), offers excellent insight into the nature of Apache culture.

5. Sioux is the most commonly used name for the powerful tribal people also known as the Lakota or Dakota, whose seven principal tribes are usually divided linguistically into three segments, the westernmost being identified as Teton, the middle group as Yankton, and the easternmost as Santee. These peoples originally inhabited woodlands east of Minnesota, where they lived in pole-frame, bark-roofed lodges, gathered wild rice, hunted woodland game, and fished, their principal means of transportation being the birchbark canoe. Moving on to the Plains – under pressure from peoples such as the Ojibwas, who obtained guns from the French first – the Sioux, who never were agriculturalists, even gave up fishing and became primarily dependent upon the buffalo. Buffalo meat constituted the major part of their diet, and from the skins the Sioux made their famous tipis (which were property of the women who set them up and took them down as the tribal parties moved). Skins were also used for clothing and blankets, as well as for inscribing "winter counts," pictographic calendric records. Buffalo bones were shaped into tools, hair into belts and bags, hooves into rattles, horns into spoons, and sinews into bowstrings and thread. Dried buffalo droppings (chips) were used as fuel.

With their mastery of wild horses, descendants of escapees from the animals the Spanish had introduced to the New World, the Sioux became in the early eighteenth century an equestrian society, killing the majority of their buffalo in communal hunts on horseback by surrounding the herd. These big hunts occurred in the summer, for in the severe Plains winters the tribe survived best by breaking up into small, self-sufficient bands. Focus of the summer reunion, besides the communal hunts, was the Sun Dance, a four-day ceremony of fasting, prayer, self-torture, and the fulfillment of religious vows but also dancing, feasting, and socializing. Deeply religious, the Sioux believed in guardian spirits, whose aid was attained through visions. Healers cured sickness with a combination of ritual performances and the use of medicinal plants.

Their culture flowered rapidly on the Plains, and by the middle of the nineteenth century the Sioux were one of the most powerful nations there, engaged in continual fighting with other Indians (frequently initiated by horse stealing). In this active, warlike society the moral purity and bravery of young men became a focal point – the highest honor accruing to those who rode into a battle and touched but did not kill an enemy – "counting coup" – although that kind of honor had to be abandoned when resisting the United States Army. The Sioux fought valiantly in defense of their territory – most famously in destroying Custer. Many of their gifted war leaders, such as Sitting Bull and Crazy Horse, were men of impressive moral dignity and spiritual wisdom.

Decimated by disease and driven to starvation by the whites' destruction of the buffalo, the Sioux reluctantly accepted reservation life. In the late 1880s they became caught up in the revivalistic Ghost Dance religion, an activity that the U.S. government savagely suppressed, most infamously by a wanton massacre (largely of women and children) at Wounded Knee in 1890. In recent years the commemoration of that massacre has become a major ceremony of the vigorously resurgent Sioux culture.

Luther Standing Bear's *My People the Sioux* (Lincoln: University of Nebraska Press, 1975), is a classic autobiography, and his *Land of the Spotted Eagle* (Boston: Houghton Mifflin, 1933) contains much information on Sioux ceremonialism. Vine Deloria Jr., one of the most vigorous spokesmen for Indian rights and recognition since the 1960s, is best known for *Custer Died for Your Sins* (Norman: University of Oklahoma Press, 1988) and *God Is Red*, now revised as *God Is Red: A Native View of Religion Updated* (Golden CO: Fulcrum, 1994). Among the huge body of works about the Sioux one may cite for its profuse illustrations Thomas Mails, *Sundancing at Rosebud and Pine Ridge* (Sioux Falls SD: Center for Western Studies, 1978). Raymond J. DeMallie, *The Twelve Grandfathers* (Lincoln: University of Nebraska Press, 1978), analyzing the book *Black Elk Speaks* (see chapter 5) is a wonderful ethnohistorical study of the famous Indian visionary's autobiographical account.

6. Originally connected with the Southern Paiutes of the Great Basin culture area, the Chemehuevis, a small hunting and gathering tribe, moved about in the open spaces of southern Nevada and California, including the Mojave Desert. Chemehuevi men hunted with bows (some of cedar and some of horn) and flint-tipped arrows, and pulled small game out of their burrows by using special crooked sticks (the *poro*). The women wove fine baskets from willow or cottonwood, and when living along the Colorado River, where they sometimes grew crops, the Chemehuevi used rafts made of reeds. Association with the Mojaves influenced Chemehuevi religious practices, such as burial of the dead but cremation of the deceased's property along with gifts, and the development of elaborate song cycles. They were assigned to a special reservation in 1907, but a few years later part of this land was flooded by the Parker Dam; in 1951 the Chemehuevi won a significant suit for reimbursement for the land taken from them.

Carobeth Laird's book *The Chemehuevis* contains a wealth of ethnographic information (she was married to George Laird, who was a Chemehuevi). A. L. Kroeber included a chapter on the Chemehuevis in his *Handbook of California Indians*, Bureau of American Ethnology Bulletin 78 (Washington DC, 1925). James A. Sandes and Larry E. Burgess, *The Hunt for Willie Boy: Indian History and Popular Culture* (Norman: University of Oklahoma Press, 1994), studies both written and filmic representations of a Paiute-Chemehuevi who in 1909, after killing an old man and running off with his daughter, became the object of a large manhunt that concluded with his suicide. To reconstruct the actual events, the authors sympathetically investigate Chemehuevi cultural practices, modes of thinking, and relation to the "land without boundaries" that the tribe inhabits.

7. Tricksters and Trickster-Transformers, of course, function in an enormous variety of cultures around the world, although recent studies suggest that the Trickster's "transforming" qualities (making him a creator of culture) tend to drop away in agriculturally based societies; there he becomes more purely a buffoonish figure of fun. The probable link of complexly creative Trickster-Transformers with paleolithic hunting-and-gathering peoples deserves more intensive investigation, since it offers unique insights into the sources of unfamiliar modes of human imagining. A comprehensive and balanced recent survey of the trickster as a worldwide phenomenon is *Mythical Trickster Figures*, ed. William J. Hynes and William G. Doty (Tuscaloosa: University of Alabama Press, 1993).

8. More than one Indian has told a version of defecating Coyote to an inquiring ethnologist as a semipolite judgment of what does – and should – happen to unimaginative data gatherers. I felt an obligation, therefore, to include a ver-

sion in this collection as evidence of my awareness that to some Native Americans all projects such as this produce nothing but talking-bulb results.

9. From Barre Toelken's essay "Poetic Retranslation and the 'Pretty Languages' of Yellowmen," in *Traditional Literatures of the American Indian*, 2d ed., ed. Karl Kroeber (Lincoln: University of Nebraska Press, 1997), 101–2; that essay includes the revised translation reprinted here, carried out by Toelken with the assistance of his Navajo friend Tacheeni Scott.

10. Barre Toelken, "Life and Death in the Navajo Coyote Tales," in *Recovering the Word*, ed. Brian Swann and Arnold Krupat (Berkeley: University of California Press, 1987), 388–401, 390. Toelken was warned by a Navajo healer that because the telling of mythic stories (and even reference to parts of them) contributes to the health of the Navajo people and their environment, Toelken's use of the story to inform non-Navajos and to benefit white scholarship might have unfortunate consequences for his family, even though he did his best to respect Navajo practices and beliefs – for example, studying his tapes and teaching this Indian material only in winter months, when Coyote stories may be told. In a subsequent essay, "From Entertainment to Realization in Navajo Fieldwork," in *The World Observed*, ed. Bruce Jackson and Edward D. Ives (Urbana: University of Illinois Press, 1996), 1–17, Toelken recounts disasters that struck the Navajo family into which he had married, including Yellowman's death, and that of two of his brothers, a daughter's injury in an auto accident that killed her daughter, and a son's "schizophrenic episode." He observes that for the Yellowman family "these facts are related because the people involved are all related, so this constellation of events cannot be merely coincidental. I doubt if they see their father's narration of Coyote stories as having *caused* a series of family injuries, but it would be unavoidable for them to see their troubles and the possible misuse of the stories as intertwined somehow" (14). Toelken concludes this troubling essay by urging that "what we lack is a concerted effort to understand fieldwork as an interhuman dynamic event," which could prevent us from "believing ourselves to be objective beneficiaries of other people's traditions" (17).

11. Gerald Vizenor, "Trickster Discourse: Comic Holotropes and Language Games," in *Narrative Chance: Postmodern Discourse on Native American Indian Literatures*, ed. Vizenor (Albuquerque: University of New Mexico Press, 1989), 187, 190, 194, 196.

12. E. H. Gombrich, *Art and Illusion* (London: Phaidon, 1960), 4–5.

13. Paul Watzwalick, introduction to *The Invented Reality*, ed. Watzwalick (New York: Norton, 1984), 10.

14. Barbara Babcock-Abrahams, "'A Tolerated Margin of Mess': The Trick-

ster and His Tales Reconsidered," *Journal of the Folklore Institute* 11 (1975): 147–86.

15. Walter J. Ong, *Interfaces of the Word: Studies in the Evolution of Consciousness and Culture* (Ithaca NY: Cornell University Press, 1977), 136, 222.

16. See, besides Ong, Stephen A. Tyler's important essay (cited in chapter 2) "The Vision Quest in the West, or What the Mind's Eye Sees," *Journal of Anthropological Research* 40 (1984): 23–40.

17. Walter J. Ong, *Orality and Literacy* (London: Methuen, 1982), 102, 169. Michael Holquist, in "The Surd Heard: Bakhtin and Derrida," in *Literature and History*, ed. Gary Saul Morson (Stanford CA: Stanford University Press, 1986), 150–51, correctly points to Bakhtin's emphasis on the "surd" as enabling him to break free of deconstructive limitations in his conception of "utterance," which subsumes distinctions between writing and speech but shifts the focus of critical attention to the physical vitality (as opposed to the inertness of texts) of addressivity-response situations.

18. As I indicated earlier, fundamental to many Native American healing methods is a principle of better integrating not merely an individual patient but also his or her community with specific environmental conditions. A widespread and deeply interesting aspect of this Indian approach, which I hope to look at in more detail in a subsequent study, is the conception of breath or breathing as "inner wind," so that the fundamental relationship of an individual to the circumambient world is through moving air. Socially acquired song or speech is for many Indians a human structuring of air movement reciprocal to the life-bringing winds of the environment. For example, at the conclusion of a nine-day Navajo healing ceremony involving hundreds of songs and chants, the patient breathes in the dawn wind. The most perceptive account of this topic I have encountered is that of David Abram, *The Spell of the Sensuous* (New York: Pantheon, 1994).

19. This point is excellently developed by Babcock-Abrahams in "A Tolerated Margin of Mess."

20. See Lawrence Aripa, "Coyote and The White Man," in *Stories That Make the World*, ed. Rodney Frey (Norman: Oklahoma University Press, 1995), 81–91.

21. Quoted in Holquist, "The Surd Heard," 150–51.

22. For me, the terrible price of being a culture hero is most poignantly epitomized by Mastamho, a Mojave culture hero who is said to have taught the Mojaves every part of their culture – from language to building houses to making pottery to recognizing what plants are good to eat, from how to farm to how to count – and even given them the use of their fingers and their mouths. Having taught them everything, he leaves his people:

> He wanted to have wings and flap them. He moved his arms four times to make them into wings. Then he said: "See, I shall be a bird. Not everyone will know me when I am a bird. My name will be Saksak. . . . He flew southward, looking for a place to sit. He settled on a sandbar. But he thought: "It is not good; I will not sit here"; and again he went on. So he went far down to the sea where the [Colorado] river empties into it. There he stayed, and lived near the river eating fish. Now he was crazy and full of lice and nits. Now he had told everything and was a bird, he forgot all that he had known. He did not even know any longer how to catch fish. Sometimes other birds kill fish and leave part of them. Then Saksak eats them, not knowing any better. He is alone, not with other birds, and sits looking down at the water; he is crazy.

From A. L. Kroeber, *Seven Mohave Myths*, University of California Anthropological Records 11 (Berkeley: University of California Press, 1948), 57, 64.

23. Babcock-Abrahams, "A Tolerated Margin of Mess," 148, 164.

24. A valuable analysis of this story provided by Elaine Jahner, "Cognitive Styles in Oral Narrative," *Language and Style* 16, no.1 (1982): 32–51, illustrates the cogency of Bakhtin's emphasis on the non-verbal context of utterances. Jahner demonstrates how circularities within the story reflect the physical situation of the traditional enactment situation. The teller would sit within a circle of auditors in a circular tipi that is one of a circle of tipis. Superimposed upon this pattern is one of stillness (embodied in the physical quietness of teller and audience) and movement (articulated through the oral narration). The superimposition enriches and complicates the development of the theme of insider/outsider, inclusion/exclusion, focused by interreflections between the two parts of the story. The inversions transform what at first appears mere sequentiality into a circle of meaning, substantively represented by the boy's return. This story's very form thus becomes the vehicle for the kind of deep cultural resonance that Toelken discovers in what appears merely an amusing tale.

25. One way to define the formal structure of myths would be to recognize modular units as "nested" as well as arranged in linear sequentiality. From this perspective the relation of episodes would always require attention to embeddedness. Such a form also accords with two-but-no-more character presentations and the omission of lavish descriptions and motive analyses. I hope in subsequent work to develop this possibility.

5
Myth as Historical Process

Sioux (Dakota)

Stone Boy

ANONYMOUS

Four brothers lived together in the same tipi. One day a strange woman came and stood outside. They sent the youngest brother out to see what it was that stood outside. The youngest brother went out to see, and came back with the information that a woman was standing there. Then the eldest brother said to the youngest, "Call her your sister and invite her inside."

When she was invited she hesitated. She kept her face hidden in her robe. The brothers were cooking buffalo tongues for their meal. They gave some of these to the woman, but she turned her back while eating them so as not to show her face. After a while the three older brothers went out to hunt. The youngest brother was curious to see the face of the woman. So he went to the top of a high hill and sat down. Then he left his robe on the hill and changed himself into a bird. He flew to the tipi and sat upon the poles at the top. He began to sing and to peck upon a pole, looking down at the woman. Now she had her face exposed, and he saw that it was covered with hair. Spread out before her was a robe with a row of scalps half way around it. The woman heard the bird pecking on the poles above, and looking up said, "You bad bird, go away."

Then she began to count the scalps in the row, and, talking to herself, said, "I will take the scalps of these four brothers and fill out this row with them in the order of their ages, beginning with the oldest."

Now when the little bird heard this he returned to the hill, resumed his former shape, and waited for his three brothers. When he saw them coming he went out to meet them. He related what he had seen. Then they planned to take a pack strap and boil it so as to make it weak and soft. When this was done they gave it to the woman and sent her for

Clark Wissler, "Some Dakota Myths," *Journal of American Folklore* 20 (1907): 199–202.

wood. Now when the woman had gone they took up the bundle she had brought with her and in which she kept the robe with the scalps and tossed it into the fire. Then the brothers went away.

The woman gathered together some wood, but every time she tried to tie it up with the pack strap the strap broke. At last she became very angry and said, "I will kill the brothers." So she returned to the tipi, but found the brothers gone and her bundle burned up. She was very angry. She thrust her hands into the fire and pulled out the robe. Then she took up a large knife, tied an eagle feather on her hair, and started in pursuit of the brothers. As she was very swift, she soon overtook them, and shaking her knife at them, said, "I will kill you." All of the brothers shot arrows at her, but could not hit her. She came up, knocked down the oldest, then the second in order, and then the third. The youngest brother stood far off, with a bow and arrows in his hands. The woman ran at him, but a crow that was flying around over his head said, "Young man shoot her in the head where the feather is." The young man did as directed and killed the woman. He beheaded her and buried the body. Then he made a fire, heated some stones, and made a sweat house. When this was done, he dragged his three dead brothers into the sweat house, where he began to sing a song and beat with a rattle. Then he poured water upon the heated stones, as the steam began to rise one of the brothers began to sigh. Then all three sighed. When the youngest brother poured more water upon the stone, the three brothers came to life again. Then they all returned to their tipi.

One day another young woman came and stood outside of the tipi as before. The youngest brother looked out and said, "My sister, come in." This woman did not hide her face. After a time she said, "Have you any brothers?" The youngest brother told her that he had.

The youngest brother cooked some buffalo tongues and gave one to the woman. She thanked him for this and they talked pleasantly together.

Now the brothers were out hunting for buffalo as before, and the youngest went out to the top of a high hill and left his robe, became a bird, and sat upon the poles on the top of the tipi. He pecked at the poles. The woman looked up and said, "Get away from here. You will spoil my brother's poles." Looking down the bird saw a row of moccasins laid out in front of the woman. She put her hand upon one pair saying to herself, "these are for the oldest." Then she took up another pair, saying, "these are for the next of age." So she went on until all were provided for. Then the bird flew back to the hill and became a boy again. When he met his brothers, he related to them what he had seen. They were all happy. They had as much buffalo meat as they could carry, and when they came into the tipi the woman said, "Oh my, you are good." At once she began to dry and cook meat.

One day the oldest brother went out to hunt, but did not return. The following day the next in order of age went out to search for him, and he never came back. Then the next went out, but he also failed to come back. Then the youngest went out to look for his brothers, and as he did not come back the woman began to cry. She went out to the top of a hill and found a nice smooth round pebble there. So she slept at that place one night and then swallowed the pebble. When she reached the tipi her abdomen has become very much distended. After a little while she gave birth to a child. It was a boy.

As this boy grew up he was always wanting a bow and arrows. And when he got them he was always shooting at birds and small animals. At last he became a tall man. Some of his uncles' arrows were still in the tipi, and one day, as he took them down, his mother related the fate of his four uncles. When the young man heard this story he said to his mother, "I shall find them."

"No, you are too young," said his mother.

"No, I am old enough," said the young man.

So the young man started out to search for his uncles. After a time he came to a high hill, from the top of which he saw a little old tipi. He went up to it and looked in at the door. He saw a very old woman inside. When the old woman saw him she said, "Come in, my grandchild; come in and break my ribs."

As the young man entered, the old woman stooped over toward the ground, and the young man kicked her with his foot until all her ribs were broken. At last, as he kicked, one of the ribs turned inward and pierced the old woman's heart. This killed her. Looking around inside the tipi, the young man saw the skeletons of many people. They were killed when breaking the old woman's ribs, because the last rib when broken turned outward and pierced the heart of the kicker. But this young man, who was called the Stone Boy, could not be killed in that way.

Among the skeletons in the tipi were those of the four uncles of the Stone Boy. He looked over the bones, then went outside, made a sweat house, and heated some stones. Then he took the bones into the sweat house, sang some songs, and beat with a rattle as his uncle had done. When he poured water on the stones and the steam began to rise, the dead all came to life. The Stone Boy addressed his uncles and said to them, "You are my four uncles who went away and never came back. Now I shall take you home with me."

One day Stone Boy said to his mother, "I am going out in this direction" (pointing to the left).

"No," said she, "you must not go that way, for it is dangerous."

"Yes, but I am going that way," said he. This was in the winter. He came to a very high hill where four girls were sliding down on the snow. "Come chase us," said they. Stone Boy sat down behind them on the piece of raw hide they were sliding with. At the bottom of the hill they ran against a bank and Stone Boy bumped the girls so hard that they were killed. Then he went home.

After a time he went on another journey, and saw an old buffalo bull hooking a rock. Stone Boy stood watching him for a while and then said, "What are you doing there?"

The buffalo replied: "A man named Stone Boy killed four girls. These girls were four white buffalo, and now all the buffalo are hunting for Stone Boy. So I am practicing my horns on this rock, because Stone Boy is very hard to kill. When winter comes, we shall go out to hunt for Stone Boy."

"I am the one you are looking for," said Stone Boy to the buffalo, and he shot an arrow into his heart.

Then Stone Boy went home, and told his four uncles that they should gather together a lot of brush, because the buffalo were coming, and they would cover the earth. With the brush they built four fences around their tipi. Then the buffalo came. Stone Boy and his uncles shot down many of them with their arrows, but the buffalo tore down one fence after the other until just one remained. But so many buffalo had been killed by this time that the leader of the herd called the others away, and Stone Boy and his uncles were left to live in peace.

Sioux (Lakota)

The Stone Boy

BAD WOUND

The Four Brothers lived together, with no woman, so they did the woman's work.

As the oldest was gathering wood, after night, something ran into his big toe. This pained him but little and he soon forgot it but his toe began to swell and was soon as big as his head. Then he cut it open and found something in it. He did not know what this was, but his brothers washed it clean and found that it was a little girl baby.

The Four Brothers kept this baby and gave it good food and fine clothes so that it grew to be a beautiful young woman. She could do all of woman's work well and quickly and never allowed anyone to leave their tipi cold or hungry. She could dress skins so that they were white and soft and make good clothing from them, upon which she put beautiful ornaments and each ornament meant something.

Many young men tried to get her to live with them but she would not leave the Four Brothers. So they told her that they would keep her always as their sister and they did everything so as to please her.

The oldest brother said, "I will go and hunt deer so that our sister may have the skins to make herself clothing."

He went away and did not return.

Then the next oldest brother said, "I will go and hunt buffalo so that our sister may have skins to makes robes for herself."

He went away and did not return.

Then the next to the youngest brother said, "I will go and hunt elk so that our sister may have meat for herself."

He went away and did not return.

James R. Walker, *Lakota Myth*, ed. Elaine A. Jahner (Lincoln: University of Nebraska Press, 1983), 140–53. Reprinted by permission of the University of Nebraska Press.

Then the youngest brother said, "Sister, our brothers have gone away and have not returned. I will go and find them."

So he went away and did not return.

When the youngest brother had been gone one moon, the young woman went to the top of a high hill to mourn and to seek a vision. While she was mourning, she saw a pebble. She looked at this pebble for a long time for it was very smooth and very white so she put it in her mouth to keep herself from being thirsty.

She fell asleep with this pebble in her mouth and swallowed it and while she slept the vision came to her in the form of the Great Beast which told her that the four brothers were kept by a stone and that a stone would find them and bring them back to her.

She told this vision to a shaman and asked him to tell her what it meant. The shaman told her that she should marry and name her son The Stone.

But she would not live with any man for she remembered the Four Brothers, how they were good and kind to her and she wished to live for them only.

Soon she grew big with child and gave birth to a boy baby. The flesh of this baby was as hard as stone and she knew that it was mysterious (*wakan*) and came from the pebble which she had swallowed.

She went far away and lived with her son alone. She taught him all the games and songs and all about roots and plants and animals and birds so that he was cunning and wise.

She gave him fine clothes and good food so that he grew up strong and brave but his flesh was hard as stone.

She would not allow him to hunt or go in a war party for she was afraid he would go away and never return like the Four Brothers.

Each moon she would go to the top of a hill and mourn.

When her son had grown to be a man, he asked her why she went to mourn each moon and she said to him, "My son, you are now a man and I will tell you why I mourn."

So she told him the story of the Four Brothers, of her coming to them, of how they went away and did not return, of his own birth and the vision of the Great Beast.

She sang to him this song.

I am a mysterious woman.
I am [not] like other women.
You are a mysterious man.

Your flesh is like a stone.
You are the Stone Boy.
You are the stone the Great Beast told of.

Then he sang to her this song.

I am the Stone Boy.
I am the stone that will aid you.
I will bring back your brothers.
My mother, I will make you happy.

He then said to her, "Mother I will go and find your brothers. I will bring them to you."

She said, "I am afraid you too will go away and never come back."

He said to her, "What did the Great Beast tell you? I am the stone."

So she made a great feast and invited a wise shaman, a wise old woman, a great brave, a great hunter and four maidens as the chief guests and all the people as common guests.

She placed the people according to the bands and her son among the chief guests, and when all were satisfied with eating, she stood before all the people and told the story of the Four Brothers, of her coming to them, of their going, of her vision, of the birth and life of her son.

She then told them to examine her son that they might know that he was mysterious (*wakan*). The people all examined the young man and when they found that his flesh was hard like stone they said he was indeed mysterious and that he was the Stone Boy.

She then told them that her son was to go in quest of the Four Brothers and she had made this feast so that the people might have a good heart towards him and she invited the chief guests so that they would help her to prepare her son for this quest with magic.

The chief guests agreed to do what she should ask of them.

The shaman gave him a charm (*pejuta wakan rca*) that would keep all harm from him.

The old woman gave him a robe on which she had painted a dream.

This dream made the robe magical so that it hid one who wore it from the sight of everything.

The warrior gave him a magical spear that would pierce anything, a magical shield that would ward off anything and a magical club that would break anything.

The hunter showed him how to find anything.

His mother made his clothes of good deer skins and the young women put ornaments on them. While ornamenting his clothes they sang love songs and the shaman conjured the ornaments (*ca hina wakan kaga*) so that they were magical.

On the sides of his moccasins they put mountains so that he could step from hill to hill without touching the valleys. On the tops they put dragon flies so that he could escape all danger. On his leggings they put wolf tracks so that he would never grow weary.

On his shirt they put the tipi circle so that he would find shelter everywhere.

He stood before the people clothed in his magical garments, his shield on his back and his spear and club in his hands. His face was toward the rising sun. Before him was his mother, and on one side, the shaman, warrior and hunter; on the other, the old woman and the four young women.

He said to his mother, "I will bring the Four Brothers back to you." And to the young women, "When I return I will take you four as my women." And to the men, "What you have taught me I will use to release the Four Brothers." And then turning his face toward the setting sun, he said to the old woman, "I go."

Then the old woman threw the robe about him and he was seen no more; but there was a wind as if the Thunderbird flew toward the setting sun and his mother fell on her face as one dead. But the people heard a voice high in the air, clear and loud like the voices of the cranes when they fly towards the region of the pines and this is what it said, "A stone shall free the Four Brothers."

When the Stone Boy went from the people he stepped from hill to hill more swiftly than the stars fall at night (falling meteors).

From each hill he looked carefully into each valley so that he saw all there was in every valley but he found nothing of the Four Brothers until he came to the high hills far toward the setting sun.

In the valleys here there was much game of every kind and in one of them he found a stone knife that he knew belonged to the oldest brother. In another valley he found a stone arrowhead that he knew belonged to the next to oldest brother. In another he found a stone axe that he knew belonged to the next to youngest brother and in another he found a stone bone breaker that he knew belonged to the youngest brother.

So he knew he was on the right way to find the brothers and looked carefully into each valley.

Beyond this, toward the setting sun, the hills became higher and higher until they were mountains.

Near the mountains he saw a valley that was barren with nothing in it but a stone, a tree and a little brown hill. He saw smoke coming from the little brown hill so he took off his robe and sat down to watch this and soon a huge coyote, larger than a buffalo, came out of the hill and began to jump up very high and yelp very loud; then the stone began to roll and bump about and the tree began to move from place to place.

The Stone Boy took off his robe and sat down to watch these things and soon a growl like thunder came from the hills beyond. When this growl sounded, the coyote jumped very high and fast and yelped and yelled and the stone moved about and bumped the ground and the tree began to move from place to place.

Then the coyote sniffed toward him and then trotted a little way and sniffed again, then yelped and howled and jumped up and down.

Then the bear came towards the hill he was on, running very fast and growling like thunder.

The Stone Boy quickly put his robe on and when the bear was almost at him he stepped to another hill and the bear stopped and looked very foolish and said "That must have been a Thunderbird passed by me."

Then the coyote sniffed toward him again and jumped up and down, and the bear ran toward the hill he was on, but when he got there the Stone Boy stepped to another hill and the bear looked very foolish and said, "I think that is a Thunderbird going by."

Then the coyote sniffed again towards the hill the Stone Boy was on and again jumped up and down and the tree walked that way and the stone came also. And the bear growled like very heavy thunder and came creeping towards the hill watching everything very closely. But when he got near, the Stone Boy stepped to another hill. Then the bear was afraid and ran back to the little hill whining and whimpering for he thought it was a Thunderbird.

Then the little old woman came out of the hill and the coyote yelped and jumped up and down and ran around and around and the branches of the tree squirmed and licked their tongues out and hissed like a great wind.

And the stone jumped up and down and every time it would come down it would shake the earth.

Then the Stone Boy stood up and took off his robe and jeered at them and mocked them and they saw him and the old woman screamed at him and the coyote yelped louder than ever and jumped up and down and the tree walked towards him, every snake hissing loud and the stone rolled and tumbled towards him and the bear came very fast towards him growling like a thunder cloud.

When the bear was very close he raised his paw to strike him and the Stone Boy shot one of the arrows through his heart and he fell dead.

Then the coyote came jumping up and down and every time he jumped up he went higher and higher and when he was near, he jumped up so as to come down on the Stone Boy, but the Stone Boy set his spear on the ground and when the coyote came down, the spear ran through his heart and killed him.

Then the stone came rolling and tumbling and smashing everything in its path and when it was near it was about to roll on the Stone Boy and smash him also, but he raised the war club he had and struck it a mighty blow and broke it into pieces.

The tree could not walk up the hill so Stone Boy went down into the valley and when he came near the tree, the branches began to strike at him, but he held up the shield the warrior had given him and when one of the branch snakes would strike it, its teeth would break off and its head would be smashed. And so the Stone Boy danced about the tree and sang and shouted until every branch had smashed itself to death on his shield.

The little old woman then went into the little hill and the Stone Boy came near it and cried out, "Ho, old woman, come out!"

But the old woman said, "My friend, I am a weak old woman. Have pity on me and come into my tipi."

So the Stone Boy found that the little hill was a strange kind of a tipi and he found the door open and went in when the woman said, "My friend, I am weak old woman, but you are welcome to my tipi. I will get you something to eat and drink."

But the Stone Boy noticed that her tongue was forked so he was wary and watched her close.

She said, "My friend you must be tired. Lie down and rest while I get food for you."

So the Stone Boy lay down and the old woman passed close to him saying, "The meat is behind you." And as she leaned over him, she stabbed him over the heart but her stone knife broke off when it struck him.

She said, "My friend, I stumbled and fell on you."

The Stone Boy said, "I will sit up so that you will not stumble over me."

So she said, "My friend, sit near the center of the tipi so I can go about you without stumbling on you."

So the Stone Boy sat near the center of the lodge and the old woman went about him and as she passed behind him, she struck him on the head with a war club, but it only bounced up without hurting him so she said, "My friend, that was a stone that fell from the top of the tipi."

So the Stone Boy said, "I will sit out by the door of the tipi so that stones will not fall on me," and he sat outside the door.

The old woman said, "My friend, you must be hungry, and I will make soup for you to drink," so she made soup with bad medicine in it and gave it to Stone Boy, who drank it.

Then the old woman said, "Ho, you are the one whom I hate. I am *Iya* the evil spirit. I hate all Indians. I destroy all Indians. I have given you that which will destroy you. You have swallowed poison. It will kill you. I am *Iya* the evil one. I know whom you seek. You were hunting for your mother's brothers. They are there in that tipi. They are like tanned skins. You will soon die and I will make a tanned skin of you. But I must have a living stone to flatten you out. But there is only one other living stone and I must find it. The living stone was my master. He is the only one I feared. He is the only one who could hurt me. No one else can do me any harm. His only relation is a living stone. He is now my master and none other.

"But you will die from the poison I have given you and I will sing your death song."

So she sang:

A young man would be wise.
A young man would be brave.
He left the place he knew.
He came to strange places.
He came to death's valley.
He came to *Iya*'s tipi.
He slew *Iya*'s son the coyote.
He slew *Iya*'s daughter the snake tree.
He broke the living stone.
He broke *Iya*'s only master.
Iya will be revenged on him.
Iya will see him die.

He slew my friend the bear.
Iya will laugh and see him die.

Then the Stone Boy said, "May I also sing a song?"

And *Iya* said, "Ho, sing what you will. It is your death song and it is music that will make my heart glad."

Then the Stone Boy sang:

The living stone was *Iya*'s master.
The living stone had but one relation.
He had a son that was little.
A pebble white as the snow.
Iya feared this pebble and stole it.
Feared it because it was white.
You will not laugh and see me die.
For this is not my death song.
I am the pebble you threw away.
I am the Stone Boy, your master.

Then *Iya* said, "How shall I know you to be my master?"

The Stone Boy said, "Do my bidding or I will punish you."

Then *Iya* said, "I am a weak old woman. Have pity on me and do not punish me."

The Stone Boy said, "Your tongue is forked and you do not tell the truth. You are not a woman. But you are an evil old man. You have pity on no one but do evil to everyone. Tell me. Where are my mother's brothers?"

Iya said, "I do not know."

Then the Stone Boy seized him by the foot and placed his foot on the ground and trod on it and he howled with pain. But the Stone Boy demanded of him to tell where his mother's brothers were and *Iya* declared that he did not know. Then the Stone Boy flattened his other foot in the same way and *Iya* sobbed and cried with pain and said he would tell all to the Stone Boy if he would not punish him any farther for he recognized that he was truly his master.

Iya said, "In ancient times I found game plentiful in the valleys about here and that good hunters and brave men came here to hunt it. These good men could not be made to do evil at their homes so I could not do them mischief. So I made a bargain with your father, the living stone and with the Great Bear and brought my son and daughter with me and we all lived here in this valley.

"The bargain was that the bear would go out among the game and when a good man came to hunt them, the bear would show himself and being so big, the hunters would chase him until they came where they could see my son who would jump up and down and scare them so that they would fall down with no strength. Then the bear would take them in his arms and bring them to my daughter who would sting them so that they would be paralyzed. Then the living stone would roll on them and flatten them out like skins and I would heap them up on my tipi poles. And as they were alive, this would always be a torment to them. In this way I could do mischief to good men.

"We often heard of the four men who lived alone and did a woman's work and who never did evil to anyone, so that I could not torment them but they would not hunt or go on the war path and we thought they would never come within our power.

"So I determined to get a woman into their tipi that they might do some evil but I could not get an ordinary woman among them. Then I tried to break off a branch from my daughter, the snake tree, and put it into their tipi but the branches would not break and the only way I could get a part of my daughter was by digging out a part of the heart of the tree. This I did and placed it near the tipi of the four men so that when one of them went to get wood he would step on it and stick it into his toe.

"But these men were so good that when they cared for this child it grew up a good woman such as they were men but I waited patiently for I knew they would not live as they had when she grew to be a woman.

"So when she was a woman, they came to hunt for her and the bear enticed them and they were caught and flattened and are now tormented on my tipi poles.

"When I threw the white pebble away, I knew that no ordinary woman could nourish it into life and growth and when your mother grew up to be a woman I did not think of her being a mysterious woman who could give life and growth to the pebble.

"So my own evil has brought the punishment on me for I know that you are my master and that you will not let me do evil anymore.

"But those who now lie on my tipi poles will still be tormented."

Then the Stone Boy said, "Tell me, how can these people that are on your tipi poles be restored to their natural conditions?"

And *Iya* said, "I will not."

The Stone Boy said, "I am your master. Tell me or I will punish you."

Then *Iya* said, "Remember I am your grandfather and do not punish me."

The Stone Boy said, "I broke my own father in pieces because he was evil. Do you think I would spare you because you are my grandfather?"

Iya said, "I will not tell you."

Then the Stone Boy said, "Give me your hand, and he took *Iya*'s hand and trod on it and it was flattened like a dried skin and *Iya* howled with pain.

Then the Stone Boy said, "Tell me or I will flatten your other hand," and *Iya* said, "I will tell you.

"You must skin the bear and the coyote and stretch their skins over poles so as to make a tight tipi. Then you must gather all the pieces of the broken living stone. You must make a fire of the wood of the snake tree and heat these stones over this fire. Then place the stones in the tipi. Then get one of the flattened people off the poles of my tipi and place it in the tipi you have built. Then place the hot stones in the tipi and pour water over the stones. When the steam rises onto the flattened persons, they will be as they were before the bear enticed them."

Then the Stone Boy did as he was told but the skins of the bear and the coyote would not make a full sized tipi so he made it low and round on top. And when he made fire of the snake tree the branches were so fat that one would heat all the stones red hot. So he had plenty of fuel to heat the stones as often as he wished.

So he placed the flattened people in the sweathouse and steamed them and they became men as they were before they were enticed by the bear.

But he did not know who his mother's brothers were, so he took the arrow he had found and called to all and asked them whose arrow it was, and one man said it was his, and he told him to stand to one side and he took the stone knife he had found and asked them whose it was, and a man said it was his, and he told him to stand to one side. He then took the wooden bowl he had found and asked them whose it was, and a man said it was his, and he told him to stand to one side. He then took the plum seed dice he had found and asked them whose it was, and a man said it was his, and he told him to stand aside.

Then he told the men he had separated to look at each other and they did so and when they had looked at each other they each embraced the other and the Stone Boy knew that they were brothers.

Then the Stone Boy took them by themselves and told them the story of the four men and the birth of his mother and of the four men going away and never coming back. Then the men said, "We are those four men," and the Stone Boy knew that they were his mother's brothers, so he told them the story of his own birth, and they said, "We believe you because we know of the birth of your mother." Then he told them of his preparation to come for them and his coming and his fight with the bear and the coyote and the stone and the snake tree and how he was master of *Iya* and they said, "We believe you because the bear did entice us and the coyote did jump up and down and the snake did bite us and the stone did roll on us and make us flat like skins and the old woman did spread us on her tipi and we were in torment."

Then the Stone Boy counseled with them as to what he should do with *Iya* and they advised him to make him flat like a skin but the Stone Boy said, "There is no snake tree to bite him."

So he came back to *Iya* and said, "You have been very evil and now I am your master and I shall punish you for all the evil you have done so that you shall always be in torment as you have kept all these people."

Iya was a great coward and he begged the Stone Boy to spare him and not punish him.

But the Stone Boy said, "I shall flatten you like a skin and spread you on poles."

Then *Iya* said, "I am *Iya* the giant and I will grow so big that you cannot flatten me," and he began to grow and grew larger and larger so that he was a great giant. But the Stone Boy began to trample on him beginning at his feet which he had already flattened and he trampled his legs so that *Iya* fell to his knees and he trampled his thighs so that *Iya* fell to his buttocks. And he trampled his hips so that great floods of water ran from him and this water was bitter and salty and it soaked into the earth and where it comes out in springs and lakes, it makes the water very bad and bitter.

Then he trampled his belly and *Iya* vomited great quantities of cherry stones and the Stone Boy said to him, "What are these cherry stones?" and *Iya* said, "They are the people that I have sucked in with my breath when I went about the earth as a giant."

The Stone Boy said, "How can I make these people as they were when you sucked them in with your breath?" and *Iya* said, "Make a fire without smoke." So the Stone Boy got very dry cottonwood and made a fire and when it was burned to coals, *Iya* said, "Get some of the hair from the Great Bear's skin," and he got hair from the Great Bear and *Iya* said, "Put this hair on the fire," and he put it on the fire.

Then there arose a great white smoke and it was like the smoke from wild sage branches and leaves.

Then *Iya* said, "Blow this smoke on the cherry stones," and the Stone Boy did so and *Iya* said, "This drives away all my power to do these people any harm."

Iya said, "Get the hair of many women," so the Stone Boy took the hair ornaments from his [jacket] and *Iya* said, "This gives you power over these people to do what you wish to them."

So the Stone Boy said to the people, "Be as you were before *Iya* sucked you in with his breath," and every cherry stone arose and was alive, some as men and some as women and children so that there were a great many people there.

These people were all very hungry and the Stone Boy said to *Iya*, "What shall I give these people to eat?" and *Iya* said, "Give them the meat of the Great Bear," so he cut off a piece of meat of the Great Bear and gave it to a woman and it grew to be a large piece and this woman cut it in two and gave half of it to another woman and immediately each of these pieces grew to large pieces and each one of these women cut their pieces in two and gave half to other women, so that every time a piece was given away, it grew to be a large piece.

The women built fires and cooked the meat and all feasted and were happy and sang songs.

[*The Songs – not recorded by Walker*]

But the people spoke many languages and they could not understand each other but the Stone Boy could speak to each one in his own language and he came to some and said to them in their own tongue, "Where was your place?" And they said, "Over the mountains." And he said to them, "Go to your people." He said this to everyone and when he said this, he gave to the oldest woman of each people a piece of the meat from the Great Bear so that they had plenty to eat while traveling.

Then the Stone Boy said to his mother's brothers, "Now we will go back to your sister, to my mother, but before we go, I will destroy *Iya* so that he may do no more mischief or hurt the people."

So he trod on *Iya*'s chest and *Iya*'s breath rushed out of his mouth and nostrils like a mighty wind and it whirled and twisted, breaking down trees and tearing up the grass and throwing the water from the lake and even piling the rocks and earth over the carcasses of the coyote and snake tree so that the Thunderbird came rushing through the air to know what all this tumult was about, and with his cloud shield he rushed into this great whirlwind and roared and flashed the lightning from his eyes and fought the whirlwind and carried it away into the sky.

Then the Stone Boy said to *Iya*, "I will now tread your head and your arms out flat like a dried skin and you shall remain forever here in this evil valley where there is no tree nor grass, nor water and where no living thing will ever come near you. The sun shall burn you and the cold shall freeze you and you shall feel and think and be hungry and thirsty but no one shall come near you."

When *Iya* was growing, he grew so large that he lay almost all across the valley and his hands were up on the hill where the Stone Boy first showed himself and when the Stone Boy told him his fate, his hands grasped for something and he felt the Stone Boy's robe. This he quickly threw over himself and immediately he became invisible. But the Stone Boy saw what he was doing and jumped quickly to trample on his head before he got the robe over himself. When the Stone Boy trampled the breath out of *Iya*, his mouth gaped wide open and he got the robe over his head before the Stone Boy could get his feet on him and when the Stone Boy did trample, he stepped into *Iya*'s mouth, and he closed his jaws like a trap and caught both of the Stone Boy's feet between his teeth.

Iya could not hurt the Stone Boy but he held the feet very tightly between his teeth and when the Stone Boy drew out one foot, he closed still on the other, so that when that one was dragged out, the moccasin was left in *Iya*'s mouth and was invisible and could not be found.

COMMENTARY

Perhaps the book about Indians that has been most popular both with Indians and non-Indians is *Black Elk Speaks*, of which more than a million copies have been sold since its publication in 1932. This autobiography of a Sioux visionary, born before the battle of the Little Big Horn, was told to and written up by a white man, John G. Neihardt. One of the most moving accounts of the destruction of Indian people appears on the book's last page, where Black Elk tells that after the 1890 massacre at Wounded Knee he reluctantly went with Chief Red Cloud to surrender to U.S. Army troops:

> And so it was all over.
>
> I did not know then how much was ended. When I look back now from this high hill of my old age, I can still see the butchered women and children lying heaped and scattered all along the crooked gulch as plain as when I saw them with eyes still young. And I can see that something else died there in the bloody mud, and was buried in the blizzard. A people's dream died there. It was a beautiful dream.
>
> And I, to whom so great a vision was given in my youth – you see me now a pitiful old man who has done nothing, for the nation's hoop is broken and scattered. There is no center any longer, and the sacred tree is dead.[1]

These words can help us to understand the retelling of the Stone Boy myth by a Lakota called Bad Wound, which was recorded about twenty years after the 1890 massacre of the Lakota at Wounded Knee, and about twenty years before Black Elk talked to Neihardt. Like Black Elk, Bad Wound had been born into a seemingly successful Lakota culture in the mid-nineteenth century, and then personally experienced the violent and drawn-out degradation of his people. Unlike Black Elk, he was given no great spiritual vision, but he was a gifted storyteller. Indeed, his version of the Stone Boy myth has been called by Claude Lévi-

Strauss the "finest, richest, and most dramatic in the whole of American oral literature."[2]

Bad Wound's telling offers special insight into the function of the most obtrusive rhetorical feature of oral – as opposed to written – narratives: repetition. Oral narratives are persistently repetitious. First, they are always retold stories. Furthermore, most are manifestly structured by repeating elements, both thematic and formal. Among the Lakota Indians, "Stone Boy" is one of their most frequently retold myths, and all other versions of which we have a record are much closer to the version collected by Clark Wissler than to Bad Wound's enactment.

But of course we know only a tiny fraction of the enactments of the Stone Boy myth. It would take a book to describe even partially what can be known and guessed about the relation of Bad Wound's telling to other versions. Actual mythic history (in contrast to schematic theorizing about myth) makes our literary history look like child's play. Bad Wound's "Stone Boy" offers fascinating insight into how the process of mythic enactment introduces such a rich complexity of profitable variations into "repeated" tellings. For the sake of simplicity of illustration I will confine my comments to the possible relations of Bad Wound's story to Wissler's and to others recorded by Ella Deloria and Marie L. McLaughlin, reminding the reader to multiply the problems and possibilities thus raised by a thousand to appreciate the intricate density of a living oral mythology.[3]

There is, to begin with, the problem of temporal relation. Deloria collected her narratives after Bad Wound's death, but the version she heard could have preceded his telling. And we are confronted by relationships among a variety of affiliated narratives, not just two stories. Thus, in Bad Wound's version the cherry stones that Stone Boy expels from Iya are people, whom the hero revives. In a story Deloria records about how the Trickster Iktomi conquers Iya, Iktomi looks into the sleeping giant's body through his mouth and there sees "all the tribes that Iya had eaten in the past, living on in contentment in their respective tribal circles. Inside Iya, they were living and having their being in exactly the same fashion as when they lived on earth." There follows a description of what is happening inside Iya: ball games and races, dancing, hunters returning with game, women taking food to the council tipi where old men were "recounting past glories. Taken all in all the sight presented a picture of the good old days" (3–4).

To evaluate adequately Bad Wound's narrative of the restoration of diverse peoples, one would need to know to what degree he was drawing on an earlier tradition such as that recovered by Deloria, or to what degree her story may be making use of Bad Wound's telling. The point is not to establish any definitive priority but to assess with some precision the fashion in which different tellers modify and revise as well as repeat, so that we can understand something of the peculiar meaning each enactment might have had for its audience. What is revealed here is the extraordinary fluidity of Native American oral mythic traditions, in which there is no fixed, definitive hierarchy of enactments but, instead, the dynamism of continuous interactiveness of affiliative tellings.

The instance just cited could be paralleled by hundreds of other particularities, especially if one searches out other versions. McLaughlin's telling is unusually intriguing because it illuminates how much of Bad Wound's "originality" consists in subtle reworkings of traditional elements. A difficult kind of subtlety for modern readers is presented (as I have already suggested about Tom Peters's telling of the girl-bear story) by omissions that we overlook but that may have been powerfully meaningful for a native audience. Bad Wound, for example, omits the episode in Wissler's version of the sledding with four white buffalo girls, which results in their death and the vengeful attack of the buffalo herd. Since white buffalo were highly valued by the Sioux, Deloria suggests a probable parallel between powerful human familial attachment of mother for son and nephew for uncles and the buffaloes' feeling for their cherished offspring. Further, the modern reader's doubt as to whether the killing was or was not inadvertent is intensified by McLaughlin's lengthy representation of the episode as involving attractive twin boys, whom Stone Boy helps to drag their sled uphill, who must overcome his reluctance (because of the danger) to slide down with them, and their bodies (after he has crushed them) are touchingly described.

A more positive subtlety (which I mention in part because I find it unusual in Indian myths and provocatively difficult to assess) appears in the handling of topography. One notices even in the austere, almost skeletal Wissler version that the youngest brother goes to "the top of a high hill" to become a bird in order to observe the strange woman, and it is from the top of another "high hill" that he perceives "the little old tipi" of the deceptive old woman. Other versions, not just Bad Wound's, make more of heights, distance, and topography. McLaughlin, for example, offers an unusual description of the strange place where the evil woman lives: "After noting the different landmarks carefully, he arose and slowly started down the slope and soon came to the creek he had seen from the top of the range. Great was his surprise on arriving at the creek to find what a difference there was in the appearance of it from the range and where he stood. From the range it appeared to be a quiet, harmless, laughing stream. Now he saw it to be a muddy, boiling, bubbling torrent, with high perpendicular banks" (183). I know of no other Indian myth that uses the landscape this way to dramatize social and psychological conditions. Study of a variety of Stone Boy tellings suggests that Bad Wound could give his enactment special historical pointedness by elaborating unusual features of both topographic representation and acts of misperception that distinguish this myth.

More readily apparent to a modern reader are his seemingly arbitrary disruptions of some expectable internal repetitions of detail. The most glaring inconsistency occurs in the listing of the artifacts Stone Boy uses to distinguish his uncles after their revival, a listing not congruent with the enumeration of the artifacts by which he had tracked them and by which we have presumed he will identify his relatives. Stone Boy finds first his eldest uncle's stone knife, then an arrowhead belonging to the next oldest uncle, then a stone axe, and finally a stone bone breaker belonging to his youngest uncle. When he identifies the resurrected uncles, however, he first seeks the owner of an arrow (not an arrow point), then the stone knife (changing order) and finally a wooden bowl and plum-seed dice – neither one of which was mentioned previously.

It is of course possible that Bad Wound simply forgot his earlier details or was indifferent to the misfitting. To read such variations as mere mistakes, however, would imply that "correctness" in a myth is always constituted by exact repetition. It is conceivable that we as print-oriented readers, unfamiliar with overt repetition as an artistic mode, see as meaningless discrepancies what Bad Wound quite consciously intended. He may have deliberately broken a conventional symmetry (microscopically echoing his transformations of the myth as a whole) so as to intensify through complication the referential significance of the traditional myth. For painful historical reasons, Bad Wound's telling developed a self-reflexive intricacy for his compatriots by using the same kind of mythic resonances we observed in the Iroquois story of Tekanawita (chapter 1), but historical circumstances required the

Sioux teller to deploy this rhetoric in a manner more challenging to his audience.

Bad Wound's identification of the Four Brothers (whom Stone Boy has never seen), for example, is a remarkably complex recognition scene. After the four revived brothers have been made to stand apart, they first look at and then recognize one another and embrace. At this point Stone Boy knows *not* that they are his uncles but only that they are brothers. He identifies them as *his* uncles only by telling the story of his mother's birth, which, in turn, enables them to recognize *him*. Narrative here establishes a complex continuity of relationships between family members who have previously had no physical contact. The uncles did not even know of Stone Boy's existence, since he was born after their imprisonment by Iya. The event, then, is not merely one of identification but also of an expansion of family interrelationships dependent on *narrative* processes of both recovery and discovery. The "recognition" dramatizes possibilities of reviving a community whose artifacts signal it to be one that integrates war, hunting, feasting, and social entertainment.

A little later Stone Boy forces Iya to disgorge cherry stones that are people the evil giant had previously swallowed. The resurrection of people from cherry stones occurs elsewhere in Lakota mythology, and both the cherry tree and water carried in a wooden bowl are in other rites associated with life continuance.[4] Bad Wound's manipulation of these traditional motifs seems oriented toward representing the restoration of the brothers as the reestablishment of balanced communal life – but under changed conditions requiring reconsideration of the inherited systems of Lakota culture, not as mere nostalgic commemoration.

Overt repetition bothers us because it has been so excluded from our own literary art. It has been our unanalyzed assumption that the structures created by aesthetic symbolism depend primarily on unapparent repetitions. Symbolic parallelisms and equivalences are significant to us because they are to some degree hidden, the form of their concealment constituting the principal material for the exercise of literary interpretation. Indian myths often seem impoverished, dull, or "primitive" because their obvious repetitions – including their self-presentation as retellings – frustrate our aesthetic pleasure in seeking out concealed linkages. This critical preconception originates in our separation of aesthetic discourse from other sociocultural practices, a separation alien to Indians.[5] We have difficulty, therefore, recognizing what Bad Wound's "distortions" of repetitive symmetry (whether in detail or in his total narrative) might signal to a Lakota audience. I suggest that his manipulations (in manner congruent with all myth telling but directed to an unusual historical crisis) carry his audience's imagination *beyond* the traditional myth so that the familiar story can help the Lakota reevaluate their shockingly new political situation at the beginning of the twentieth century. Bad Wound's version displays how myth tellings can not only reflect but also direct shifts in the conditions of culture. His revision of the traditional Stone Boy story makes productive use of the new tensions and ambiguities created by the catastrophes the Lakota people have undergone.

The Lakota difficulties were part of the larger disaster for all Native Americans produced by the European invasion of the New World. On no part of indigenous cultures was that impact greater than on religious belief and practice. Some Plains Indians at the end of the nineteenth century, to cite but one relevant example, were driven to abandon ceremonies involving buffalo, because there were no more buffalo. Across the continent the overwhelming power of Europeanized culture, especially because it brought with it diseases against which traditional religious medicine seemed ineffective, forced Indians to question the validity of their tribal cultures' powers. One response was the emergence of the Ghost Dance at the end of the nineteenth century.

The Ghost Dance was a revivalistic religious movement that swept through Indian tribal groups across the country in the 1880s; indeed, the killings at Wounded Knee were precipitated by the U.S. government's determination to suppress the Ghost Dance among the Sioux. The basic doctrine of the Ghost Dance was that the whole Indian race, living and dead, would soon be reunited upon a regenerated earth – repopulated with vast herds of buffalo – to live a life of happiness, free from death, disease, and hunger. The white race, being alien and secondary, was to have no part in this regeneration and would be eliminated.[6]

Bad Wound's "Stone Boy" belongs to the time after the suppression of the Ghost Dance and the seeming destruction of traditional Lakota lifeways: the extermination of the buffalo, the massacre at Wounded Knee, the confinement to a nonhunting, near-starvation life on the reservation. Perhaps the most impressive evidence of how directly Bad Wound's telling addresses these terrible circumstances is his startling omission of what is the celebratory conclusion of all other versions: Stone Boy and his uncles defeating hordes of attacking buffalo. Bad Wound concludes instead with the strange ambiguity of the evil giant Iya disappearing into invisibility, taking with him one of Stone Boy's moccasins.

The conventional Stone Boy story is surely to be interpreted as an imaginative figuration of the triumphant origin of buffalo-based Lakota culture, which flourished on the Great Plains only at a relatively late period – probably the eighteenth century – after the Lakotas had left behind their original woodland habitat and lifeways. By transforming this traditional myth of an earlier new beginning, Bad Wound in effect urges his people to recognize that they must once again radically alter an established mode of life. Bad Wound's hero triumphs, to be sure, but not over buffalo; rather, he renders impotent one of the Lakota's own traditional evil monsters – now apparently linked to the destructive intrusiveness of white civilization. Stone Boy's victory, moreover, is not definitive: evil Iya carries into undiscoverability one of his moccasins, a prime artifact of Indian culture and one particularly significant in a story that begins with an infected toe, empowers the hero with magical footwear allowing him to step from mountain to mountain, and ends with his trampling upon evil.[7]

Bad Wound's artistry appears in his linking of that strange conclusion to an almost hyperconventional opening: "The Four Brothers lived together," seemingly a reference to a large body of Lakota stories about brothers, most frequently four in number. This traditionality adds potency to the innovative surprise of the first sentence's second part: "so they did the woman's work." I know of no other Lakota version of the Stone Boy story that with such abruptness dramatizes a reversal of gender roles. The force of this surprise may be difficult for anyone to appreciate who is not familiar with the many Lakota myths built around representations of conventionalized gender roles, or with the usual Stone Boy beginning (illustrated by Wissler's version), which presents first a bad female visitor, then a good female visitor to the brothers' tent.

Bad Wound begins his story instead with the girl born from the eldest brother's toe. The girl is, we will discover, the evil Iya's granddaughter; she comes from the heartwood of his offspring, the mobile tree with branches of snakes. Genealogically, then, she is evil, an equivalent of the bad female visitor of the traditional tale. The brothers – *really* doing woman's work – rear her and care for her with such solicitude and love, however, that she grows into a wonderfully competent woman who refuses to leave the brothers by marrying, returning in kind their intense but disinterested affection: "they did everything so as to please her." An exhibition of nurture overcoming nature could not be more boldly dramatized. By behaving like women, not like men in the traditional Lakota conception, the brothers create a good woman out of a female emissary of evil.

This development of the traditional myth permits newly complicating ironies. The brothers are destroyed by reassuming their traditional masculine role *for the benefit of their sister*. The oldest goes to hunt deer "so that our sister may have the skins to make herself clothing"; the next brother goes to hunt buffalo so that she can make a robe for herself; the third goes to hunt elk so that she can have meat. As we learn later, Iya had despaired of capturing the "good men who could not be made to do evil at their homes." Only by making a bargain with Stone Boy's father, the living stone, and the Great Bear was Iya able to entice these good men to hunt where they could be captured with the aid of the giant leaping Coyote and the mobile snake-tree, both Iya's children. Evil succeeded because men pursued accepted masculine roles to benefit a woman whose worthiness had been created by their willingness to act like women.

After the disappearance of her brothers, the woman mourns them and seeks a vision in a traditional Lakota manner. The vision, which comes after she swallows a white pebble, informs her that the brothers are imprisoned by a stone and that a stone will return them to her. This incident develops innovatively a fundamental Lakota belief at the root of the traditional Stone Boy story: namely, faith in the sacred power of certain stones.[8] In other versions I know, this belief is simply taken for granted, as a given, and is not dramatized. Bad Wound, however, by narrativizing the Lakota conviction that mysterious power inheres in particular stones, brings this article of faith under conscious scrutiny. Normally it was Lakota men, not women, who treasured sacred stones, and men did not swallow them. In Bad Wound's story the sacred potency of stone is enhanced, not diminished, and the mystery of its power dramatized by self-conscious evaluations of conventional practices.

The woman, acting in accord with convention, asks a shaman to explain her vision but then rejects his quite intelligent interpretation –

that she should marry and name her son "Stone." The shaman undervalues the extraordinary sacredness of this granddaughter of Iya, who, inseminated by the white pebble, gives birth to Stone Boy and chooses to bring him up by herself. She teaches him, however, not only about the natural world but also "games and songs": that is, elements of Lakota culture. When the boy announces his determination to recover his uncles, the woman gives a feast and invites "all the people," thus reaffirming her link (through acculturation, not genetics) to traditional Lakota ways. The Lakota guests respond by bestowing on the boy gifts appropriate to the givers, each of whom is an essential figure in Lakota society: shaman, warrior, hunter, old woman. Each gift of a Lakota artifact increases the power of the already powerful boy of stone to the point of invulnerability.

His climactic triumph is the defeat of Iya, who, attempting to beguile Stone Boy after the demolition of his helpers, presents himself disguised as a "weak old woman": that is, concealed within the figure of the traditional myth, the woman who killed men by encouraging them to kick her. The hero, however, having been empowered by a wise old Lakota woman, is not deceived. The contest between Iya and Stone Boy would resonate richly for a Lakota audience, since Iya's actions would recall the many deceptively dangerous women that appear everywhere in Lakota mythology, enticing men to their destruction through the offer of sex or poisoned food. But none of these dangerous women, so far as I know, mocks her potential victim in the way Iya mocks Stone Boy. Unaware of the boy's invulnerability, the evil giant ironically fulfills his traditional repute as stupid by advertising his malevolence. This malevolence is given a peculiar twist by his assertion: "I hate all Indians. I destroy all Indians." The specification brings into the open a possibility that Iya's evil is *now* to be associated with the destructiveness of white culture. The connection strengthens when Bad Wound represents Iya's traditional power (he was feared for his habit of twisting and distorting the features of his victims' faces) through a peculiar maltreatment of his Indian victims, a physical torture that seems to imply also distortion of their social being. What Stone Boy first perceives as a small hill turns out to be a horror: a "tipi" constructed of the flattened, tanned bodies of Indians whom Iya has captured.[9] His victims are not dead but painfully mummified and forced to form a grisly parody of the Lakota home. This grim mockery, along with Iya's overt hatred of Indians, his forked tongue, and his offer of poisoned drink, allows a possible linking of the traditional Lakota monster to the monstrousness of white culture's assaults on *all* Native Americans; the association is strengthened by the recovery of people from cherry stones, all speaking mutually unintelligible languages. The vision here may owe something to the influence of the Ghost Dance, yet the profundity of Bad Wound's enactment, it seems to me, is that his Iya, whatever his new "connotations," also remains completely the traditional Lakota myth figure of stupid evil. Bad Wound, that is to say, does not simplify the difficulties of the Lakota situation by demonizing white culture. Iya's power to flatten Stone Boy, for example, depends upon his recovering the "living stone," a purely Lakota power. From Stone Boy's countersong against Iya, moreover, we learn that the "living stone" had one relation, "a son that was little": a white pebble that Iya first stole, then feared "because it was white," and foolishly threw away. Stone Boy, the son of that white pebble, is the destroyer of his "father," who was "the living stone." Stone Boy is Iya's master because he has killed his own father: he reaffirms the potency of Lakota culture by destroying part of his and its traditional power.

Just as Bad Wound breaks free of conventionalized Lakota definitions of good and bad women, so he celebrates Lakota ways without saying a single good thing about Western society, but also without relying on the tempting antithesis of good/Lakota opposed to bad/white. Bad Wound achieves this remarkable feat by representing whatever may be devastating in white culture as definable dramatically through forces familiar to his audience in their traditional belief system. Iya's human tipi is a development of his conventional power to distort bodies. Bad Wound's reaffirmation of Stone Boy as *the* Lakota hero, to cite an even more salient illustration, depends on connecting him genealogically through his mother, Iya's granddaughter, to a traditional Lakota image of monstrousness. This lineage suggests that the Lakota do possess the strength in their own right to control malign *external* forces, because the threatening evil is identified with an overcomable power already defined *within* Lakota tradition.

The imaginative complexity of Bad Wound's story embodies an essential validating of Lakota life (even to representing Stone Boy as a savior of other Indians), while demonstrating that its vitality under current circumstances will be sustainable only through reexploration of its cherished traditions. This reinvigoration through critical recursiveness is perhaps best exemplified by Stone Boy's bringing back to full life the mummified bodies of his uncles and other Indians through his re-creation of the sweathouse – the physical core of his people's curative religious practices, as is suggested by its double use in Wissler's version. Yet Bad Wound's is a story of "the first sweathouse," *reconstituted*, even as the uncles are revitalized: the frame and cover of the medicinal hut, the sticks that heat the rocks, and the heated rocks themselves are all made from pieces of the evil beings who had paralyzed and tortured Stone Boy's relatives; Lakota society is to be restored by sweating out, by retransforming, natively malign elements.

In accord with many traditional myths, Stone Boy accomplishes this restoration by following instructions given by his victim, illustrating that the cause of disease must be the source of recovery (this conventionality now made to reflect the special historical purpose of Bad Wound's version). Absolutely unique, so far as I know, is the final trampling of Iya, when, with the wind driven from this chest and his head being smashed, he seizes Stone Boy's feet in his mouth. The unexplained ambiguity of the conclusion is contrary to usual Lakota narrative practice. Bad Wound leaves the final meaning in doubt by closing with an "original" event, because the success of the Lakota at renewing their culture must be uncertain, since such success truly lies in the future (in traditional Stone Boy stories the so-called future was, of course, the buffalo-hunting present). The final ambiguity, nevertheless, returns us to the beginning of this unusual version of the familiar story. Iya, underestimating the Lakotas (and validating the correctness of their traditional view of him as stupid), had not believed that his granddaughter, the offspring of the snake-tree, was capable of giving "life and growth to the pebble." That capability came, as we've seen, from culture, not nature: his granddaughter's power rested upon the nurturing given her by the brothers, who were not, however, constrained by conventional gender roles. This is why it is appropriate (if startling) that Stone Boy's triumphant reaffirmation of his culture comes about through destroying his own ancestors. What the Lakota call the mysteriousness and we call the sacredness of the stone derives not from its belonging to some "other" realm but, to the contrary, from its centrality to the Lakotas' cultural world, which for them is inseparable from the natural world – a world ever renewable because intrinsically mutable.

It is crucial that we who read, not hear, Bad Wound's story recognize that his narrative skill appears principally in his adapting a traditional myth in response to the political circumstances of the Lakotas. A primary function of myths is to assist a people in productively dealing with the uncertainties that inevitably arise from the interplay of diversified historical developments, especially when these are intensified by the pressure of ferocious attacks from external forces. What the Lakotas need to survive the destructive impact of Western civilization, Bad Wound's retold story urges, is neither a retreat to revivalistic Ghost Dance mysticism nor rigid adherence to an orthodoxy of beliefs but a probing reassessment of the religious core of their culture. Only a very skillful, subtle, and intricate storytelling can articulate both the need for and the confidence required to accomplish such a renewal.

Bad Wound does not promise success. His story ends not triumphantly, as traditional versions do, but mysteriously, bafflingly. Iya is crushed, but drawing Stone Boy's cloak of invisibility over him, he vanishes, somehow gaining for himself his adversary's magical garment even as he swallows the victor's moccasin. This is perhaps Bad Wound's most skillful transmutation of his source, which celebrated victory over the buffalo as the establishment of Lakota Plains culture. Bad Wound projectively offers the potency of possible renewed culture to his audience's strength of imagination – and practice. He brings his people to the edge of what lies hidden within their own future behavior.

Because that future has now reached our time, I began by quoting the eloquent words concluding *Black Elk Speaks*, words that help to explain why the book became, as Vine Deloria has several times observed, almost a bible for young Indians and has sold a million copies. But the words I reproduced were in fact not Black Elk's; they were Neihardt's. What Black Elk actually said is less immediately inspirational but, in the light of Bad Wound's retelling of "Stone Boy," I think both comprehensible and spiritually expressive. What Black Elk actually told Neihardt was this:

> You have heard what I have said about my people. I have been appointed by my vision to be an intercessor of my people with the spirit powers and concerning that I had decided that sometime in the future I'd bring my people out of the black road into the red road of life. From my experience . . . and recalling the past from where I was at that time, I could see that it was next to impossible, but there was nothing like trying.
>
> At that time I could see that the hoop was broken and all scattered out and I thought, "I am going to try my best to get my people back into the hoop again." . . . it was up to me to do my utmost for my people and everything that I did not do for my people would be my fault. . . . If I were in poverty my people would

also be in poverty, and if I were helpless or died, my people would die also. But it was up to me to scheme a certain way for myself to prosper for the people. If I prosper, my people would also prosper. I am just telling you this, Mr. Neihardt. You know how I felt and what I really wanted to do is for us to make that tree bloom. On this tree of life we shall prosper. Therefore my children and yours are relative-like and therefore we shall go back into the hoop and here we'll co-operate and stand as one. . . . Our families will multiply and prosper after we get this tree to blooming.[10]

These words tell us that like Bad Wound, Black Elk had rejected Ghost Dance revivalism as an adequate response to the devastation of his culture. Unlike Bad Wound, however, he put his faith in assimilation. In the light of what he really said to Neihardt, it should not surprise us that in the earlier decades of this century Black Elk was an active and effective catechist for the Roman Catholic Church – although the publication of *Black Elk Speaks* disturbed some of the Jesuits with whom he worked, since the only religious experiences described in the book are Lakotan, not Christian. Bad Wound seems to have been more conservative: the vision embodied in his version of "Stone Boy" is not Black Elk's assimilationist one. Bad Wound, appropriately using a traditional mode of mythic revision, recommends renewal of an independent Lakota culture through a process of cultural self-transformation equivalent to (and as equivalently disruptive as) their change from a woodland to a buffalo-dependent Plains people.

A century after the seeming destruction of the Sioux, with their culture steadily regaining strength and self-respect, I hesitate to judge which of these impressive men was the wiser. I have no doubt, however, that the very difference between their stories proves that Lakota dreaming did not perish in the bloody mud of Wounded Knee, in part because culture can be imagined in many forms, and the power of imagining culture is more wondrously vital than we have taught ourselves to believe.

NOTES

1. *Black Elk Speaks*, as told through John G. Neihardt (1932; New York: Pocket Books, 1972), 230.

2. Claude Lévi-Strauss, *The Origin of Table Manners* (New York: Harper & Row, 1978), 380. On the popularity of the Stone Boy myth among the Lakota, see Elaine Jahner, "Stone Boy: Persistent Hero," in *Smoothing the Ground: Essays on Native American Oral Literature*, ed. Brian Swann (Berkeley: University of California Press, 1983), 171–86.

3. Ella Deloria, *Dakota Texts*, Publications of the American Ethnological Society 14 (Washington DC, 1932), which includes, besides a specific Stone Boy myth, others that are closely affiliated with it, as well as several that treat the stupid ogre Iya; Marie L. Mclaughlin, *Myths and Legends of the Sioux* (Bismarck, ND: Bismarck Tribune, 1916).

4. The relevance to Lakota ceremonial practices of the "new" identifiers Bad Wound uses are suggested by the rites that prepare a girl for womanhood after her first menstruation. A holy man puts balls of sage in the eye sockets of a buffalo skull and then, as Black Elk described the ceremony, places "a wooden bowl of water in front of the buffalo's mouth. Cherries were placed in the water, for these represent the fruits of the earth, which are the same as the fruits of the two-leggeds. The cherry tree you see is the universe, and it stretches from Earth to Heaven; the fruit which the tree bears, and which are red as are we two-leggeds, are as all the fruits of our Mother, the Earth" (Nicholas Black Elk, *The Sacred Pipe: Black Elk's Account of the Seven Rites of the Oglala Sioux*, ed. Joseph Epes Brown [Norman: University of Oklahoma Press, 1989], 123).

5. I have addressed our specific separation of religious and aesthetic discourse in an essay from which my present discussion derives: Karl Kroeber, "Religion, Literary Art, and the Re-Telling of Myth," *Religion and Literature* 26, no. 1 (1994): 9–30.

6. The classic account of James Mooney, *The Ghost-Dance Religion and the Sioux Outbreak of 1890* (1896; University of Nebraska Press, 1991), which in-

cludes some beautiful song translations, should now be supplemented by Raymond J. DeMallie, "The Lakota Ghost Dance: An Ethnohistorical Account," *Pacific Historical Review* 51 (1982): 385–405; and Alice Kehoe, *The Ghost Dance: Ethnohistory and Revitalization* (Fort Worth TX: Holt, Rinehart & Winston, 1989).

7. Again I cannot resist pointing out that Bad Wound, in true myth teller's fashion, makes dramatic use of an apparently trivial feature in the traditional story. As Wissler's version shows, the bad woman takes scalps, whereas the good woman offers moccasins, footwear made by women from skins of animals killed by male hunters. Bad Wound's development of the moccasin motif suggests to me that the detail in the original story was already more meaningful to the Lakotas than a modern reader is likely to recognize.

8. A description and interesting examples are provided by Frances Densmore, *Teton Sioux Music*, Bulletin of the Bureau of American Ethnology 61 (Washington DC, 1918), 204–44. Paul B. Steinmetz, *Pipe, Bible, and Peyote among the Oglala Sioux* (Knoxville: University of Tennessee Press, 1990), 18, comments on the relation of sacred stones to the Sioux Yuwipi ceremony (which focuses on the sweathouse).

9. This is another fascinating artistic development of a conventional motif, since traditional tellings probably refer to the literal fact that poor old women often dwelt in overused, discarded skin tipis that had been much "tanned" by years of smoke; see Deloria, *Dakota Texts*, 36.

10. Quoted in Raymond DeMallie, *The Sixth Grandfather* (Lincoln: University of Nebraska Press, 1980), 294, from the virtually stenographic notes that Neihardt's daughter took of her father's conversations with Black Elk.

INDEX